Spoken Language Comprehension

Issues in the Biology of Language and Cognition
John C. Marshall, editor

Spoken Language Comprehension:

An Experimental Approach to Disordered and
Normal Processing

Lorraine Komisarjevsky Tyler
with Howard Cobb and Naida Graham

The MIT Press
Cambridge, Massachusetts
London, England

This book was set in Palatino by Asco Trade Typesetting Ltd., Hong Kong and printed and bound in the United States of America.

Library of Congress Cataloging-in-Publication Data
Tyler, Lorraine Komisarjevsky, 1945–
  Spoken language comprehension : an experimental approach to disordered and normal processing / Lorraine Komisarjevsky Tyler with Howard Cobb and Naida Graham.
    p.   cm.—(Issues in the biology of language and cognition) Includes bibliographical references and index.
  ISBN 0-262-20088-0
  1. Aphasia. 2. Psycholinguistics. 3. Comprehension. I. Cobb, Howard. II. Graham, Naida. III. Title. IV. Series.
  RC425.T95   1992
  616.85'52—dc20   91-41317
                                                                    CIP

. . . dedicated to the ones I love.

Contents

Foreword

How to Track Comprehension (Failure)

John C. Marshall

Aphasic language disorder frequently involves severe impairments of comprehension. In cases where the patient realizes (in part at least) that he or she does indeed have problems with understanding spoken (or written) language, the condition is frustrating for patients and their families alike. Some slight appreciation of the difficulty can be obtained by recalling the acute fiascos of travel in lands where one has no mutually comprehensible language; failure to understand what is happening around one can be even more of a hindrance than inability to speak appropriately. This analogy between aphasic comprehension and limited command of a language that we know but dimly is sometimes drawn by the patients themselves. Elvin and Oldfield (1951) describe a young man with a deep penetrating injury to the left temporal lobe who "on becoming aware of his surroundings ... thought that he must be in a foreign country as speech had no meaning."

Comprehension failure without self-awareness (as in many cases of Wernicke's aphasia) can be even more disturbing. It is thus not too surprising that some patients should "blame" their (normal) co-communicators for the breakdown of dialogue; patients who "accuse" the examiner of talking gibberish are not (always) correct in this assessment.

Yet, despite the manifest importance of understanding "receptive" aphasia, the scientific study of comprehension (and its failures) has often been impeded by the indirectness of traditional testing. Conventional approaches such as forced-choice picture-pointing presuppose an adequate grasp of the pictures themselves and the ability to "translate" between verbal and pictorial representations. Furthermore, such tests determine in advance the range of miscomprehensions that can occur; it is the examiner, not the patient, who delineates the response set.

When the patient is allowed "free" praxis in the form of verbal response to a linguistic communication, it is often difficult to disentangle comprehension failure from expressive failure. Similarly, correct compliance with requests to perform an action to verbal command (Caplan and Hildebrandt 1988) presupposes relevantly intact praxis.

Finally, it should be noted that all traditional techniques for the assessment of comprehension in aphasia are "off-line" in the sense of Marslen-

Wilson and Tyler (1980). It is not merely that the standard methods allow (or require) some significant delay between the relevant parts of the signal and the patient's response (although all do). Rather, these tasks assess only the endpoint of comprehension in (at least) two senses: first, no response is output before the entire message has been input, and second, that response (which is often a complex function of understanding) must be both compiled (Hamburger and Crain 1984) and executed before the examiner can "see" evidence of comprehension (or failure *somewhere* along the line).

In short, the unfolding of comprehension in time cannot be observed in the standard paradigms. The *process* of understanding cannot be tracked as each successive word (or syllable) adds to and modifies the representation of the signal formed up until that time.

The great virtue of the studies pioneered by Lorraine Komisarjevsky Tyler is that they *do* allow us to watch the build-up of a linguistic representation in real time. The elaboration of structural descriptions as they follow (almost immediately) behind the unfolding acoustic signal can be tapped.

Such "on-line" investigations of comprehension processes usually involve reaction-time techniques where the response must be made as quicly as possible to a target detected in the speech stream. Stimulus materials are manipulated so that, in the normal case, detection of the target item can be facilitated (or retarded) by the preceding linguistic context.

The relevant techniques, which include phoneme- and word-monitoring, speeded naming, and lexical decision (all in sentential or discourse contexts), are now widely used in the investigation of *normal* understanding processes; and they allow (many critical aspects of) comprehension to be assessed within 500–1000 msec of the presentation of the relevant signal. I was initially skeptical that such methods could be usefully employed with aphasic patients. Since very long and varied reaction times are characteristic of many patients when they undertake off-line tasks, I had assumed that one-line tasks would generate more noise than signal.

I was wrong ("the proof of the pudding ..."). What Tyler has shown is that the on-line approach, with particular emphasis on word-monitoring and "gating" techniques (a form of naming in response to partial physical cues) can provide solid evidence about the real-time assignment of linguistic structures in aphasic patients. This book documents the grounds for this assertion in considerable detail; it brings together the results of an extensive research program, assesses the validity of the paradigm, and derives totally new insights into the (psychological) locus of comprehension disorder in a wide range of aphasic pathologies.

It should not be thought that Tyler's techniques are an *alternative* to traditional testing; there are, after all, good reasons for wanting to know whether patients can appropriately manipulate and deploy the *final* output of comprehension processes. But on-line studies are nonetheless essential.

They show how the successive stages of comprehension emerge over time; they locate the early indications of breakdown; and they sometimes reveal that these initial representations are intact (and hence that malfunction must arise after the "automatic" processes of structural assignment are complete).

In sum, then, Tyler expounds a major advance in understanding mis-understanding.

References

Caplan, D., and Hildebrandt, N. 1988. *Disorders of Syntactic Comprehension.* Cambridge, MA: MIT Press.

Elvin, M. B., and Oldfield, R. C. 1951. Disabilities and progress in a dysphasic university student. *Journal of Neurology, Neurosurgery and Psychiatry* 14, 118–128.

Hamburger, H., and Crain, S. 1984. Acquisition of cognitive compiling. *Cognition* 17, 85–136.

Marslen-Wilson, W., and Tyler, L. K. 1980. The temporal structure of spoken language understanding. *Cognition* 8, 1–71.

Acknowledgments

In the spring of 1988 William Marslen-Wilson first suggested that I write a book describing the neuropsychological work that had been going on in our lab for the past 10 years. I initially rejected the idea out of hand, but he can be very persuasive. I rejected the idea primarily because I felt daunted by the amount of data collected over the years and the scale of the story. In the end I was convinced that no other public format was suitable for this particular body of research. The story—partial though it might be—had to be told in its entirety and not in selective slices suitable for journal articles.

Although I started writing the book in the early summer of 1988, there were two long breaks in its progress, when my son, Jack, and my daughter, Lydia, arrived. My delight in the children amply compensated for any frustration I felt during those periods in being unable to continue with the book. I eventually completed the manuscript in July 1990 and finished the final revisions in January 1991. From the vantage point of being able to leaf through a completed manuscript, I can say that I have enjoyed writing this book. Despite the difficulties, it has been stimulating and thought-provoking. I believe that the psycholinguistic approach to the study of language disorders which I have described here enables us to ask a different set of questions about the nature of language disorders, questions that point the way to a deeper understanding of the underlying functional bases of aphasia.

First of all, I wish to thank the patients who endured the many years of testing necessary to develop the processing profile. Without their cooperation, the entire enterprise would have been impossible. Equally important has been the role of the Medical Research Council in providing the long-term support that allows this kind of research program to be carried out. To develop the type of detailed analyses of individual patients that I describe in this book takes years of testing and would have been impossible if we had been solely dependent upon short-term funding. In our dealings with the MRC over the years, we have received special help from John Woodhead-Galloway, Ann Horn, Megan Davies, and David Cox. I thank them for their help and support.

I also thank a number of people who have worked with me over the years and who, in their various ways, helped me to write this book. First, the members of the MRC Speech and Language Group at the University of Cambridge (Paul Warren, Susan Behrens, Rachel Spence, and Ruth Ostrin). Two members of the group—Howard Cobb and Naida Graham—deserve special thanks for the care and effort they put into many of the studies described in this book and also for their patience and gentleness with the patients. Without their contributions, this book could not have been written. It is for this reason that I have included their names on the title page. Second, I thank William Marslen-Wilson for the endless discussions we have had about various aspects of this work and for his encouragement throughout the past few years. Finally, I thank Jack and Lydia for being their utterly delightful selves. I hope they will read this book one day.

Spoken Language Comprehension

PART I

A Psycholinguistic Processing Approach to the Study of Aphasia

Chapter 1
Processes and Paradigms

The purpose of this book is to illustrate a particular approach to the study of language-comprehension disorders in aphasic patients. The approach focuses on the real-time analysis of spoken language, on the processes and representations involved in the immediate interpretation of the speech input. It asks detailed questions about when and how different types of mental processes take place as each utterance is heard and about the types of representations that are constructed as a result of these mental processes. This approach provides the basis for a detailed examination of the ways in which these processes and representations break down in aphasia.

The general framework for this research is the "cohort model" of spoken language comprehension in normal listeners (Marslen-Wilson 1973, 1975, 1987; Marslen-Wilson and Welsh 1978; Marslen-Wilson and Tyler 1975, 1980; Tyler and Wessels 1983, 1985). The model has, first of all, the advantage of being based entirely upon data about *spoken* language comprehension. This makes it the appropriate starting point for a program of research into the breakdown of spoken language comprehension in aphasia. Its second advantage is that it attempts to address the full range of mental processes and representations involved in translating the speech signal into a meaningful representation of what is being said. Naturally, the model is currently more specific about some aspects of the process than others. It contains a detailed model of lexical processing, which covers the processes and representations involved in mapping the speech input onto representations of the phonological form of a word and accessing its semantic and syntactic properties (i.e., its lexical content) (e.g., Marslen-Wilson and Welsh 1978; Warren and Marslen-Wilson 1989; Marslen-Wilson and Zwitserlood 1989; Lahiri and Marslen-Wilson 1991; Tyler and Wessels 1983). It also makes specific claims about the basic structure of higher-level processing, stating that higher-level representations are constructed incrementally as each word of the utterance is heard and that both syntactic and semantic information are used immediately in the construction of higher-level representations (Marslen-Wilson and Tyler 1975, 1980, 1987).

The third advantage of the cohort model—and, indeed, the main reason it is the framework we use for the study of aphasic disorders—is that it distinguishes between *intermediate* and *final* representations of a spoken utterance. In the process of interpreting the speech input, a set of processes operate to construct different types of intermediate representations word by word as the speech input is heard. We can think of this as a set of layers, with each layer corresponding to a different type of representation and the top layer being the final representation. The processes involved in constructing these representations are automatic, not under voluntary control nor available to conscious awareness. Similarly, the intermediate representations themselves are not normally available to conscious awareness. When listeners hear an utterance spoken in their native language, they cannot choose to hear it as anything other than a meaningful utterance of their language, although for this to happen the utterance will have undergone a complex sequence of transformations: the acoustic-phonetic properties of the speech signal will have been encoded into individual words; the semantic and syntactic properties of those words will have been combined into syntactically and semantically well-formed phrases, and so on. But listeners cannot normally gain access to these intermediate representations. They do not "hear" the utterance as a string of separate words, just as they do not hear it as a string of grammatical formatives. What they "hear" is the final representation—a pragmatically coherent utterance in which the details of the intermediate representations have been lost. It is only this final representation that listeners can, in principle, gain conscious access to. This implies that the intermediate representations are qualitatively different from the final propositional representation (cf. Marcel 1983, 1988[1]).

To determine whether a patient's language-comprehension deficit is due to problems with the construction of intermediate representations rather than to problems with the properties of the final representation, we have to use very different experimental paradigms from those standardly used in aphasia research.

If it is indeed the case that the intermediate representations are not available to conscious awareness, any task that requires the listener to make some type of explicit response about properties of the utterance will necessarily involve processes other than those required to generate the intermediate representations. If we are to tap at all directly these intermediate representations—and given that they form the core of the comprehension system, we need to be able to do so—then the task cannot be one that requires any type of explicit decision about, or reflection upon, the properties of the representation. Thus, we have to use tasks that implicitly tap into the representations in which we are interested.

Furthermore, for a task to tap the intermediate representations the listener constructs, it must also require the listener to produce a response closely tied in time to relevant stretches of the speech input. We have termed those tasks that tap into intermediate representations *on-line* tasks (Marslen-

Wilson and Tyler 1980; Tyler and Marslen-Wilson 1982) and those that tap the properties of the final representation *off-line* tasks.

A number of tasks, such as associative priming, word monitoring and lexical decision—if used appropriately—can satisfy the requirement of implicitly tapping mental representations. For example, the word-monitoring task becomes an implicit measure of language function when the monitoring target word occurs immediately *after* the relevant stimulus, so that the listener's awareness of the properties of the target is not at issue. Rather, we are interested in how monitoring latencies to the target word are affected by what has been heard prior to that word. For example, in the sentence,

> Sally couldn't believe that John used so much butter. He was the most *wastage* COOK she had ever met.

the target word *cook* occurs after the derived word *wastage*. It is processing of the derived word that we are actually interested in. We measure the ease with which listeners process this word with respect to the previous context by obtaining monitoring latencies to the following word *cook*. Using the word-monitoring task in this way provides an implicit measure of language processing. If instead we had been interested in the subject's processing of the target word *cook*, then the task would not be implicit.

The gating task (Grosjean 1980; Tyler and Wessels 1983, 1985) does not provide an implicit measure of processing in the same way as the word-monitoring task. We ask subjects to listen to fragments of a word and say what word they think they're hearing. We assume that the words subjects produce under these circumstances reflect the set of words that are automatically activated whenever the subject hears a speech stimulus. In this sense, the task taps into intermediate representations.[2] The fact that in the gating task subjects produce a word in response to a fragment of speech input has led some people to argue that it does not tap into automatic, nonconscious processes and representations. I disagree with this for the following reasons. First, since it is possible to answer a question without having prior consciousness of the answer (Marcel 1988), it may, in the same way, be possible for listeners to produce a response in the gating task without prior awareness of the word. Second, as Marslen-Wilson (1985) has claimed to account for the behavior of close shadowers, the process of initiating a spoken response does not have to to be a conscious activity. In gating, it is very often the case that the word just seems to "pop out" in response to a fragment of speech.

However, given that subjects typically have time to reflect on their word choice (but see Tyler and Wessels 1985 for a fast, timed version of the gating task), there is a metalinguistic component in the task. Subjects can, in principle, read their response off the "top layer" representation. Therefore, the task cannot be taken as an uncontaminated reflection of intermediate representations.

An on-line task can satisfy the requirement of a close temporal relationship between speech stimulus and response in one of two ways—either by requiring the listener to produce a fast response immediately after the critical part of the stimulus has been heard (as in the word-monitoring task) or by stopping the input at a specified point and requiring the listener to make a response on the basis of partial information (as in the gating task). The more time that is allowed to elapse between stimulus and response (either because subjects are given plenty of time to respond, or because the word that they have to respond to occurs a long time after the relevant stretch of speech input has been heard), then the more plausible it is that the response will be affected by those aspects of the representation of which they can become aware.

The word-monitoring task, as I use it in the studies reported in this book, is a typical example of the way an on-line task can be used to tap into interim linguistic representations. It does so by measuring processing difficulty. We typically place the target word the subject is listening for *immediately* after one or other type of linguistic violation. If monitoring latencies are longer than to when there is no disruption, this means that the information must have been available and necessary for the listener to develop the appropriate representations. Thus, elevated reaction times suggest that constructing the appropriate linguistic representation is made more difficult when that particular type of linguistic information is disrupted in some way. By introducing different types of linguistic violations and seeing under what conditions latencies increase, we can make inferences about the kinds of information a listener uses to interpret an utterance, and when these different kinds of information become available during the comprehension process.

In the monitoring task, there is also a close temporal relationship between the speech stimulus and the subject's response. This is achieved by eliciting a fast reaction time in response to a target word. In gating, the close temporal relationship is achieved by presenting fragments of each word so that the listener's response is determined by a specific stretch of speech input, and in monitoring by eliciting a fast reaction time in response to a target word. In both cases, the listener's response cannot be affected by anything downstream of the stimulus. In this way, the experimenter can relate quite precisely the properties of the stimulus to the subject's response.

A number of other tasks typically used in psycholinguistic experiments fall into the on-line category. Tasks such as cross-modal naming (as used by Tyler and Marslen-Wilson 1977), cross-modal lexical decision (as used by Swinney 1979; Seidenberg et al. 1982), and phoneme monitoring (laying aside for the moment the inherent problems associated with this task) as used by Foss and Gernsbacher (1983) are implicit measures of processing. In addition, in all cases, the word the subject responds to is closely related temporally to the linguistic variable(s) of interest, and therefore the tasks are tapping intermediate representations rather than the final representation.

We can contrast these types of on-line task with off-line tasks. In general, off-line tasks share three characteristics. First of all, they rarely attempt to tie the response to particular aspects of the speech stimulus. This means that it is often impossible to be sure that the listener's response is determined solely by the linguistic variables one is interested in. Take, as an example, the sentence–picture matching task. Here, subjects are presented with a sentence (either spoken or written) and a set of pictures. Their task is to match the sentence to the appropriate picture. Since they are under no time pressure to respond, other, nonlinguistic variables may also affect performance (cf. Black, Nichols, and Byng 1991). Second, all off-line tasks require the listener to be aware, in some way, of the utterance they have heard; they are all explicit measures of language comprehension. Third, they invariably access the final linguistic representation the listener constructs.

There has never been a systematic attempt to classify tasks according to the extent to which nonconscious and metalinguistic components are involved, although it is crucially necessary given the fact that some patients show comprehension deficits only when tested on tasks which require a significant degree of conscious awareness (Tyler 1988; chapters 16 and 17). Tasks like associative priming and word monitoring (where the monitoring target word occurs after the relevant stimulus and so the listener's awareness of the properties of the target is not what is being measured) are likely to have a minimal metalinguistic component, whereas tasks like anomaly detection, grammaticality judgments, and acting out all heavily involve metalinguistic awareness.

Perhaps one of the surprising things about research into disorders of language comprehension is the extent to which it relies almost exclusively on data from off-line tasks. This means that much of the data on aphasic deficits are restricted to telling us about those aspects of representations the patient can explicitly reflect on. They are unable to tell us about those representations of which the patient is unaware. And yet these, as we have argued elsewhere (e.g., Marslen-Wilson and Tyler 1987), form the core of the comprehension system. To study only those aspects of linguistic representations of which the listener is aware undoubtedly gives a distorted view of aphasic deficits (see Tyler 1988).

Experimental tasks that are used to explicitly tap linguistic representations in aphasic patients do not form a homogenous set. Tasks vary in a number of ways. I will focus here on how they differ with respect to conscious awareness. I believe that, in this respect, the tasks commonly used to test for comprehension deficits in aphasic patients fall into two broad categories.

First, there are tasks such as *sentence–picture matching* and *acting out*, where the final product of the intermediate processes and representations can become available to conscious reflection when the task demands it. The point is that the listener has some degree of control over this. He or she can in some sense decide whether or not to reflect on the representation in order to carry out the task. This is the more traditional kind of conscious awareness which has been discussed in terms of "a mechanism of limited capacity which may be directed toward different types of activity" (Posner and Snyder 1975).

Second, there are explicit tasks that are based on the patient's awareness that a linguistic procedure has not successfully run through its operations. The best example of this is *grammaticality-judgments*, where the listener hears an utterance and has to say whether it is a grammatical/acceptable sentence of his or her native language. In this task, when there is an error in the operations of a procedure, this information percolates automatically to the listener's awareness. The subject has no control over whether to be aware that an error has occurred.[3] If it is indeed the case that errors in the operation of an automatic process automatically become available to consciousness, then the grammaticality-judgment task potentially offers more insight into the nature of intermediate linguistic representations than tasks such as sentence–picture matching and acting out. Errors arise from the breakdown of processes and the resulting inability to construct intermediate representations. To the extent that subjects can accurately reflect on the nature of the error, then the task can reveal something about the properties of intermediate representations. However, this potential may be obscured by the processes involved in deciding whether an error has occurred, and the time intervening between the occurrence of an error and the judgment response.

Let me elaborate on the differences between these two types of tasks in more detail. The normal processes that translate the speech input into a meaningful representation are obligatory. They operate in a particular and fixed way on the speech input. When these processes run through normally, we are not aware either of them or of their intermediate products. However, when they cannot—because there is some kind of error in the input which does not permit the normal procedure to run successfully—then the listener becomes aware of his or her inability to construct the correct representations. This does not mean that the listener necessarily knows what type of error has occurred, but only that the normal process has not been successful. The grammaticality-judgment task is of this type. The listener can make the correct judgment on the basis of being aware that "something has gone wrong"—that is, a procedure has not been able to run through its normal operations. This is a very different task from those such as sentence–picture matching and acting out in that the listener has no voluntary control over whether he or she will become aware of the error.

These two types of tasks elicit different kinds of awareness on the part of the listener. In both cases, the listener becomes aware of linguistic representations, but the way in which he or she does so differs. In this book, I am primarily interested in exploring deficits in the nonconscious processes involved in language comprehension, but in two chapters (9 and 12) I also report judgments made on the same materials. This enables us to evaluate the evidence with respect to the distinction between implicitly and explicitly accessed linguistic knowledge. Moreover, we also find evidence in support of the distinction between different kinds of conscious awareness.

Finally, experimental tasks also vary in the *cognitive demands* they place on the subject, in the extent to which his or her response depends largely on general cognitive processes rather than linguistic ones. The Token Test clearly falls into this category. There is a large nonlinguistic problem-solving component to this task, although this has never been systematically investigated. When a patient performs badly on this task, we cannot be confident that poor performance is due purely to problems with linguistic processes and representations.

Other tasks, such as various types of matching tasks and acting-out tasks also suffer in this respect. For example, it has been claimed that the acting-out task, which is frequently used to study language deficits, runs the risk of seriously underestimating performance because it involves a number of different cognitive components. This concern about the testing of adult aphasics using the acting-out task is supported by recent work using this task with young children. Crain (1982; Gorrell, Crain, and Fodor 1989) has found that standard use of the acting-out task did not accurately reflect the syntactic knowledge that young children have. He claimed that this was because the task not only measured linguistic knowledge, but also placed various unspecified cognitive demands on the subject. This means that people can perform badly on the task for a number of reasons, and not only because they are unable to comprehend a particular linguistic structure. It seems that the acting-out task is not good for trying to determine the extent to which brain damage affects a particular aspect of the language-comprehension process. Although the extent to which a task requires general cognitive, as opposed to linguistic, processes is an important issue, it is rarely taken into account when considering the appropriateness of a task for asking questions about language comprehension deficits in aphasics. I do not want to give the impression that such tasks are completely without value; if a patient can act out or match certain types of grammatical constructions but not others, then this can tell us something about the nature of the deficit. The difficulty lies in being able to identify the specific processes and representations that are impaired.

In contrast, then, to most research in aphasia, the research on the spoken-language-comprehension deficits I describe in this book focuses primarily on the ways in which the nonconscious processes and representations involved in the immediate, on-line analysis of spoken language are impaired in aphasic patients. Using on-line tasks, we hope to reduce the possibility that a patient's performance is contaminated by compensatory and adaptive strategies (cf. Caplan 1987).

Processing Profiles

Together with a variety of colleagues over the years (Paul Warren, Susan Behrens, and William Marslen-Wilson), we have developed a set of experimental tests designed to detect specific deficits in the principal categories of real-time spoken-language comprehension—acoustic-phonetic, lexical, syntactic, semantic, and prosodic. These tests all use experimental paradigms that tap the processes involved in constructing various types of representations of the speech input. These paradigms have been extensively used with normal listeners and have been modified so as to be appropriate for aphasic patients. For some of our tests, we also collect off-line data, using different versions of the grammaticality judgment task. This allows us to compare performance on on-line and off-line tasks for the same set of experimental materials.

Taken together, the results of these tests form a *processing profile* for each aphasic patient. Each processing profile provides a detailed picture of a particular patient's ability to perform all the appropriate on-line analyses on the speech input—analysing the speech signal, using the speech input to make contact with the appropriate lexical representations, making available the syntactic and semantic properties of words, and constructing the appropriate types of higher-level (syntactic, semantic, pragmatic, prosodic) representations. In addition, the processing profile also includes a comprehensive set of probes into the nature of the final representation the patient is able to construct of the speech input.

The advantage of the processing profile is that it provides a detailed picture both of where the patient performs normally and of where his or her performance is disrupted. This is invaluable if we wish to know what the limits of the patient's deficit are. Take, for example, the case of a patient who is tested only for her ability to process morphologically complex words. If this patient shows a selective deficit for the syntactic aspects of complex words but is not tested for her ability to process other aspects of syntax, then we do not know whether her problems with morphologically complex words are due to some general problem with syntax or confined to a particular aspect of complex words. To be able to understand the nature of any aphasic deficit, we need to know how a patient performs on a range of tests of various aspects of comprehension and build a detailed picture of what is preserved and what is impaired.

In summary, then, the particular approach we take to the study of language-comprehension deficits allows us to gain more direct access to the mental processes and representations involved in understanding spoken language. This in turn allows us to build a picture of the processing performance of an individual patient, going from the initial analyses of the sensory signal right up to the process of interpreting an utterance in its discourse context. To be successful, this research needs to be firmly rooted in a detailed model of normal language comprehension, which specifies the entire range of processes and representations involved in spoken-language comprehension. At present, no such model is available. But, as I have argued above, the cohort model of spoken-language comprehension offers a sufficiently well developed account of a number of the basic properties of the language comprehension system to enable us to use that model as our framework for studying aphasic deficits.

Within this framework we can ask the following basic questions about each patient's comprehension deficit. First, what specific aspect of the processing system is functioning abnormally? Developing a processing profile for each patient allows us to pinpoint where, in the sequence of processing operations involved in spoken-language comprehension, the patient's performance breaks down. We can, for example, determine whether a patient's comprehension deficit is due to some specific problem with the lexicon, and, if so, whether it is due to an inability to access either the appropriate phonological form of a word or its semantic and/or syntactic content. If the access process is unimpaired, then the patient may be having problems integrating lexical content into the developing representation of the utterance.

Second, the methodologies we use are better suited than conventional aphasia-testing methods to determine whether a patient's deficit is due to a *loss* of stored information or to some difficulty with the *access* of this information. So, for example, the question of whether "anomia" is due to a loss of the appropriate lexical representation or to an inability to access it can be illuminated using the gating task. If a patient can produce appropriate words in response to a fragment of the word, then we know that the phonological representation for that word is not lost and that the problem lies in the patient's inability to access the form appropriately in other contexts.[4]

Third, we can determine whether a patient's comprehension deficit is due to a breakdown in the nonconscious processes and representations underlying the real-time analysis of a spoken utterance, or in the ability to reflect consciously on the final, top-level representation. We can do this by comparing performance on tasks which tap on-line processes with those which tap conscious processes.

Fourth, if a patient has not lost the relevant representation and if access is unimpaired, our approach enables us to find out whether the problem lies instead in an inability to *use* particular types of information to build representations or to integrate the products of different types of analysis.

Finally, if one aspect of the patient's processing system is selectively impaired, we can examine the implications this has for the rest of the processing system. We can determine whether the impaired system compensates for the deficit and, if so, how.

This psycholinguistic approach to the study of aphasic deficits depends on in-depth, detailed analyses of individual patients, as opposed to carrying out experiments on a group of patients who have been categorized as falling into the same aphasic category. The approach runs the risk of encountering extreme variability between patients. Patients who one might assume, on the basis of standard tests, to have similar comprehension problems often look very different when their comprehension deficits are probed in detail. How can we interpret this variability? How can we tell which aspects of the variability are due to chance co-occurrence of symptoms and which result from the same functional deficit?

Brain lesions are rarely so specific that they produce only a single functional deficit. Typically they produce a cluster of deficits. Two patients may thus have some functional deficits in common, and some not. The important issue is to determine which symptoms co-occur by chance and which are due to the same underlying deficit. Probably the only way we can do this is to assume that if two symptoms co-occur by chance there will be considerable variation between patients. It is only those symptoms that co-occur because they are functionally related that should be reliably observed across patients (Caplan 1987). The detailed analyses of patients' comprehension deficits that I describe in this book enable us to see which patterns of co-occurrences of deficits are reliable and which vary across patients.

Structure of the Book

This book does not aim to present an exhaustive list of the studies that could be done and need to be done so that we can understand the functional basis of various types of comprehension disorders. My purpose in writing the book is more modest. I attempt to show how a particular kind of model of spoken-language comprehension in the unimpaired adult—a model that attempts to capture some of the important characteristics of spoken-language comprehension—can be used to ask a different kind of question about language disorders. My hope is that, because the model specifies the processes involved in constructing intermediate representations, it can be used to guide the kinds of questions we ask about aphasic disorders. In so doing, we can focus on an important but neglected aspect of the comprehension process: How the processes involved in the immediate construction of various types of linguistic representations break down in acquired aphasia.

The book consists of 17 chapters organized into seven parts. The first part contains three chapters, this introduction being the first. Chapter 2 summarizes the studies which are described in detail in chapters 3–14. It is intended to provide a reference point for the reader. It gives a concise description of what each study tests, how it does so (the methodology used), and the way in which unimpaired subjects perform on the test. The purpose of the chapter is to provide an overview of the research so that readers can find their way around the book and select those studies they want to read about in greater detail in subsequent chapters. Chapter 3 gives general background information on the 13 patients we have tested in depth over the years.

Parts 2, 3, 4, and 5 each contain chapters describing studies that deal with different aspects of spoken language comprehension. Each chapter contains a considerable amount of methodological and statistical detail. I have included information about how the materials for each study were selected, the criteria employed, the pre-tests carried out, and the data analyses on all the control groups and the patients. My intention is to provide sufficient detail about the methodology and the subjects (both control subjects and patients) that the book can be used as a handbook, enabling readers to select those studies that are appropriate for asking questions about the nature of comprehension deficits in their own patients.

The actual sequence of chapters follows, in a general way, the sequence of events involved in processing a spoken utterance, from initial access of lexical representations to the final stages of interpretation. I use the word "sequence" in its loosest sense here. I do not intend to suggest that the language-comprehension system is organized so that there is a great deal of serial processing in the system. Quite the contrary. There is considerable evidence in support of massive parallelism. But, obviously, some types of processes must precede others. For example, the form representation of a word must be contacted before its semantic and syntactic content can be activated.

Part 2 contains five chapters, each of which describes a study designed to test whether the initial phases of lexical processing—the access of the phonological form of a word—are impaired. These studies test whether a

patient can use the sensory input to contact the appropriate form representation of either a morphologically simple (chapters 4 and 5) or complex
(chapters 6, 7, and 8) word. The experiments described in Section 3 (chapter
9) investigate the next phase of the process: the access of lexical content.
Lexical content is defined as the semantic and syntactic properties of
a word's specification in the mental lexicon. In this chapter a patient's
ability to use this kind of information to construct representations is contrasted with the same patient's ability to reflect consciously on those
representations.

Two studies testing whether patients are able to construct higher-level
representations are described in part 4. The first study (chapter 10) evaluates
whether patients can construct global representations of the syntactic and
semantic properties of an utterance, and chapter 11 describes an experiment
that assesses whether they use various types of processing information
(syntactic, semantic, and prosodic) to construct local structures such as noun
phrases and prepositional phrases that are semantically, syntactically, and
prosodically coherent. Testing for a patient's ability to use prosodic information is particularly important when we are discussing spoken, as opposed
to written, language comprehension.

Because many patients have difficulty in processing morphologically
complex words, I have included a series of tests designed to explore various
aspects of the processing of such words. Chapters 6, 7, and 8 in part 2
establish whether a patient can map the sensory input onto the appropriate
phonological form of a morphologically complex word. The studies described in part 5 all deal with issues related to the access of the semantic
and syntactic properties of complex words. These studies explore the
processing of morphologically complex words when they appear in various
types of sentential contexts. The first chapter in this section describes a
general test of a patient's ability to process inflected and derived words in
context. If a patient has problems with either inflected or derived words,
the reason for his or her problem can be investigated in greater detail by
testing the patient on the studies reported in chapters 13–15. Chapters 13
and 14 deal with the processing of inflected words. In these studies we try
to tease apart the syntactic (chapter 13) and semantic (chapter 14) implications of inflected words in order to see whether a patient has problems with
one or other type of information. If a patient has problems with both
inflected and derived words, we need to be sure that the patient doesn't
have some general difficulty with word endings. Chapter 15 describes a
study that tests for a generalized deficit in the ability to process word
endings that are not either inflectional or derivational but occur in morphologically simple words.

Although the research described in this book is mainly concerned with
the processes involved in the immediate construction of intermediate repre-

sentations of the speech input, we are also interested in those patients who show a contrast between performance on tests that tap these on-line processes and on those that tap off-line, metalinguistic processes. Two chapters present data from on-line and off-line tasks, using the same experimental stimuli (chapters 9 and 12). This allows us to contrast a patient's ability to construct various types of linguistic representations with his or her ability to reflect consciously on those representations.

Chapter 16 gives examples of two detailed processing profiles: one of a nonfluent patient (BN) and the other of a fluent patient (RH) and eight summary profiles. Concluding comments are given in chapter 17. Finally, Appendix A gives general background information about the control subjects, and Appendix B gives some methodological information about the word monitoring task.

Terminology

Throughout the book I occasionally label patients with the classification they received on the basis of standard tests. I provide these labels purely as an aid to those readers who find them useful. I wish at the outset to make it clear that I do not myself subscribe to the view that these labels describe (or explain) the nature of the patient's deficit. In fact, it should become clear throughout this book that patients who are classified according to standard tests as being members of the same aphasic category have very different comprehension deficits. This is one of the points I discuss at length in chapter 17.

Chapter 2

Overview and Summary of Processing-Profile Experiments

This chapter consists of a summary of each of the experiments described in detail in parts 2, 3, 4, and 5. The aim is to enable readers to review briefly the entire set of studies described in the book and select those of special interest to read about in greater detail in the relevant chapter.

I begin each part with a general overview placing the set of studies within that section in their wider context. I then summarize the motivation for each individual study, the materials and methodology used, and the results from control subjects. The organization of the sections follows, in a general way, the sequence of events involved in spoken-language comprehension. The studies described in part 2 attempt to tap the processes involved in the initial phases of the comprehension process—the access of the phonological form of a word. We need to establish that these processes are unimpaired before examining deficits at later stages of the comprehension process. The studies in this section involve both morphologically simple and complex words.

If a patient has no difficulty mapping the sensory input onto representations of the phonological form of a word, the next question is whether the patient is able to access the word's syntactic and semantic content (part 3). Successful access of these properties in the on-line processing of spoken language is tested for in chapter 9. In the same chapter I also describe two types of acceptability judgment on the same materials. This is followed by part 4, which outlines two tests of a patient's ability to construct different types of higher-level representations. Finally, in part 5, I describe three studies that examine a patient's ability to process different aspects of morphologically complex words and integrate them into the higher-level sentential context. The last study involves distortions at the end of morphologically simple words, which acts as a control condition for the morphology experiments in that section.

Part II   The Access of Lexical Form

Morphologically Simple Words

To understand spoken language, listeners first have to use the sensory input to make contact with representations of lexical form (i.e., the phonological forms of words). It is only when this process of lexical access is achieved that the syntactic and semantic properties of words become available for the construction of a higher-level representation of the utterance. The first question we need to ask of aphasic patients is whether they have any problem with the initial phases of analysing the sensory input for the purpose of accessing lexical form. We need to establish that this process is unimpaired before going on to determine whether there are problems elsewhere in the system.

One important factor that needs to be taken into account when asking this question concerns the morphological structure of the words the patient is hearing. In English, all open-class words (nouns, verbs, and adjectives) can have a morphological structure of greater or lesser complexity, due to the addition of one or more affixes—e.g., *jump/jumping; manage/management*. Because many aphasic patients have particular difficulty producing morphologically complex words, it is important to determine whether the access process is impaired for both morphologically simple and morphologically complex words.

The way in which the lexical mapping process is conceived of in our model is as follows. In the process of recognizing a word, the speech signal is continuously projected onto representations of lexical form. At the beginning of a word, this means that the sensory input will activate all of the words which share the same initial sound sequence. So, for example, the sequence *bla..* will activate all of the words the listener knows beginning with that sequence (*black, bland, blanket*, etc.). This set of activated words gradually decreases in size as more and more of them fail to match the accumulating sensory input. This process of attrition continues until only a single activated word matches the sensory input. It is at this point of separation from all other activated candidates (that is, the word's set of competitors)—which is the first possible point at which a word can be confidently identified—that a listener first recognizes the word. It is in this sense that the lexical mapping process can be thought to be highly efficient. Numerous studies with normal listeners have provided evidence for this model (Marslen-Wilson and Welsh 1978; Marslen-Wilson 1987; Tyler 1983).

This model provides a useful framework for establishing whether patients have any problems with the initial analysis of the sensory input. First, can a patient use the sensory input to identify the individual speech sounds in words correctly? Second, does the patient recognize a word at the point at which it separates from all other words? If the answer is yes to both of these questions, then we can be confident that a patient does not have problems with this early analysis process.

Chapter 4: Identifying Speech Sounds: Phoneme Discrimination Test

Motivation
The phoneme-discrimination test evaluates a patient's ability to identify speech sounds correctly. Previous research on phoneme discrimination has tended to use non-words or nonsense syllables because this is seen as a "pure" test of phonemic processing. Because our interest was in how the speech input makes contact with lexical representations, we examined various phonological contrasts as they occur in naturally produced real words. Our test included a wide set of single-feature contrasts occurring in different positions in a word, in order to provide a comprehensive test of the patient's ability to discriminate phonemes in different contexts. It was short enough to be administered to the patient in a single session. The test consisted of word-pairs that were either the same or different. The "different" pairs involved a single-feature change. We used both consonant and vowel contrasts (although consonants are standardly tested in aphasia research, vowel contrasts are usually ignored). We also varied the position in the word of the consonant contrasts. They were presented in both word-initial and word-final position. We did this because the phonetic realizations of word-initial and word-final phonemes differ, and this may lead to differences in discriminability, depending upon the exact location of a phoneme within a word.

Stimuli and Method
The test used 204 word-pairs. We varied place of articulation and voicing for a set of plosive and fricative contrasts. The unvoiced plosives and fricatives test for the effects of hearing loss (which is usually confined to the high frequencies), since the discriminability of these phonemes relies upon sensitivity to high-frequency information. We also varied place of articulation for a set of nasals. The vowel contrasts included most of the English vowels. They varied along both front-back and height dimensions. After hearing each word-pair, subjects judged whether they were the same. The percentage of correct responses establishes the extent to which a patient can correctly discriminate different kinds of phonemes in different lexical contexts.

Control Results
Unimpaired listeners have no difficulty performing this task with a high level of accuracy. Moreover, the task is sensitive to high frequency hearing

loss; subjects with significant degrees of hearing loss find phonemes carrying high-frequency information difficult to discriminate.

Chapter 5: Recognizing Words from Fragments

Motivation
One important characteristic of the way in which neurologically unimpaired
listeners process spoken words is their ability to recognize a word at the
point at which it separates from all other candidates (these are referred to
as the "competitors" of the test word). This may be well before the end of
the word, especially for words of more than one syllable. One way of
determining whether aphasic patients are able to process the speech input
in the same way is to determine empirically the point at which they
recognize a spoken word and compare this to the point at which normal
listeners recognize it. We can do this by means of the gating task (Grosjean
1980; Tyler and Wessels 1983, 1985; Tyler 1984).

   In the gating task, subjects hear an initial fragment of a word (e.g., the
initial *gr...* of the word *grumble*) and try to determine what word they think
they are hearing. They hear progressively longer fragments of the word,
(e.g. *gru..*, *grum...*, *grumble.*) producing a response to each fragment, until
they have heard the whole word. By asking subjects to respond after each
successive fragment, we can build up a picture of the way in which the
sensory input is mapped onto lexical representations over time. This allows
us to determine directly the amount of the word that needs to be heard
before it can be recognized. This task is useful, then, for assessing the way
in which the sensory input is mapped onto the appropriate lexical representations, and the point at which a word can be correctly identified.

Stimuli and Method
We used 24 polysyllabic monomorphemic words. Half of the words separated from their competitors early in the word, and half late. We varied the
concreteness/abstractness of the word and its form-class. Each word was
divided into increasingly larger fragments, starting from the beginning of
the word. Each fragment increased in duration by 50 msec. One fragment
at a time was presented to subjects who, after hearing it, said what word
they thought they were hearing.

Control Results
Neurologically unimpaired listeners process the speech input efficiently in
the sense that they need less sensory input to recognize a word with an
early separation point compared to one which has a late separation point.
If an aphasic patient shows the same pattern, then we can be confident that
he or she is mapping the sensory input onto lexical representations in the
same way as normal listeners.

Morphologically Complex Words

In English, words become morphologically complex when affixes are added to word-stems. These affixes can be either derivational or inflectional. English inflectional morphology has a primarily grammatical function. It includes, for example, suffixes that mark tense and number on verbs (as in *struggle/ struggling/ struggles*), suffixes that mark plural on nouns (e.g., *shoe/ shoes*) and comparative suffixes attached to adjectives (*dirty/dirtier/dirtiest*). It can, however, also have a semantic function in the sense that it can mark time and reference. Derivational morphemes, in contrast, function primarily to alter the meaning of the base-forms to which they are attached—as in *manage/management, nation/nationhood, paint/repaint*. English derivational morphology includes both prefixes (such as *re-, ex-, pre-*) and suffixes (such as *-ment, -ness, -ence*), whereas the inflectional morphology is confined to suffixes (such as *-ed, -s, -est*).

Chapter 6: Recognizing Words from Fragments: Morphologically Complex Words

Motivation
Many patients have difficulty in comprehending morphologically complex words, especially inflected words (Miceli and Caramazza 1987; Goodglass and Berko 1960). In order to locate the basis for these difficulties, we first have to determine whether the initial process of mapping the sensory input onto morphologically complex form-based representations is itself unimpaired. For words occurring in isolation, this means establishing that complex words are recognized at the point at which they separate from other words in the language. We can do this by using the gating task, as in the study described in chapter 5.

Stimuli and Method
The stimuli consisted of six derived words (e.g., *childish*), six inflected words (e.g., *planting*) and six morphologically simple words (e.g., *table*) for comparative purposes. All words were bisyllabic. We used the gating task to estimate the point at which each suffixed word was correctly identified (see chapter 5).

Control Results
Unimpaired subjects map the sensory input onto morphologically complex words so as to identify such words at the point at which they separate from the other words in the language. For a word like *breakable*, this means that it is identified as the second [b] is heard. This is the point at which it separates from words like *breakage*. If patients can access the phonological

form of a complex word in a normal manner, then they should show the same pattern of results.

Chapter 7: Auditory Lexical Decision for Suffixed Words

Motivation

Another way of determining whether the form mapping process is unimpaired is to see whether patients can accurately distinguish between morphologically complex real words and non-words that are composed of an illegal combination of a real stem and affix (e.g., *manage + ly*).

Stimuli and Method

We used 74 real-word test items—21 derived forms, 24 inflected forms, and 29 morphologically simple words. The morphologically complex real words were made into non-words by illegally combining a real stem and a real suffix (e.g., *wastely*). The morphologically simple words were made into non-words by changing the last syllable (e.g., *nylon* became *nylup*). The real word and non-word versions of each item appeared in different experimental lists.

We used an untimed version of the auditory lexical decision task in which subjects hear a list of words and non-words and after each item say "yes" if the sequence is a real word and "no" if it is not. The proportion correct tells us the extent to which the processes involved in accessing the form of a morphologically complex word are intact.

Control Results

Control subjects were very accurate. They correctly rejected almost all of the non-words and accepted the real words. Complex words did not pose any special problems. If patients cannot contact the appropriate form representation of a suffixed word, they will tend to confuse real words and non-words. Their performance on the two sets of suffixed words will tell us whether a patient has greater problems with one type of word rather than the other.

Chapter 8: Auditory Lexical Decision for Prefixed Words

Motivation

This study is the same as the one above, except that it used prefixed rather than suffixed words. We developed this study because patients may have problems with one type of complex word rather than the other and therefore a test of both is needed. We varied the semantic transparency of the prefix in relation to the stem so that the relationship between the prefix and its stem was either opaque (e.g., *invest*) or transparent (e.g., *rebuild*). This was in case a patient had more or less difficulty discriminating a prefixed word from a non-word as a function of the semantic relationship between the stem and the prefix.

Stimuli and Method
We used 200 test items—100 non-words and 100 real words. Half of the real words were morphologically simple and half contained a derivational prefix. We also varied the semantic transparency/opacity of the stem and prefix. As in the study described in chapter 7, we used an untimed auditory lexical decision task.

Control Results
Unimpaired listeners have no difficulty with this task and are very accurate. Moreover, their level of accuracy does not vary as a function of the semantic transparency/opacity of the stem and prefix.

Part III   Accessing Lexical Content

If we establish that a patient's comprehension deficit does not stem from problems in accessing lexical form, the next question is whether the access of lexical content is unimpaired. By lexical content, we mean the syntactic and semantic properties of a word that are stored as part of the specification of that word in the mental lexicon.

Chapter 9: Verb-Argument Structures

Motivation
We can ask whether a patient can access the syntactic and semantic properties of words by focusing on the processing of verbs. The representation of verbs includes both syntactic and semantic information, each of which constrain the possible arguments which a verb can take. One major type of syntactic constraint on possible verb-argument structures (subcategorization constraints) involves restrictions on whether the verb can be followed either by a noun phrase, by an adjectival phrase, or by nothing (in its intransitive use). A verb's lexical entry also specifies the semantic properties of permissible arguments. This type of selectional rule includes information such as [+ Animate] or [+ Abstract].

We can contrast subcategorization and selectional constraints, which we can assume to be lexically coded, with a different type of constraint on verb-argument structures—namely, pragmatic constraints. Pragmatic information is assumed to involve a process of interpreting information that is lexically represented with respect to real-world knowledge. This contrast between what we can reasonably assume to be lexically represented (selection restrictions and subcategorization information) and what must be inferred from lexically represented knowledge (pragmatic information) provides an interesting set of contrasts for examining the ability of aphasic patients to access and use different types of information associated in different ways with lexical representations.

A number of experiments with normal listeners show that all three types of information have an immediate effect on constraining the argument structure of a verb (Marslen-Wilson, Brown, and Tyler 1988; Tyler 1985; 1988).

Stimuli and Method
The experimental stimuli consisted of sets of sentences where each sentence contained an object noun preceded by a verb (italicized in the examples). The relationship between the verb and its argument noun was either normal, as in

(i)   The crowd was waiting eagerly. The young man *grabbed the guitar* and ...

or the noun violated pragmatic constraints, as in

(ii)   The crowd was waiting eagerly. The young man *buried the guitar* and ...

or it violated selectional restriction constraints, established by the verb, as in

(iii)   The crowd was waiting eagerly. The young man *drank the guitar* and ...

or it violated subcategory constraints, as in

(iv)   The crowd was waiting eagerly. The young man *slept the guitar* and ...

The violation was always caused by the verb stem alone. The inflection was always appropriate for the prior context. This contrasts with the morphology experiments (chapters 11–13) where the verb stem is appropriate for the context and the suffix is not. We used three different tasks with these materials:

The Word-Monitoring Task   The subject monitors for a prespecified target word (always the noun following the test verb; *guitar* in the examples above) and presses a response key when he or she hears it. We contrast the subject's latency to respond to the target word when it occurs in an utterance containing some type of linguistic violation with the baseline condition (i), which contains no violation. If latencies are slower in an utterance containing a linguistic violation than in the baseline condition, we can argue that listeners must have been attempting to use the linguistic information in the disrupted utterance. If they had not been, then there would have been no reason for latencies to have increased when that particular type of linguistic information was disrupted. This task enables us to determine whether a patient can access and use different types of lexical information to immediately build the appropriate verb-argument structure. It also has the advantage of being simple to administer with patients.

End-of-Sentence Acceptability Judgment Task   In this task, the subject hears a spoken sentence and, when the sentence ends, the patient indicates whether or not it was grammatical and meaningful by saying "good" or "bad." This enables us to compare a patient's performance on an on-line and off-line task using the same experimental materials. Will there be any difference between performance on this type of task, which is standardly used to test aphasic patients, and performance on the word monitoring task? Are patients sensitive to the different types of anomaly, in the ways suggested by their latencies in the word-monitoring task?

Anomaly Detection Task   If patients have to wait until the end of a sentence before judging whether or not it is an acceptable sentence of English, their performance might be poor, not because they cannot make the correct judgment but because they cannot remember the sentence in sufficient detail. We can avoid this potential problem by having the patient make their judgment as soon as the violation is detected, rather than wait until the end of the sentence.

Control Results

Word-Monitoring   We measured the immediate consequences for verb-argument relations of various types of violation by looking at latencies to the target word, which always immediately followed the test verb. The time taken to respond to the target reveals whether the subject is able to access the syntactic and semantic properties of words and immediately use this information to constrain permissible verb-argument structures. It also reveals the extent to which subjects immediately interpret the speech input with respect to their knowledge of the world. For unimpaired listeners, when the target word occurs in a sentence where the verb-argument relations are normal, as in (i) above, latencies to respond to the target word (*guitar*) were faster than when verb-argument relations are violated either semantically, syntactically or pragmatically. Thus, any type of violation of verb-argument relations disrupts processing in normal listeners, and this results in longer reaction times in the word-monitoring task. This shows that listeners use all three types of information to constrain immediately their incremental interpretation of the utterance.

If an aphasic patient shows the same pattern, we can assume that he or she is able to access the appropriate type of information in the lexicon and use it to constrain verb-argument relations. If, however, the patient is unable to use a particular type of information, word-monitoring responses will not be disrupted over the baseline condition.

End-of-Sentence Acceptability Judgment Task   Normal listeners have no problems in performing this task with almost perfect accuracy for all types of verb-argument violation.

Anomaly Detection Task   Normal listeners detect all three types of violation without any difficulty.

Part IV   Constructing Higher-Level Representations

In the process of understanding spoken language, listeners have to construct a representation of each entire utterance they hear. We know from research on neurologically unimpaired listeners that this representation is constructed word-by-word as the utterance is heard, and that syntactic and semantic information is used both to construct local phrases and to construct a representation spanning an entire utterance (Marslen-Wilson and Tyler 1975, 1980; Tyler and Warren 1987).

Chapter 10: Global Sources of Processing Information

Motivation
The purpose of this study was to look at a patient's ability to construct global representations spanning an entire utterance. We modeled our study on earlier research by Marslen-Wilson and Tyler (1975, 1980) which tracked the availability of syntactic and semantic information as it accumulated over time across the entire course of a sentence. To do this, the experiments used the word-monitoring task and asked listeners to monitor for target words occurring at various word-positions across three different kinds of prose materials—normal sentences, anomalous sentences (where the syntactic structure was intact but the material was meaningless), and scrambled strings of words (where there was neither syntactic nor semantic structure). Varying the word-position of the target and the presence or absence of syntactic and semantic structure allowed us to track the availability of different kinds of processing information across an entire utterance.

    Marslen-Wilson and Tyler (1980) found that word-monitoring latencies to targets occurring in normal prose were consistently faster than those in anomalous prose which, in turn, were consistently faster than in scrambled strings. More important, they found that latencies got progressively faster with later target-word positions in both normal and anomalous prose sentences, but not in scrambled strings. They argued that this was because the global semantic and/or syntactic structure in normal and anomalous prose develops across the sentence and increasingly facilitates word identification.

This experiment was adapted for use with patients. It provides us with a general picture of a patient's ability to develop syntactic and semantic representations across an entire spoken utterance.

Stimuli and Method
We manipulated the availability of different types of processing information by presenting listeners with sentences which were either syntactically and semantically well-formed, as in

> (i)   Everyone was outraged when they heard. Apparently, in the middle of the night some thieves broke into the *church* and stole the crucifix.

or semantically anomalous but syntactically well formed, as in

> (ii)   Everyone was exposed when they ate. Apparently, at the distance of the wind some ants pushed around the *church* and forced an item.

or unstructured strings of words, as in

> (iii)   They everyone when outraged heard was. Of middle apparently the some the into the broke night in thieves *church* and crucifix stole the.

We also manipulated the position of the target word (*church* in the example above) in the sentence. It could occur toward the beginning, middle, or end of the sentence. Monitoring latencies to targets occurring in different word positions enables us to track the availability of syntactic and semantic information as it accumulates as more of the sentence is heard.

Control Results
For unimpaired listeners, latencies get progressively faster in normal (i) and anomalous (ii) prose as more of the sentence is heard. If a patient also shows faster latencies for later word-positions in both types of prose material, then we can conclude that he or she is able to use syntactic and semantic information in the process of interpreting an utterance. However, if latencies do not get faster in one or other type of prose, then we can argue that the patient is unable to use a particular type of information in comprehending an utterance. Unimpaired listeners also show overall faster monitoring RTs (response times) to normal prose compared to anomalous prose, which in turn is faster than scrambled strings. The overall difference in latencies between the three types of prose provides a measure of the general extent to which patients can use semantic and/or syntactic information as they comprehend a sentence.

Chapter 11: Local Sources of Processing Information

Motivation

Many patients are unable to develop a normal representation of a spoken utterance. In particular, we have found a number patients who do not show a word-position effect in anomalous prose (see previous study), indicating that they are not using syntactic information appropriately as they process an utterance. And yet these same patients invariably produce overall faster RTs to anomalous prose than to scrambled prose. For these patients, faster RTs in anomalous prose might be due to their residual ability to construct local phrases using the syntactic and prosodic information available in anomalous prose. This study is designed to determine whether a patient can construct local phrases using prosodic and syntactic information.

Stimuli and Method

To determine whether a patient has problems in organizing the speech input into prosodically and syntactically structured phrases, we use sentences that are structured into local units defined in terms of "phonological phrases" (Selkirk 1980; Nespor and Vogel 1982; Gee and Grosjean 1983). These are short phrases that have prosodic and syntactic coherence. By disrupting the internal prosodic and syntactic coherence of these phrases independently, we can determine whether the patient uses each type of linguistic structure in the process of interpreting an utterance.

To examine the patient's ability to use syntactic and prosodic structure independently of the meaning of the utterance, the materials consist of anomalous prose sentences that are meaningless but grammatically well formed. Each anomalous prose sentence is structured into phonological phrases (these are indicated by the slashed lines in the examples below). Each sentence contains a critical phonological phrase (italicized in the examples). The word which the patient has to monitor for is the final word (the "head") of a phonological phrase (in bold in the examples).

In one condition, the internal structure of the critical phonological phrase remains intact, as in

(1)   Anomalous Prose/ Undisrupted: An orange dream/ was loudly watching/ the house/during smelly lights/ because within these signs /*a slow* **kitchen**/ snored/with crashing leaves.

This constitutes the baseline condition, against which we evaluate the effect of the various disruptions. The first of these is the prosodic disruption condition. Here we disrupt the prosodic structure of the critical phonological phrase, while leaving syntactic structure undisturbed, as in

(2)   Anomalous Prose/ Prosodic disruption: An orange dream/ was loudly watching/ the house/ during smelly lights/ because within these signs/ *a slow //* **kitchen** *in mist*/ snored/ with crashing leaves.

The second type of disruption is a syntactic disruption, where we violate constraints on word order within the critical phonological phrase, as in

(3)   Anomalous Prose/ Syntactic disruption: An orange dream/ was loudly watching/ the house/ during smelly lights/ because within these signs/ *slow very* **kitchen** / snored/ with crashing leaves.

This leaves local prosody intact and allows us to measure the effect of disrupting local syntactic structure alone.

Control Results
For normal listeners, monitoring RTs to the target word are slowed down when either the syntactic or prosodic structure of the phonological phrase is disrupted. However, when the prosodic structure is disrupted, listeners' ability to process the utterance is much more severely disturbed than when the syntactic structure is disrupted. This shows that listeners do indeed use the prosodic structure of a spoken utterance in the process of comprehending it. We can use this test to determine whether a patient is able to use prosodic and syntactic information to structure the input into locally coherent structures in the same way.

Part V   Processing Morphologically Complex Words in Utterances

Many patients have difficulty in processing morphologically complex words, and much research effort has been devoted to explaining the nature of their deficit (Bradley 1978, Bradley, Garrett, and Zurif 1980, Miceli and Caramazza 1989). Patients' problems with morphologically complex words have figured prominently in theoretical accounts of particular types of aphasic deficits (see Goodglass and Menn 1985, Berndt 1987, Berndt and Caramazza 1980). However, there have been few systematic investigations of the various possible causes of this deficit. This is what we try to do with the following sequence of tests.

We first need to establish whether a patient with problems in the morphological domain has any difficulties in mapping the sensory input onto the appropriate form-based representations. This is evaluated in chapters 6, 7, and 8. If performance on these tests is normal, then we have to look elsewhere for our explanation. One possibility is that the patient is unable to access the syntactic and semantic properties of affixes in developing a meaningful representation of an utterance.

To evaluate this possibility, we need to see how the patient processes morphologically complex words in utterances. Because there was little existing research on this topic using either unimpaired or aphasic listeners, we developed from scratch a series of tests that probe different aspects of morphological processing. The first study (chapter 12) examines the processing of derived and inflected words in sentential contexts. This is a general test of the patient's abilities in this domain. The other studies explore specific aspects of the relationship between different types of morphologically complex words and the contexts in which they occur.

Chapters 13 and 14 probe more deeply into the processing of inflected words, and chapter 15 examines the patient's sensitivity to distortions of word-endings, where these distortions are not morphological (e.g., the non-word *syruff*, which is constructed from the real-word *syrup*). This test is particularly important if the patient fails to show any sensitivity to the morphological manipulations in any of the previous studies. We need to know whether such a patient is generally insensitive to the endings of words (whether suffixes or not) when they appear in context, or whether he or she has a selective impairment for morphological suffixes.

All the tests in this section use materials containing test words (either simple or complex words) that are disrupted in various ways. Each test word is followed by a target word for which the listener has to monitor. Monitoring RTs to the target word should increase if the listener is sensitive to the type of disruption initiated by the test word. This enables us to measure the extent to which a patient is immediately sensitive to the contextual appropriateness of derivational and inflectional suffixes and to deviations in word-endings in morphologically simple and complex sequences.

Chapter 12: Processing Derived and Inflected Words in Context

Motivation
The purpose of the study is to determine whether a patient can evaluate the contextual implications of derived and inflected words when they appear in sentence contexts.

Stimuli and Method
The test sentences contained a derived or inflected test word (*wasteful* and *causing* in the examples below). The stem of the word was always appropriate for the context, but the suffixed word varied with respect to its contextual appropriateness. It was either appropriate for the context, inappropriate for the context, or a non-word consisting of an illegal combination of a real stem and real suffix. This contrasts with the test words in chapter 9, where the stem was sometimes contextually inappropriate but the inflection was always appropriate. We used two different tasks on these stimuli. One was the word-monitoring task in which the subject always had to monitor for the word (noun or adjective) immediately following each suffixed test word

(*cook* in example 1 below). The second task we used was the end-of-sentence judgment task. An example set of sentences are:

Derivations:

(1.1)   Appropriate: Sarah could not understand why John used so much butter. He was the most *wasteful cook* she had ever met.

(1.2)   Inappropriate: Sarah could not understand why John used so much butter. He was the most *wastage cook* she had ever met.

(1.3)   Non-word: Sarah could not understand why John used so much butter. He was the most *wastely cook* she had ever met.

Inflections:

(2.1)   Appropriate: I have to be careful when eating ice-cream. It often *causes pain* in my loose filling.

(2.2)   Inappropriate: I have to be careful when eating ice-cream. It often *causing pain* in my loose filling.

(2.3)   Non-word: I have to be careful when eating ice-cream. It often *causely pain* in my loose filling.

Control Results

Word-Monitoring Task   For normal listeners, monitoring latencies are slower when the suffixed word is inappropriate for the context. Latencies are slowest of all when the target follows a non-word. This shows that listeners access the syntactic and semantic properties of a suffixed form and immediately use this information as they interpret an utterance. Moreover, the results for the derivational and inflectional items are the same. This suggests that the relationship between the prior context and the form of a suffixed word is similar for both derived and inflected words. If a patient's latencies do not increase when a suffixed word is contextually inappropriate, this is evidence that he or she is not sensitive to the contextual appropriateness of suffixed words.

Latencies in the non-word condition are particularly important if a patient's latencies in the appropriate and inappropriate conditions do not differ. This raises the question of whether the patient is processing the suffix. However, if latencies in the non-word condition are slowed down, this suggests that the suffix is being processed.

The results of this study also reveal whether or not a patient has selective problems with either derivational or inflectional morphology.

Finally, because the suffixed test words are the same suffixed words used in chapter 7, we are able to compare a patient's ability to process those words when they occur as isolated forms and when they occur in a normal sentential context.

End-of-Sentence Acceptability Judgment Task   Control subjects are very accurate in making the correct judgment for all types of stimuli. They show no differences between derived and inflected forms.

We can compare performance on these materials with those in chapter 8 where the inflected form is always contextually appropriate but the stem is sometimes inappropriate. If a patient shows sensitivity to the contextual appropriateness of stems but not of affixes, we can conclude that he or she has a selective deficit for the semantic and syntactic properties of affixes.

Chapter 13: Inflectional Morphemes as Syntactic Structural Devices

Motivation

The inflectional morphology is an aspect of language structure that is especially important to examine in detail because many aphasic patients show selective deficits in producing and/or comprehending inflectional morphemes. This is assumed to be due to the primarily syntactic role of inflectional morphemes, which are bound up with the syntactic organization of the utterance in which they appear. Unfortunately, there has been little explicit discussion, in either the linguistic or the psycholinguistic literature, about the actual processing role of bound morphemes in utterances. Consequently, we know very little about exactly how they might function in utterances. Therefore, before testing patients, we needed to obtain the appropriate normative data.

In this study we examined the way in which the inflectional morphology functions in particular syntactic contexts to determine the syntactic structure of the utterance. We asked whether inflectional morphemes immediately constrain the syntactic structure of the utterance in which they occur.

Stimuli and Method

The materials consisted of test sentences of the form: NP + V + NP. The second noun was always the target word which the subject had to monitor for. The test sentence was either presented in isolation, or it was preceded by a context sentence, as in:

> (i)   Eric spent hours sitting by his easel. He was *painting boats* down by the riverside.

The verb of interest (*painting* in the example above) was always inflected. The nature of the inflection constrained the syntactic structure of the sentence. When the inflection was the [-ing] form as above, the sentence had to be in the active voice. This, in turn, generated a structural preference for a noun phrase to follow. However, when the inflection was the [-ed] form as below, the sentence had to be in the passive voice. This prohibited a noun phrase as a legal continuation.

(ii)   Eric spent hours sitting by his easel. He was *painted boats* down by the riverside.

To evaluate the role of the suffix alone in determining the syntactic structure of the utterance, we had to take into account the potential structural preferences introduced by the number, gender, and animacy of the first NP in the test sentence as well as the syntactic and semantic properties of the verb stem. These also bias towards the active or passive reading and thus interact with the role of the suffix. To examine these biases, we distinguished three sentence types: where the combined biases of initial NP and verb stem are toward the active reading; where they are toward the passive reading; where they are neutral. This allows us to see whether the syntactic structural effect of the inflection is modulated at all by biases generated by the previous words in the test sentence.

Control Results
For normal listeners, RTs to the target word were faster when it followed an inflected verb requiring the active voice ([-ing]) rather than the passive voice ([-ed]). This means that the inflectional suffix can immediately constrain the syntactic structure of the utterance, and this is reflected in the appropriateness of the following noun. The appropriateness effect is not affected by the presence or absence of a context sentence ("Eric spent hours sitting by his easel" in the example above). The only effect which the discourse context has is to make it generally easier to identify the target word. The biases generated by the first NP and the verb stem had no effect on RTs. These were always faster to the target noun if it was consistent with the syntactic structure of the sentence as determined by the inflectional suffix. If a patient has problems exploiting the syntactic functional role of inflectional morphemes, then RTs should be unaffected by the structural constraints imposed by the verb inflection.

Chapter 14: Inflectional Morphemes as Anaphoric Devices

Motivation
Because the inflectional morphology marks tense, aspect, and number, it can serve an anaphoric or deictic role, maintaining time and reference within a discourse. Because this is very different from its syntactic role, we need to determine whether either or both are implicated in a patient's problems with the inflectional morphology. In this study, then, we examine the anaphoric role of the inflectional morphology. In particular, we look at the way in which tense markers are used in the on-line processing of an utterance.

Stimuli and Method
The test sentences contained a tensed verb. In half of the sentences the tense of the verb was consistent with the tense established by the prior

context, and in the other half it was inconsistent. The target word (*coats* in the example below) immediately followed the tensed verb. In the example below, the tense established by the context is consistent with that of the verb in (1). In (2) there is a mismatch between context tense and verb tense.

(1) Consistent tense: Ellen finds it incredibly boring working in the laundry. She sews on buttons and *patches coats* all day long.

(2) Inconsistent tense: Ellen finds it incredibly boring working in the laundry. She sews on buttons and *patched coats* all day long.

Control Results
For normal listeners, a mismatch between context and verb tense disrupts processing. This is reflected in longer RTs when the verb tense is inconsistent with the context tense. If a patient is insensitive to inflectional morphemes marking tense, then latencies will be unaffected by the mismatch between context and verb tense.

Chapter 15: Distortions at the Ends of Morphologically Simple Words

Motivation
If a patient shows no effect of the contextual appropriateness of various types of derived and inflected words, and no effect of the morphological legality of a non-word, we need to establish whether this is due to the patient's general insensitivity to the ends of words or to a selective impairment for morphological suffixes. In this test we examine the patient's sensitivity to deviant word-endings in morphologically simple words.

Stimuli and Method
We constructed sentences containing morphologically simple test words (*nylon* in the example) that were either intact or become non-words in the final syllable, as in the example below:

(i) John always got the most hideous presents from Aunt Mary. This year it was a *nylon tie* which he knew he'd never wear.

(ii) John always got the most hideous presents from Aunt Mary. This year it was a *nylup tie* which he knew he'd never wear.

As in chapters 11–13, we use the word-monitoring task, and target words (*tie* in the example above) occur immediately after the test word.

Control Results
RTs to targets occurring after a deviant word are slower than when the word is intact. This shows that listeners are immediately sensitive to the deviation in the final syllable of the test word. If a patient shows a similar increase in monitoring latencies when the test word is deviant, but shows

no sensitivity to the various manipulations in the series of tests using morphologically complex words, then we can be confident that he or she does not have a general inability to process the ends of words. Rather, the patient must have a selective deficit for processing suffixed words in context.

Summary

The studies summarized here test for deficits in many of the major categories of spoken-language comprehension. They also enable us to contrast a patient's ability to carry out the relevant analyses involved in the real-time construction of linguistic representations with his or her ability to perform on standard tests of language-comprehension deficits. The results of all of these studies taken together enable us to draw a processing profile for each patient, specifying his or her pattern of impaired and preserved abilities in the domain of spoken language comprehension. Examples of processing profiles are given in chapter 16.

Chapter 3
Patient Details

Patient 1:   PK

Date of birth: 1945
Date of onset: April 1984
Began testing: April 1985
Previous occupation: Architect

General details:
Hearing loss: 12.9 db
Phoneme discrimination: 4.9% errors
Digit span: 4 digits
Digit matching task: 5/6 correct on 4 digits; 3/6 correct on 5 and 6 digits
Simple RT: 242 msec (compared to 161 msec for mid-age controls)

Standard aphasia tests:
Trail Making Test: 72 seconds
Token Test: 9/36 correct (severe impairment)
BDAE (administered October 1984):

• auditory comprehension: $z = +.5$
• repetition: normal
• Spontaneous speech: His output is fluent, well-intoned, and grammatically correct. He does, however, show a severe word-finding problem. In addition, he tends to produce verbal (semantic) paraphasias.

Samples of spontaneous speech

a.   Cookie theft picture (11/3/89)
PK: Right you have a mother, daughter and a son. The son and daughter are in the process of picking out coconut coco jam umm ... high level and to get up there he has gone on a eh ... one two three pinned sort of ... it's a kind of very tall um ... what do they call it a tall table not table er chair. And he has climbed up to get the um ... the eh ... um ... anyhow gone up to get two, one for his ... one one for his eh daughter no his um son no no his eh younger son keep on and the chair has slipped. Sorry that is all that was in that one. Um ... the wife is busy washing up and she seems to have forgotten the eh sink and whereas one would normally pull out the plug she has left it in and it's all poured down the front and on the floor um. . . . That's it.

b.   Elicited conversation (11/3/89)
(The experimenter is asking about Guy Fawkes Night.)
NG: I hear everybody has bonfires and firecrackers. Do you know what it is?

PK: Once a year it's the um ... very very many years ago it was a member of the government I think or I kee ... I keep using the words anyway who tried to blow up the king the government and they managed to get way under the umm ... underneath the er what do you call them the er things which go way you've got the standard house you've got a place underneath where they ... just lots of beer and everything else keep them.

NG: The cellar.

PK: The cellar and under the cellar used to be large bo eh ... eh what do they call them um places where they used to keep um ... barrels of eh ... used to blow up umm....

NG: Explosives?

P: Explosives and he set this up to blow up the whole of the umm ... people who used to stand in eh government and by a mere chance somebody found out, caught him and did he he died naturally and eh from ever since it been called the umm ... November November the s ... I don't know there is a song from it and umm ... it's on the it's not Saturday it's on Sunday the actual date and um everybody builds a ... that is a good day to have fireworks and everything just let them off into the air into the place and eh ... and he quite happy.

Z-SCORE PROFILE OF APHASIA SUBSCORES

NAME: PK

DATE OF EXAM: OCT 1984

| | | -2.5 | -2 | | -1 | | 0 | | +1 | | +2 | +2.5 |

SEVERITY RATING 0 1 (2) 3 4 5

FLUENCY
Artic. Rating 1 2 3 4 5 6 7
Phrase Length 1 2 3 4 5 6 7
Verbal Agility 0 2 4 6 8 10 12 (14)

AUDITORY COMPREH.
Word Discrimin. 15 20 25 30 35 40 45 50 55 60 (65) 70 72
Body Part Ident. 5 10 (15) 20
Commands 0 5 10 15
Complex Material 0 2 4 6 (8) 10 12

NAMING
Responsive Naming 0 5 10 15 20 25 30
Confront. Naming 5 15 25 35 45 55 65 75 85 95 105
Animal Naming 0 2 4 6 8 10 12 14 16 18 20 23
Body Part Naming 0 5 10 15 20 25 30

ORAL READING
Word Reading 0 5 (10) 15 20 25 30
Oral Sentence 0 2 4 6 8 10

REPETITION
Repetition (wds.) 0 2 4 6 8 10
Hi Prob. 0 2 4 (6) 8
Lo Prob. 0 2 (4) 6 8

PARAPHASIA
Neolog. 0 2 4 6 8 10 12
Literal 0 2 4 (6) 8 10 12 14 16
Verbal 0 2 (4) 6 8 10 12 14 16 18 20 22 24
Extended 0 2 4 6 8 10 12 14 16

AUTOM. SPEECH
Autom. Sequences 0 2 4 (6) 8
Reciting 0 (1) 2

READING COMPREH.
Symbol Discrim. 4 6 8 (10)
Word Recog. 2 4 (6) 8
Compr. Oral Spell 0 (2) 4 6 8
Wd. Picture Match 0 (2) 4 6 8 10
Read. Sent. Parag. 0 2 4 6 8 10

WRITING
Mechanics 0 1 2 (3)
Serial Writing 0 5 10 15 20 25 30 35 (40) 45 47
Primer. Dict. 0 2 4 (6) 8 10 12 14 15
Writ. Confront. Naming (0) 2 4 6 8 10
Spelling To Dict. (0) 3 5 7 9 10
Sentences To Dict. (0) 2 4 6 8 10 12
Narrative Writ. (0) 1 2 3 4

MUSIC
Singing 0 1 2
Rhythm 0 1 2

PARIETAL
Drawing to Command 1 3 5 7 9 11 13
Stick Memory 1 3 5 7 9 11 13 14
Total Fingers 40 60 80 100 120 140 152
Right-Left 0 2 4 6 8 10 12 14 16
Arithmetic 0 4 8 12 16 20 24 28 32
Clock Setting 1 2 3 4 5 6 7 8 9 10 11 12
3 Dim. Blocks 0 1 2 3 4 5 6 7 8 9 10

| | -2.5 | -2 | | -1 | | 0 | | +1 | | +2 | +2.5 |

Patient 2:   JA

Date of birth: 1915
Date of onset: March 1985
Began testing: July 1986
Previous occupation: Engineer

General details:
Hearing loss: 30.8 db
Phoneme discrimination: 12.7% errors
Digit span: 3 digits
Digit matching task: 4/6 correct on 4 digits; 4/6 correct on 5 and 6 digits
Simple RT: 424 msec (compared to 293 msec for old-age controls with poor hearing;
range: 160–524 msec)
Other details: Color-blind for red and green

Standard aphasia tests:
Trail Making Test: 120 seconds
Token Test: 21/36 correct (moderate impairment)
BDAE (administered June 1985):

• auditory comprehension: $z = +.5$
• repetition: Single word repetition within normal range. Very poor at repeating
phrases.
• Spontaneous speech: His speech is limited to short, syntactically simple sentences,
with a relatively normal intonational contour. His articulatory agility is also normal. His
major problem lies in finding the correct word.

Sample of spontaneous speech

Elicited conversation (7/9/86)
E: What did you do before you were ill?

JA: Um, well … I … um … now … eh … just gone you see.

E: You thought of it and its gone?

JA: I … um … this is … but … oh … see its … that is.

E: Can you think of something that's related to it?

JA: Yes … eh … engineering

E: And you worked here in Cambridge?

JA: No, oh, now there's see got see its right down south … Cambridge, eh Cambridge
… no.

Z-SCORE PROFILE OF APHASIA SUBSCORES

NAME: JA

DATE OF EXAM: JUNE 1985

-2.5   -2   -1   0   +1   +2   +2.5

SEVERITY RATING
0   1   2   3   4   5

FLUENCY
Artic. Rating   1   2   3   4   5   6   7
Phrase Length   1   2   3   4   5   6   7
Verbal Agility   0   2   4   6   8   10   12   14

AUDITORY COMPREH.
Word Discrimin.   15   20   25   30   35   40   45   50   55   60   65   70   72
Body Part Ident.   5   10   15   20
Commands   0   5   10   15
Complex Material   0   2   4   6   8   10   12

NAMING
Responsive Naming   0   5   10   15   20   25   30
Confront. Naming   5   15   25   35   45   55   65   75   85   95   105
Animal Naming   0   2   4   6   8   10   12   14   16   18   20   23
Body Part Naming   0   5   10   15   20   25   30

ORAL READING
Word Reading   0   5   10   15   20   25   30
Oral Sentence   0   2   4   6   8   10

REPETITION
Repetition (wds)   0   2   4   6   8   10
Hi Prob.   0   2   4   6   8
Lo Prob.   0   2   4   6   8

PARAPHASIA
Neolog.   0   2   4   6   8   10   12
Literal   0   2   4   6   8   10   12   14   16
Verbal   0   2   4   6   8   10   12   14   16   18   20   22   24
Extended   0   2   4   6   8   10   12   14   16

AUTOM. SPEECH
Autom. Sequences   0   2   4   6   8
Reciting   0   1   2

READING COMPREH.
Symbol Discrim.   4   6   8   10
Word Recog.   2   4   6   8
Compr. Oral Spell   0   2   4   6   8
Wd. Picture Match   0   2   4   6   8   10
Read. Sent. Parag.   0   2   4   6   8   10

WRITING
Mechanics   0   1   2   3
Serial Writing   0   5   10   15   20   25   30   35   40   45   47
Primer. Dict.   0   2   4   6   8   10   12   14   15
Writ. Confront. Naming   0   2   4   6   8   10
Spelling To Dict.   0   3   5   7   9   10
Sentences To Dict.   0   2   4   6   8   10   12
Narrative Writ.   0   1   2   3   4

MUSIC
Singing   0   1   2
Rhythm   0   1   2

PARIETAL
Drawing to Command   1   3   5   7   9   11   13
Stick Memory   1   3   5   7   9   11   13   14
Total Fingers   40   60   80   100   120   140   152
Right-Left   0   2   4   6   8   10   12   14   16
Arithmetic   0   4   8   12   16   20   24   28   32
Clock Setting   1   2   3   4   5   6   7   8   9   10   11   12
3 Dim. Blocks   0   1   2   3   4   5   6   7   8   9   10

-2.5   -2   -1   0   +1   +2   +2.5

Patient 3:   BN

Date of birth: 1944
Date of onset: March 1984
Began testing: May 1985
Previous occupation: Chemical engineer

General details:
Hearing Loss: 5.5 dB
Phoneme discrimination: 3.9% errors
Digit span: 4 digits
Digit matching task: 6/6 correct on 4 digits; 5/6 correct on 5 and 6 digits
Simple RT: 143 msec (compared to 161 msec for mid-age controls)

Standard aphasia tests:
Trail Making Test: 53 seconds
Token Test: 11/36 correct (severe impairment)
BDAE (administered January 1985):

• auditory comprehension: $z = +.5$
• repetition: Normal repetition of single words, poor repetition of phrases.
• Spontaneous speech: BN's speech is very limited. He has problems with articulation, which makes it hard for him to produce even the limited amount of speech he does. The fragments below are very typical, with long pauses between words (usually nouns) and no grammatical structure. His speech lacks intonational contour, it is effortful, and he typically produces single word utterances.

Samples of spontaneous speech

a.   Cookie theft picture (11/3/89)
BN: Eh ... man ... no ... no ... nay man cookies right, fall over um ... fall over ... stool ummmm water eh water ... eh ... over right, and eh ... um ... greemin reamin umm....

NG: What else is she doing?

BN: Dreamin say ... look no water umm....

NG: Is she?

BN: Ohh ... oh god ... woman no ... woman ... woman ordin ... ordin tachin.

b.   Elicited conversation (11/3/89)
NG: Can you tell me about your family?

BN: Eh ... Why eh Joy eh teacher um full time umm umm ... David and Mark eh eh um school um and um ... don't know um.

NG: How old are your boys?

BN: Oh dear ... I can't (*he traces out the number with his finger*).

NG: Fourteen yes....

BN: And er ... (*he traces out the number with his finger*).

NG: And eleven.

BN: Yes.

NG: And they go to school, the same school.

BN: No eh they no eh ... oh dear I live eh I live and eh country ... Rampton.

NG: Where you live?

BN: Oapingdon and Doddingdon Lane.

NG: OK, did you do anything during the summer holiday with your boys?

BN: Oh eh ... Majorca Majorca.

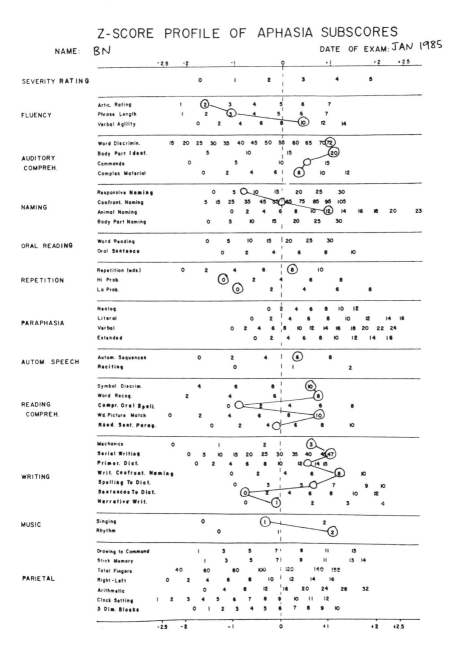

Patient 4:   VS

Date of birth: 1938
Date of onset: November 1978
Began testing: February 1983
Occupation: Housewife

General details:
Hearing loss: 21.7 db
Phoneme discrimination: 12.7% errors
Digit span: 3 digits
Digit matching task: 6/6 correct on 4 digits; 5/6 correct on 5 digits; 4/6 correct on 6 digits
Simple RT: 348 msec (compared to 161 msec for mid-age controls)

Standard aphasia tests:
Trail Making Test: 72 seconds
Token Test: 11/36 correct (severe impairment)
BDAE (administered February 1983):

• auditory comprehension: $z = +.5$
• repetition: Normal repetition of single words, poor repetition of phrases.
• Spontaneous speech: Her speech output is limited to short, syntactically simple utterances which are amelodic. She also has some articulatory problems.

Sample of spontaneous speech

Elicited conversation (4/14/89)
NG: Where did you used to live?

VS: Edge Road Edge Road ... I can't say that ... Mill Road Millweal Millwall like that ... Millwall Millwell like that foowall football.

NG: Oh, football.

VS: Yeh Yeh not London Enchroad ... I ink it where Millwall

NG: It's a football team?

VS: Yeh yeh like that when Ised we we we ... Oh I can't say that (*she writes on a piece of paper with her left hand*).

NG: Old Kent....

VS: Kent Road

NG: Oh, Old Kent Road.

VS: Yeh yeh where we wer wer lived.

NG: Did you like it there?

VS: Yeh it's nice there but now I thought it's nice nice here. Harry said I like it ere like that. Yeh it's hot now in it?

Z-SCORE PROFILE OF APHASIA SUBSCORES

NAME: VS

DATE OF EXAM: FEB 1983

Scale across top: -2.5 -2 -1 0 +1 +2 +2.5

SEVERITY RATING: 0 1 2 3 4 5

FLUENCY
- Artic. Rating: 1 2 3 4 5 6 7
- Phrase Length: 1 2 3 4 5 6 7
- Verbal Agility: 0 2 ○ 4 6 8 10 12 14

AUDITORY COMPREH.
- Word Discrimin.: 15 20 25 30 35 40 45 50 55 60 ○ 65 70 72
- Body Part Ident.: 5 10 15 20
- Commands: 0 5 10 15
- Complex Material: 0 2 4 6 ○ 8 10 12

NAMING
- Responsive Naming: 0 5 10 ○ 15 20 25 30
- Confront. Naming: 5 15 25 35 ○ 45 55 65 75 85 95 105
- Animal Naming: 0 2 ④ 6 8 10 12 14 16 18 20 23
- Body Part Naming: 0 5 ○ 10 15 20 25 30

ORAL READING
- Word Reading: 0 5 ○ 10 15 20 25 30
- Oral Sentence: 0 2 ○ 4 6 8 10

REPETITION
- Repetition (wds): 0 2 4 6 ○ 8 10
- Hi Prob.: 0 ○ 2 4 6 8
- Lo Prob.: ⓪ 2 4 6 8

PARAPHASIA
- Neolog.: 0 2 4 6 8 10 12
- Literal: 0 2 4 6 8 10 12 14 16
- Verbal: 0 2 4 6 8 10 12 14 16 18 20 22 24
- Extended: 0 2 4 6 8 10 12 14 16

AUTOM. SPEECH
- Autom. Sequences: 0 ② 4 6 8
- Reciting: 0 1 2

READING COMPREH.
- Symbol Discrim.: 4 6 8 ⑩
- Word Recog.: 2 4 6 ○ 8
- Compr. Oral Spell: 0 ○ 2 4 6 8
- Wd. Picture Match: 0 2 4 6 ○ 8 10
- Read. Sent. Parag.: 0 2 ④ 6 8 10

WRITING
- Mechanics: 0 1 2 ③
- Serial Writing: 0 5 10 15 20 ○ 25 30 35 40 45 47
- Primer. Dict.: 0 2 4 6 8 10 ○ 12 14 15
- Writ. Confront. Naming: 0 2 4 ○ 6 8 10
- Spelling To Dict.: ⓪ 3 5 7 9 10
- Sentences To Dict.: ⓪ 2 4 6 8 10 12
- Narrative Writ.: ⓪ 1 2 3 4

MUSIC
- Singing: 0 1 2
- Rhythm: 0 1 2

PARIETAL
- Drawing to Command: 1 3 5 7 9 11 13
- Stick Memory: 1 3 5 7 9 11 13 14
- Total Fingers: 40 60 80 100 120 140 152
- Right-Left: 0 2 4 6 8 10 12 14 16
- Arithmetic: 0 4 8 12 16 20 24 28 32
- Clock Setting: 1 2 3 4 5 6 7 8 9 10 11 12
- 3 Dim. Blocks: 0 1 2 3 4 5 6 7 8 9 10

Scale across bottom: -2.5 -2 -1 0 +1 +2 +2.5

Patient 5:   JG

Date of birth: 1929
Date of onset: November 1980
Began testing: February 1983
Previous occupation: Groundskeeper

General details:
Hearing loss: 22.1 db
Phoneme discrimination: 8.3% errors
Digit span: 3 digits
Digit matching task: 6/6 on 4 digits; 6/6 correct on 5 digits; 3/6 correct on 6 digits
Simple RT: 185 msec (compared to 263 msec for old-age controls with good hearing; range: 154–379 msec)

Standard aphasia tests:
Trail Making Test: 67 seconds
Token Test: 10/36 correct (severe impairment)
BDAE (administered October 1981):

• auditory comprehension: z = −.75
• repetition: Normal repetition of single words, poor repetition of phrases.
• Spontaneous speech: He produces short utterances, consisting of one or two words. His speech is hesitant and effortful.

Samples of spontaneous speech

a.   Cookie theft picture (11/23/89)
NG: Could you just describe for me what's happening in this picture?

JG: Yeh. The boy is fallin down because the chocolate in in ... then the stool is woompy and the water is a ... taps is on and drippin down. And a ... and the boy girl and the father eh father no the ... yeh far father ha ha ha. And ... a an boy and and still it's carryin on an and an an the y know. There is water an there is runnin an that boy and y know ... this ole boy.

b.   Elicited conversation (11/23/89)
JG: Forty years married German girl ... in urm ah ur amber and wed in ambe ... y'see um. And a ... yer see yersit oh and a an ... two free years um ... gaged and then pratenise, 'cos of the war and anda then France er Belgium, Ireland and then all of 'em fighting and married to the German girl ... ah amber think so yeh, and then arrived in in ... and ah then ah ohr the young girl me ell my wife's, uh twenty, thirty, forty years and ah yer know forty, no an and then a a ... yer know iz good yer know.

NG: Didn't your friend marry a German girl as well?

JG: Yes, yes oh yeah oh yes and a, oh yeah and a, not quite, ah one ta twenty, thirty, one he wed yeh. So it's hard y'know its good and ah and then a and then a,'e ... ah, I can't say it ... ah then they price a bus bus is one two pence no ah'there is one two pence old money so thats one 'p darford 'n and one dare is oh pree pree ah money. Ah one two twenty, wi there and back can't say it ... ah little village then y know ... and one car 'n one bike in warrington. Now it's cars and cars and cars but one car and one bike in Warrington oh yeah and a then the ... oh the lived there and school opposite and no cars or nothin but then and then the school is ah ... not a in school is closed in another one er y know not so clouded and a y know yeah and then ... ah some eight nine ten eleven twelve ... fourteen work work.

Z-SCORE PROFILE OF APHASIA SUBSCORES

NAME: JG   DATE OF EXAM: OCT 1981

		-2.5	-2	-1	0	+1	+2	+2.5

SEVERITY RATING — 0   1   (2)   3   4   5

FLUENCY
- Artic. Rating: 1   2   3   4   5   (6)   7
- Phrase Length: 1   2   3   4   (5)   6   7
- Verbal Agility: 0   (2)   4   6   8   10   12   14

AUDITORY COMPREH.
- Word Discrimin.: 15 20 25 30 35 (40) 45 50 55 60 65 70 72
- Body Part Ident.: (5)   10   15   20
- Commands: 0   5   (10)   15
- Complex Material: 0   2   4 (6) 8   10   12

NAMING
- Responsive Naming: 0   5   10   15 (O) 20   25   30
- Confront. Naming: 5 15 25 (35) 45 55 65 75 85 95 105
- Animal Naming: 0   2   4   (6)   8   10   12   14   16   18   20   23
- Body Part Naming: 0   5   10 (O) 15   20   25   30

ORAL READING
- Word Reading: 0   5 (O) 10   15   20   25   30
- Oral Sentence: (O)   2   4   6   8   10

REPETITION
- Repetition (wds): 0   2   4   6   8 (O) 10
- Hi Prob.: 0   (2)   4   6   8
- Lo Prob.: 0   (2)   4   6   8

PARAPHASIA
- Neolog.: (0)   2   4   6   8   10   12
- Literal: 0   2   4 (O) 6   8   10   12   14   16
- Verbal: 0   2   4   6   8   10   12 (14) 16   18   20   22   24
- Extended: (0)   2   4   6   8   10   12   14   16

AUTOM. SPEECH
- Autom. Sequences: 0   2   4 (O) 6   8
- Reciting: 0   (1)   2

READING COMPREH.
- Symbol Discrim.: 4   6   (8)   10
- Word Recog.: 2   4 (O) 6   8
- Compr. Oral Spell: (O)   2   4   6   8
- Wd. Picture Match: 0   2   4   6   8   (10)
- Read. Sent. Pareg.: 0   2   4   6 (O) 8   10

WRITING
- Mechanics: 0   1   (2)   3
- Serial Writing: 0   5   10   15   20   25 (O) 30   35   40   45 47
- Primer. Dict.: 0   2   4   6 (O) 8   10   12   14   15
- Writ. Confront. Naming: (O)   2   4   6   8   10
- Spelling To Dict.: (O)   3   5   7   9   10
- Sentences To Dict.: (O)   2   4   6   8   10   12
- Narrative Writ.: (O)   1   2   3   4

MUSIC
- Singing: 0   1   (2)
- Rhythm: 0   (1)   2

PARIETAL
- Drawing to Command: 1   3   5   7   9   11   13
- Stick Memory: 1   3   5   7   9   11   13   14
- Total Fingers: 40   60   80   100   120   140   152
- Right-Left: 0   2   4   6   8   10   12   14   16
- Arithmetic: 0   4   8   12   16   20   24   28   32
- Clock Setting: 1   2   3   4   5   6   7   8   9   10   11   12
- 3 Dim. Blocks: 0   1   2   3   4   5   6   7   8   9   10

	-2.5	-2	-1	0	+1	+2	+2.5

Patient 6:   CH

Date of birth: 1914
Date of onset: November 1980
Began testing: May 1982
Previous occupation: Glass worker
Died: 1988

General details:
Hearing loss: 55.9 db
Phoneme discrimination: 19% errors
Digit span: 4 digits
Digit matching task: 6/6 correct on 4 and 5 digits; 5/6 correct on 6 digits

Standard aphasia tests:
Trail Making Test: 76 seconds
Token Test: 18/36 correct (moderate impairment)
BDAE (administered July 1981):

• auditory comprehension: $z = +.5$
• repetition: normal at repeating single words; slightly below normal at phrases
• Spontaneous speech: His speech output is slow and hesitant. He produces short utterances which are grammatically simple.

Samples of spontaneous speech

a.   Elicited conversation (2/3/83)
E: When did you first become ill?

CH: I don't remember. Two years ago last November. Queen Mary's. I was a glass worker.

E: Tell me about your family.

CH: My family is my wife and son and daughter. Son not married. In about '35 or 6, I can't remember. And my daughter's married. She got little one. She's got ... girl ... boy! Two years and a month. Little devil ... Once a week.

b.   Elicited conversation (7/26/85)
HC: Do you want to tell me about your holidays, 'cause I know you're going ... I don't know where you're going.

CH: Mm, first of August, the first of August ... I be going to Guernsey ... a lovely time there.

HC: How are you going, and how long are you staying?

CH: Hairoplane

HC: Where from?

CH: Gatwick

HC: How long does it take?

CH: A ... a ... a ... hour

HC: And what will you do when you get there?

CH: I ... I ... I ... eh ... I ... get out of a, airplane, and go to to to to ... I can't I can't say that.

CH: Yes

HC: What do you like to see, anything special?

CH: No, no, I love to see to see anything special but I haven't been there before.

Z-SCORE PROFILE OF APHASIA SUBSCORES

NAME: CH

DATE OF EXAM: JULY 1981

		-2.5	-2	-1	0	+1	+2	+2.5

SEVERITY RATING — 0 1 (2) 3 4 5

FLUENCY
- Artic. Rating — (1) 2 3 4 5 6 7
- Phrase Length — 1 2 3 4 5 (6) 7
- Verbal Agility — 0 2 4 6 8 10 12 14

AUDITORY COMPREH.
- Word Discrimin. — 15 20 25 (30) 35 40 45 50 55 60 65 70 72
- Body Part Ident. — 5 10 15 (20)
- Commands — 0 5 10 15
- Complex Material — 0 2 4 6 8 10 12

NAMING
- Responsive Naming — 0 5 10 15 20 25 30
- Confront. Naming — 5 15 25 35 45 55 65 75 85 95 105
- Animal Naming — 0 2 4 6 8 10 12 14 16 18 20 23
- Body Part Naming — 0 5 10 15 20 25 30

ORAL READING
- Word Reading — 0 5 10 15 20 25 30
- Oral Sentence — 0 2 (4) 6 8 10

REPETITION
- Repetition (wds.) — 0 2 4 6 8 10
- Hi Prob. — 0 2 4 6 8
- Lo Prob. — 0 (2) 4 6 8

PARAPHASIA
- Neolog. — 0 2 4 6 8 10 12
- Literal — 0 2 4 6 8 10 12 14 16
- Verbal — 0 2 4 6 8 10 12 14 16 18 20 22 24
- Extended — 0 2 4 6 8 10 12 14 16

AUTOM. SPEECH
- Autom. Sequences — 0 2 4 6 (8)
- Reciting — 0 1 (2)

READING COMPREH.
- Symbol Discrim. — 4 6 8 (10)
- Word Recog. — 2 4 6 8
- Compr. Oral Spell. — 0 2 (4) 6 8
- Wd. Picture Match — 0 2 4 6 8 (10)
- Read. Sent. Parag. — 0 2 4 6 8 10

WRITING
- Mechanics — 0 1 (2) 3
- Serial Writing — 0 5 10 15 20 25 30 35 40 45 47
- Primer. Dict. — 0 2 4 6 8 10 12 14 15
- Writ. Confront. Naming — 0 2 4 6 8 10
- Spelling To Dict. — 0 3 5 7 9 10
- Sentences To Dict. — 0 2 4 6 8 10 12
- Narrative Writ. — 0 1 2 3 4

MUSIC
- Singing — 0 1 (2)
- Rhythm — (0) 1 2

PARIETAL
- Drawing to Command — 1 3 5 7 9 11 13
- Stick Memory — 1 3 5 7 9 11 13 14
- Total Fingers — 40 60 80 100 120 140 152
- Right-Left — 0 2 4 6 8 10 12 14 16
- Arithmetic — 0 4 8 12 16 20 24 28 32
- Clock Setting — 1 2 3 4 5 6 7 8 9 10 11 12
- 3 Dim. Blocks — 0 1 2 3 4 5 6 7 8 9 10

| -2.5 | -2 | -1 | 0 | +1 | +2 | +2.5 |

Patient 7:   GS

Date of birth: 1927
Date of onset: March 1978
Began testing: January 1983
Previous occupation: Computer operator/clerk

General details:
Hearing loss: 29.6 db
Phoneme discrimination: 10.3% errors
Digit span: 3 digits
Digit matching task: 5/6 correct on 4 and 5 digits; 3/6 correct on 6 digits
Simple RT: 360 msec (compared to 293 msec for old-age controls with poor hearing; range: 160–524 msec)

Standard aphasia tests:
Trail Making Test: 46 seconds
Token Test: 29/36 correct (no significant impairment)
BDAE (administered January 1983):

• auditory comprehension: $z = +1$
• repetition: only very slightly worse than normal
• Spontaneous speech: She produces speech slowly and carefully. Her utterances are short and relatively simple.

Samples of spontaneous speech

a.   Cookie theft picture (11/9/89)

NG: Could you describe what's happening in this picture?

GS: The picture's of a kitchenette um eh mother and two children a boy and a girl um she's got the tap running and the water running over the floor. She's um she's washing, driving, dry up. The boy's on the stool to get the cookies and he goin to fall um any minute (laughs). The girl the girls wants um a cookie um the window's open an you see the garden an the path and eh another window there an trees an grass and bushes eh ...

NG: That was very good. Well done.

b.   Elicited conversation (11/9/89)

NG: So could you tell me a bit about your vacation in the Canary Islands?

GS: Well I never been before, um eh it's really hot and I like that um I had a um a bungalow for self for self cating um we not cook we eat out um um really nice um um hm ... I can't think of the word ... pretty um the ... place where bungalows um oh I can't ... em ...

NG: Were you near the beach?

GS: Yes yes. Oh not really um 10 minutes away um we had a pool there really near to us and eh not a lot of people but nice um ...

NG: Did you do any sightseeing?

GS: Ah yes. We went to other village um on the bus there. And we had /s/ saw um oh ... um ... would've been oh oh I can't think (laughs). Um (pause) oh I tell you about the next holiday i'kaind?

Z-SCORE PROFILE OF APHASIA SUBSCORES

NAME: GS

DATE OF EXAM: JAN 1983

| | -2.5 | -2 | -1 | 0 | +1 | +2 | +2.5 |

SEVERITY RATING — 0   1   (2)   3   4   5

FLUENCY
- Artic. Rating — 1   2   3   (4)   5   6   7
- Phrase Length — 1   2   3   4   5   (6)   7
- Verbal Agility — 0   2   4   (6)   8   10   12   14

AUDITORY COMPREH.
- Word Discrimin. — 15   20   25   30   35   40   45   50   55   60   65   70 (72)
- Body Part Ident. — 5   10   15   (20)
- Commands — 0   5   10   (15)
- Complex Material — 0   2   4   6   8   10 (○) 12

NAMING
- Responsive Naming — 0   5   10   15   20   25 (○) 30
- Confront. Naming — 5   15   25   35   45   55   65   75   85   90 (○)05
- Animal Naming — 0   2   4   6   8   10   12 (○)14   16   18   20   23
- Body Part Naming — 0   5   10   15   20   25   (30)

ORAL READING
- Word Reading — 0   5   10   15   20   25 (○) 30
- Oral Sentence — 0   2   4   6   8 (○) 10

REPETITION
- Repetition (wds) — 0   2   4   6 (○) 8   10
- Hi Prob. — 0   2   (4)   6   8
- Lo Prob. — 0   2 (○) 4   6   8

PARAPHASIA
- Neolog. — 0   2   4   6   8   10   12
- Literal — 0   2   4   (6)   8   10   12   14   16
- Verbal — 0   2   4 (○) 6   8   10   12   14   16   18   20   22   24
- Extended — 0   2   4   6   8   10   12   14   16

AUTOM. SPEECH
- Autom. Sequences — 0   2   4   (6)   8
- Reciting — 0   (1)   2

READING COMPREH.
- Symbol Discrim. — 4   6   8   (10)
- Word Recog. — 2   4   6   (8)
- Compr. Oral Spell — 0   2   4   (6)   8
- Wd. Picture Match — 0   2   4   6   8   (10)
- Read. Sent. Parag. — 0   2   4   6 (○) 8   10

WRITING
- Mechanics — 0   1   2   (3)
- Serial Writing — 0   5   10   15   20   25   30   33 (○)40   45 47
- Primer. Dict. — 0   2   4   6   8   10   12   14 (15)
- Writ. Confront. Naming — 0   2   4   6   8 (○) 10
- Spelling To Dict. — 0   3   5 (○) 7   9   10
- Sentences To Dict. — 0   2   4   6   8   10   12
- Narrative Writ. — 0   1   2   3   4

MUSIC
- Singing — 0   1   (2)
- Rhythm — 0   1   (2)

PARIETAL
- Drawing to Command — 1   3   5   7   9   11   13
- Stick Memory — 1   3   5   7   9   11   13   14
- Total Fingers — 40   60   80   100   120   140   152
- Right-Left — 0   2   4   6   8   10   12   14   16
- Arithmetic — 0   4   8   12   16   20   24   28   32
- Clock Setting — 1   2   3   4   5   6   7   8   9   10   11   12
- 3 Dim. Blocks — 0   1   2   3   4   5   6   7   8   9   10

| | -2.5 | -2 | -1 | 0 | +1 | +2 | +2.5 |

Patient 8:   JW

Date of birth: 1933
Date of onset: May 1981
Began testing: February 1983
Previous occupation: Fitter with British Rail

General details:
Hearing loss: 34.1 db
Phoneme discrimination: 22% errors
Digit span: 2 digits
Digit matching task: 3/6 correct on 4, 5 and 6 digits
Simple RT: 334 msec (compared to 293 msec for old-age controls with poor hearing; range: 160–524 msec)

Standard aphasia tests:
Trail Making Test: 330 seconds
Token Test: 12/36 correct (severe impairment)
BDAE (administered January 1983):

• auditory comprehension: $z = 0$
• repetition: normal on single words; below normal on phrases
• Spontaneous speech: His speech is very effortful and limited. He rarely produces more than single words and he does that with considerable difficulty.

Samples of spontaneous speech

a.   Cookie theft picture (11/9/89)
NG: Could you describe what's going on in this picture?

JW: Mm kkk and a um cook cookers cookers um jar um yeh and a um s..s..s an a um sips sips an a um at um lady is a um goal … no um um … flate plate um (*mumbles*) an at um [tæ:l] oh yeh an at yeh yeh right um.

NG: Good. Very good.

b.   Elicited conversation (11/9/89)
NG: So is this usual, is this weather normal for this time of year?

JW: Yeh, yeh yeh.

NG: Do you like winter?

JW: Nah

NG: Why not?

JW: No'hm don't know um.… March March is um yeh.

NG: Do you like summer?

JW: Yeh yeh

NG: Yeh

JW: Yeh yeh yeh urm. That'm vverr verry … Yus, do dry do dry an eh um August and eh um, March (cough) March m just as dry and eh um August and um boon no.

Z-SCORE PROFILE OF APHASIA SUBSCORES

NAME: J W

DATE OF EXAM: JAN 1983

Patient 9:   DE

Date of birth: 1954
Date of onset: June 1970
Began testing: May 1983
Occupation: Storekeeper

General details:
Hearing loss: 7.0 db
Phoneme discrimination: 3% errors
Digit span: 3 digits
Digit matching task: 6/6 correct on 4 and 5 digits; 4/6 correct on 6 digits
Simple RT: 121 msec (compared to 161 msec for mid-age controls)

Standard aphasia tests:
Trail Making Test: 39 seconds
Token Test: 24/36 correct (moderate impairment)
BDAE (administered June1983):

• auditory comprehension: z = +.75
• repetition: Good repetition of single words, poor repetition of phrases.
• Spontaneous speech: His speech is slow and hesitant. He rarely produces more than single-word utterances which primarily consist of content words.

Samples of spontaneous speech

a.   Cookie theft picture (11/4/89)
NG: So if you could just describe what's going on here.

DE: Right ... children first ... alright ... like chair tip over wrong ... you got cookies high up ... wrong again, right ... like ask um ... Lady right washing um ... dry up, right ... washing right ... right ... Full up with water ... right ... turn it off right ... wrong ... overflowing right ... on the floor ... everywhere on the floor, and that's it.

b.   Elicited conversation (11/4/89)
NG: Can you tell me a bit about what you do at work?

DE: Right I I ... I Kirby and Warrick Pharmaceuticals at Mildenhall ... they've got a warehouse right ... they got a forklift driver as well right ... altogether....

NG: And what else do you do?

DE: All like ... that you got ... um ... project um ... Osy like ... like ... umm ... All right ... right ... you got umm ... boxes right ... um ... got stuff out to ... um ... pharmaceuticals like um ... like customers ... um you like UK customers um ... like chemists and things ... like that ... um ... Oh over the counter sales ... over the counter sales ... like um lactocalamine ... um tiga ... and things like that um ... and other different ... department like ... different further down um ... right like stretchers and things ... like that as well ... different departments as well.

NG: And so what are you in charge of?

DE: Oh ... OTC right umm ... over the counter sales right ... that's it right ... every Monday to Friday ... and that's it ... I ... umm ...

Z-SCORE PROFILE OF APHASIA SUBSCORES
NAME: DE   DATE OF EXAM: JUNE 1983

Patient 10:   FB

Date of birth: 1921
Date of onset: September 1979
Began testing: February 1983
Previous occupation: Solicitor

General details:
Hearing loss: 37.9 db
Phoneme discrimination: 19% errors
Digit span: 4 digits
Digit matching task: 6/6 correct on 4 and 5 digits; 5/6 correct on 6 digits
Simple RT: 221 msec (compared to 293 msec for old-age controls with poor hearing; range: 160–524 msec)

Standard aphasia tests:
Trail Making Test: 65 seconds
Token Test: 11/36 correct (severe impairment)
BDAE (administered November 1980):

• auditory comprehension: z = +.5
• repetition: Moderate repetition of single words, poor repetition of phrases.
• Spontaneous speech: His speech is fluent, with normal intonational contour. It is fairly typical of a fluent patient in that it is semantically "empty" and contains paragrammatisms.

Samples of spontaneous speech

a.   Cookie theft picture (11/9/89)
NG: Describe for me what's going on in that picture.

FB: Oh yes it obviously the first thing that you see here is is is of course the the the wife if you like or or the mother of the two children um is eh all all the waters is gone over over her sink erm and she still showin that them an she hasn't even bothered about that obviously with that because she's she's still sort of em em em cleanin cleanin washin washin … the the the plate um but I would've thought sh what she what she what she should've done should eh put put the plate allon some some there took took and took and took the um got away with the got away with the er away from from the water but there you are. Ha ha ha. Now you wan't eh …

NG: What's happening over here?

FB: Yeh now yes now the two children one one the boy is on on on the top of a of a of a stool and he's goin over over yes goin over the the stoo stool what shall I say we get stool the stool the stool the stool stool stool he's turnin no not turnin what what … I can't think of the word. But don't don't don't don't but any whatever whatever ee's doin anyway ees ees tryin to get the the cookies as it were from the from the jam er the cookie jar that was it from from the from the now thats … cupboard the cupboard that's right. Erm that naughty ol [t :t?tɪnohwWt] he he he look he look he almos there he looks like like the peazer peazer ha ha ha ha ha. The peazer the peazer the peazer peazer peazer what the I can't think what we call there there now can't even think one the other there y are. Anyway thats what he was he was turnin turnin away erm from the from the stool … erm no there' y are.

b.   Elicited conversation (11/9/89)
NG: I I I can tell you th that on on Saturday on Saturday we are going to Malta a we had been to Malta for time free years er for a week each time and its marvellous in that sense is the fact that erm don't do nothing else. Because what happens erm I'm I an association that that I belong to mostly in in in England but we have we have a circle we have a circle in Malta and in fact we've got a new circle to start again in in in erm in

Malta and erm a azay what what we go there and for the whole week erm for example we've gotum, one evenin' we go to the house one of the houses of of the members there other times we go into a coach and we for example one day we normally go into Gozo which is another little another little erm island with with Malta not very far only only about top half an hour between one the other erm on the on the boat ah ...

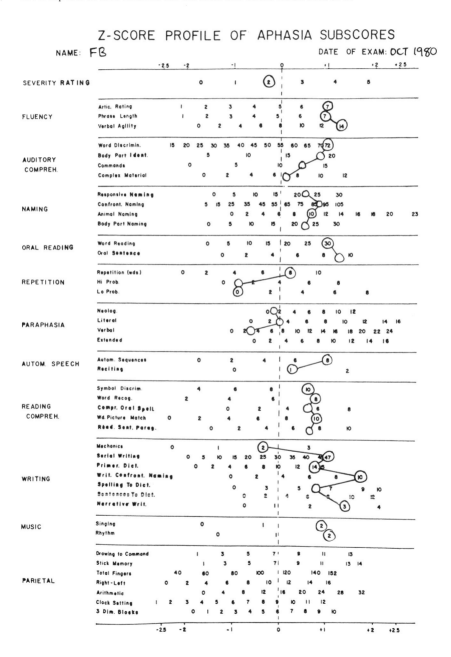

Z-SCORE PROFILE OF APHASIA SUBSCORES

NAME: FB

DATE OF EXAM: OCT 1980

Patient 11:   RH

Date of birth: 1920
Date of onset: October 1977
Began testing: February 1983
Previous occupation: Estimator
Died: 1989

General details:
Hearing loss: 30.0 db
Phoneme discrimination: 11% errors
Digit span: 3 digits
Digit matching task: 6/6 correct on 4 digits; 5/6 correct on 5 digits; 3/6 correct on 6 digits
Simple RT: 215 msec (compared to 293 msec for old-age controls with poor hearing; range: 160–524 msec)

Standard aphasia tests:
Trail Making Test: 205 seconds
Token Test: 7/36 correct (very severe impairment)
BDAE (administered February 1983):

• auditory comprehension: $z = -.5$
• repetition: Poor repetition for both single words and phrases.
• Spontaneous speech: His speech is fluent with a relatively normal intonational contour. It contains many paragrammatisms and paraphasias.

Samples of spontaneous speech

a.   Elicited conversation (2/21/83)
E: How was the party last Monday?

RH: No.

E: Didn't you go?

RH: No, because he was ... it was rather going but he went to me and he ... it was alright ... I was OK. But suddenly and he—it is form me, OK. I have to wait.

E: How long have you lived here?

RH: Oh there, just about down there, you know.

E: Five weeks?

RH: Yes, down there. Yes and then I went from there and then right over—oh dear—I forget the place. It was quite good, you know.

b.   Elicited conversation (2/13/85)
(Experimenter asks RH about coming to the Speech Therapy Department after having his stroke.)
HC: Yeah, and then you came to this place ...

RH: Yes ... well of course when they came there, I ... em ... he came there. I didn't know [xet] there and I didn't know anything for it, any. I suppose we were there, when I went 1 2 3 4 5 and he looked there and said well so and so and so and so. Now if you look here and I see, and then he said right, the next one I went there, so this is right, then the next one I'm going, for him.

HC: What's this then? Is he teaching you to count or ...

RH: Yeah … 1 2 3 4 5 6. Before. But the first, when I first went there, went there, and I didn't know anything. I didn't know anything and then he started—he's trying something, and was trying that …

HC: Trying to get you to say …

RH: And I was OK and try. And then I … you know, bad [*laughs*].

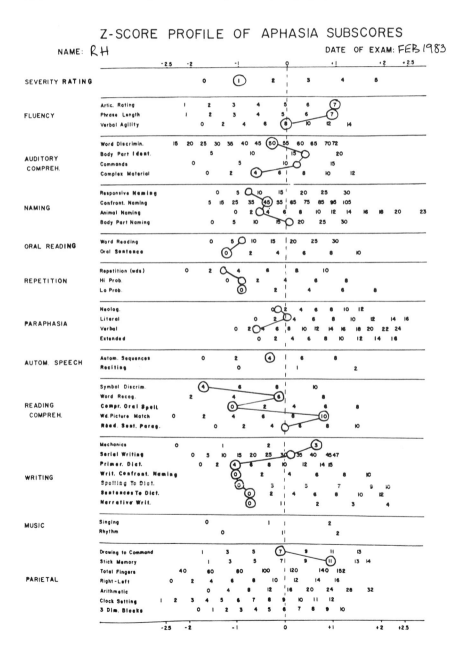

Patient 12:   WA

Date of birth: 1909
Date of onset: August 1986
Began testing: July 1987
Previous occupation: Landlord

General details:
Hearing loss: 37.9 db
Digit span: 4 digits
Digit matching task: 6/6 correct on 4 digits; 5/6 correct on 5 digits and 2/6 correct on 6 digits
Simple RT: 232 msec (compared to 293 msec for old-age controls with poor hearing; range: 160–524 msec)

Standard aphasia tests:
Trail Making Test: 135 seconds
Token Test: 30/36 correct (no significant impairment)
BDAE (administered September,1986):

• auditory comprehension: z = 0
• repetition: slightly below normal on both single words and phrases
• Spontaneous speech: WA's speech is fluent and well-intoned. He occasionally produces paraphasias. He rarely produces an utterance that is both grammatically and semantically well-formed.

Samples of spontaneous speech

a.   Cookie theft picture (11/7/89)
WA: I ... I set there's a some the washing ups carryin on but the the the the the tch ohh the bowl is overflowed ppp ... poorin with the tap which asn't kay come off (pause) ort that runs well uh uh uh oh also there is there is a cookie jar with a boy an a girl handin them out one on a boy has (pause) has given the girl as long as is is still unstable because the not easel uhm it not chair its desk, chair (pause). Desk chair desks not the chair oh oh I oh I can't describe ... the not the chair, tch ohh tch ohh I can't remember.

NG: The stool.

WA: The stool oh yes that's it the stool is un say, un, is the stool is not safe with the chair with the man with the boy oh (pause) I.

b.   Elicited conversation (11/7/89)
(The experimenter is talking to WA about some money he won.)
WA: Ever since we were in the pub. We had twelve hundred, twelve hundred, one thousand two hundred we won. It was a syndicate, eight of us. Half a crown each.

NG: Where did you win this?

WA: When when I I [k] was at the pub ... and a then one chap he's he got married, and, his wife said "oh that's waste of money, you paying this and paying that," and ah so, he packed up so, I said to 'im, Margaret "I oh don't pack, pack pack it up" I said "I'll pay that extra alf a crown" it was ... eight 'alf, it was in, not in ... it was ... English ... its not ... not, dec decimal it was before then.

NG: Oh uhm hmm.

WA: Eh ... before then befor' and a so he said "oh she's 'is wife said I've packed it up, and ah on the thirrrd time uhm we got it up ... (laughs) and his wi' wife wanted, he could come and come in with it still. I said oh I said ... so es funny that was, thats the last time we won, and Tony 'as won ... one and then the ... the chap comes round, on every Tuesday ... pick it up, pick it up and the money, and then he he, does it all, Littlewoods.

NG: What are these (*pointing at football-pool coupons*)?

WA: Ah a' agents you know oh well, 'es an agent you know, 'e 'e comes, all West Street one, um on [nonlinguistic sounds] catch me and then Mrs Mrs Green Mrs Green ... next door but one and then Tony well they don't with with Tony he puts mine and that we do ogether that twos the, money together save 'im, save 'im knocking at the door at 29. And 'is oh 'ee does 'East Street West Street ah 'is um oh he's got a fair area. Clayton's Way and different different parts.

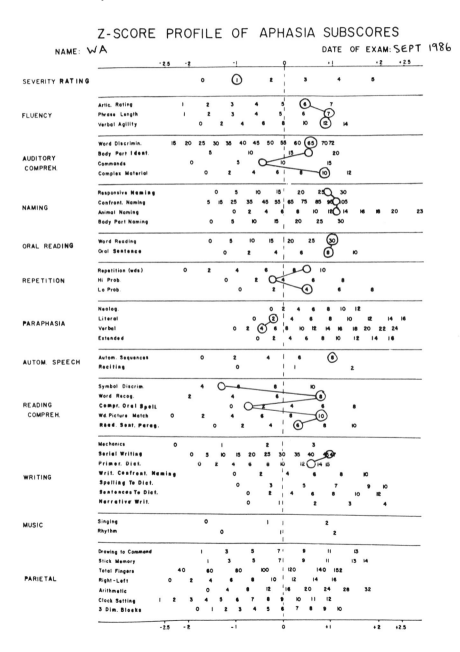

Patient 13: Geo S

Date of birth: 1926
Date of onset: February 1983
Began testing: May 1985
Previous occupation: Chargeman for British Rail
Died: 1987

General details:
Hearing loss: 28.3 db
Phoneme discrimination: 17% errors
Digit span: 3 digits
Digit matching task: 6/6 correct on 4 digits; 4/6 correct on 5 digits; 3/6 correct on 6 digits
Simple RT: 272 msec (compared to 293 msec for old-age controls with poor hearing; range: 160–524 msec)

Standard aphasia tests:
Trail Making Test: 61 seconds
Token Test: 6/36 correct (very severe impairment)
BDAE (administered May 1986):

• auditory comprehension: $z = -1.5$
• repetition: poor for both single words and phrases
• Spontaneous speech: He speaks very slowly and hesitantly. He produces mostly a sequence of nouns, occasionally preceded by a modifier.

Sample of spontaneous speech

Elicited conversation (3/25/85)
(The experimenter is asking Geo S about his cars)
E: Did you have them all at the same time?

Geo S: No, well yes ... I did ... four cars ... and ... and ... yes ... four cars but not very good, one don't like it but two ... not bad.

E: You were in the Navy. Can you tell me about it?

Geo S: Navy, yeh, yeh I, I did ... eh ... Navy, what?

E: Well, what did you do? Where did you go?

Geo S: Not very much! Because eh ... I don't ... I ... I. Oh dear.

Z-SCORE PROFILE OF APHASIA SUBSCORES

NAME: Geo S

DATE OF EXAM: MAY 1986

| | -2.5 | -2 | -1 | 0 | +1 | +2 | +2.5 |

SEVERITY RATING — 0 ① 2 3 4 5

FLUENCY
- Artic. Rating — 1 ② 3 4 5 6 7
- Phrase Length — 1 ② 3 4 5 6 7
- Verbal Agility — 0 2 4 6 8 10 12 14

AUDITORY COMPREH.
- Word Discrimin. — 15 20 25 30 35 40 45 50 55 60 65 70 72
- Body Part Ident. — 5 10 15 20
- Commands — 0 5 10 15
- Complex Material — 0 2 4 6 8 10 12

NAMING
- Responsive Naming — 0 5 10 15 20 25 30
- Confront. Naming — 5 15 25 35 45 55 65 75 85 95 105
- Animal Naming — 0 2 4 6 8 10 12 14 16 18 20 23
- Body Part Naming — 0 5 10 15 20 25 30

ORAL READING
- Word Reading — 0 5 10 15 20 25 30
- Oral Sentence — 0 2 4 6 8 10

REPETITION
- Repetition (wds) — 0 2 4 6 8 10
- Hi Prob. — 0 2 4 6 8
- Lo Prob. — 0 2 4 6 8

PARAPHASIA
- Neolog. — 0 2 4 6 8 10 12
- Literal — 0 2 4 6 8 10 12 14 16
- Verbal — 0 2 4 6 8 10 12 14 16 18 20 22 24
- Extended — 0 2 4 6 8 10 12 14 16

AUTOM. SPEECH
- Autom. Sequences — 0 2 4 ① 6 8
- Reciting — 0 1 2

READING COMPREH.
- Symbol Discrim. — 4 6 8 10
- Word Recog. — 2 4 6 8
- Compr. Oral Spell — 0 2 4 6 8
- Wd. Picture Match — 0 2 4 6 8 10
- Read. Sent. Pareg. — 0 2 4 6 8 10

WRITING
- Mechanics — 0 1 2 3
- Serial Writing — 0 5 10 15 20 25 30 35 40 45 47
- Primer. Dict. — 0 2 4 6 8 10 12 14 15
- Writ. Confront. Naming — 0 2 4 6 8 10
- Spelling To Dict. — 0 3 5 7 9 10
- Sentences To Dict. — 0 2 4 6 8 10 12
- Narrative Writ. — 0 1 2 3 4

MUSIC
- Singing — 0 1 2
- Rhythm — 0 1 2

PARIETAL
- Drawing to Command — 1 3 5 7 9 11 13
- Stick Memory — 1 3 5 7 9 11 13 14
- Total Fingers — 40 60 80 100 120 140 152
- Right-Left — 0 2 4 6 8 10 12 14 16
- Arithmetic — 0 4 8 12 16 20 24 28 32
- Clock Setting — 1 2 3 4 5 6 7 8 9 10 11 12
- 3 Dim. Blocks — 0 1 2 3 4 5 6 7 8 9 10

| | -2.5 | -2 | -1 | 0 | +1 | +2 | +2.5 |

PART II

The Process of Contacting Form Representations

Chapter 4
Phoneme-Discrimination Test

Overview

This test was designed to assess whether a patient can correctly identify speech sounds when they occur within real words. Subjects had to make same/different judgments about pairs of words containing critical phonemes (both consonants and vowels) that differ by a single feature. The test covered a wide range of single-feature contrasts that occur both word-initially and word-finally. One set of consonant contrasts involved changes in place and the other involved changes in voice. Within the set of place contrasts, we had voiced and voiceless plosives, voiced and voiceless fricatives, and nasals. In the voice contrasts, we had voiced and voiceless plosives and fricatives. We also included a set of vowel contrasts.

Background

The phoneme-discrimination test, coupled with an audiological test, provides information about the basic acoustic-phonetic capabilities of aphasic patients. We designed the present test because no existing test met our requirements. Some are extremely short, testing only syllable-initial stop consonants and others, although extensive, use synthesised speech.

The major motivation for our test was to establish whether a patient can identify speech sounds for the purpose of accessing lexical representations. There are two reasons why this is important. First, before attributing a patient's deficit to some higher-level analysis process, we have to be sure that the early stages of acoustic-phonetic analysis are unimpaired. Second, it has been claimed (Luria 1970) that the comprehension deficit experienced by some patients is due to their inability to discriminate between similar phonemes (e.g. Caramazza, Berndt, and Basili 1983). A test such as the one described here provides a simple way of evaluating this claim.

Previous research has tended to use non-words or nonsense syllables because this is seen as a purer test of "phonemic level" processing. Since our primary interest was in how the speech input contacts representations of lexical form, we examined various phonological contrasts as they occur in naturally produced real words.

A number of factors determined the design of the present test. First, we wanted to examine a wide range of single-feature contrasts in naturally produced real words. Second, the test had to be administered in a single session and could not be too demanding for the patient. In order to obtain a representative sample of speech sounds, we tested both consonant and vowel contrasts. Although consonants are standardly tested in phoneme-discrimination tests, vowel contrasts are usually ignored in the aphasia literature. In addition, we varied the word-position of the consonant contrasts. They were presented in both word-initial and word-final position. This was because the realizations of, and cues to, word-initial and word-final phonemes differ. Hence, discriminability may vary between pairs consisting of word-initial contrasts and those with word-final contrasts.

For the consonant contrasts, we varied both place of articulation and voicing for a set of plosive and fricative contrasts. We also varied place of articulation for a set of nasal contrasts. For a subset of our materials, the feature contrasts were vulnerable to high-frequency hearing loss. These were the unvoiced plosive and fricative contrasts, whose discriminability depends on high-frequency information. Since many older patients suffer from significant hearing loss, particularly involving the high frequencies, the inclusion of these materials enables us to examine the effects of hearing loss upon a patient's ability to identify various types of speech sounds.

Design and Materials

The test set was based upon 34 word pairs, representing 25 single feature consonant contrasts and nine vowel contrasts. Each of these contrasting word pairs was matched with a "same" word pair, where the two words were identical. This produced a total of 68 word pairs. Each word pair was presented three times so that we could obtain three responses from the subject for each pair. This resulted in a test block of 204 word pairs, preceded by a ten-item practice block. The distribution and nature of the contrasts are shown below.

The set of Place contrasts included the plosives /p t k b d g/, the nasals /m n/, and the fricatives /f v s z ʃ/. The place and the fricative sets were subdivided into voiced and voiceless contrasts.

The sample of fricatives was dictated by the phonotactic contrasts of English. We needed contrasts that could occur in both word-initial and word-final position. The vowel contrasts were selected as a sample of the English vowels. They varied along both front-back and height dimensions, giving a reasonably large set of contrasts.

Table 4.1
The distribution of consonant contrasts

Place contrasts		Word-initial	Word-final
i) Plosives			
a) Voiced	/b/-/d/	2	2
	/b/-/g/		
b) Voiceless	/p/-/t/	2	2
	/t/-/k/		
ii) Fricatives			
a) Voiced	/v/-/z/	1	1
b) Voiceless	/s/-/f/	2	2
	/s/-/ʃ/		
iii) Nasals	/m/-/n/	1	1
	/n/-/ŋ/	*	1
Voice contrasts			
i) Plosives			
a) Voiced	/p/-/b/	2	2
b) Voiceless	/t/-/d/		
ii) Fricatives			
	/f/-/v/	2	2
	/s/-/z/		
	Total	12	13

* The /n/-/ŋ/ contrast cannot occur word initially in English.

Table 4.2
The set of vowel contrasts

pɪt	pɛt	cɒt	cʌt
bɛg	bæg	lɒk	lʌk
pɪck	pæck	pɑk	pɔk
dɑrt	dərt	spɒt	spɔt
brʊd	brɔd		

The following vowels were contrasted in cvc environments. ɪ ɛ, ɪ æ, and ɛ æ were pairs of front vowels height; ɑɔ, ɑ ə, ɒ ʌ, ɔ ʌ, ɔ ə, and u ɔ were pairs of mid and back vowels that varied along the dimension of height and rounding. These contrasts were contained within monosyllabic nouns or adjectives that were all high frequency, familiar words.

There were a total of 68 test words. These words were recorded, in a soundproof booth, by a female native speaker of English on a Revox B77 MkII tape recorder. The words were digitized at 20 kHz sampling rate and stored on computer disc. These digitized words were then recorded back onto a Revox B77 tape recorder in the correct word pairings and in the correct sequence. This procedure ensured that the same token of a word was used in all contrasts featuring that word.

The 204 word pairs were presented in a pseudorandomized order, so that a repetition of any specific word pair was separated by at least 20 word pairs. There was a one-second interval between the two members of each pair, and a three-second interval between each word pair. The pairs were recorded in blocks of ten, separated by two tones. A practice block of ten word pairs preceded the 204 test items.

The control groups were all tested in the laboratory. The younger subjects were tested in groups of four in individual testing booths. The old controls were tested in pairs. The stimuli were presented over headphones, and subjects were asked to indicate in the booklet provided whether the words in the pair were the same or different. The booklet was divided into blocks of ten test pairs to coincide with ten item blocks on the tape. Completion of each block of ten responses was followed by the double tone signal. This allowed subjects to check that they had not missed any items.

The patients were tested individually at the Speech Therapy department of the Queen Mary Hospital, Sidcup, or in their own home. The experimenter recorded the responses of each patient, who gave verbal "same/different" responses.

Results

The percentage error rate in each condition was calculated for each subject group. A summary of the data is shown in table 4.3.

A consistent pattern of results emerges across the four groups. Performance is worse overall for the groups with poorer hearing. The old controls with poor hearing, and the aphasic patients who had a similar degree of hearing loss, performed considerably worse than the young controls and old controls who had no significant hearing loss. For all the groups, the major difficulties occurred with the place contrasts—error rates in both the voice and the vowel contrasts were much lower.

Table 4.3
Percentage error rates

	Different		Same
	Word-initial	Word-final	
Consonants			
Place			
Young	2.3	0.9	0.4
Old NHL	6.7	8.9	1.5
Old HL	35.8	42.9	5.7
Patients NHL	6.2	1.9	10.0
Patients HL	39.7	45.2	4.8
Voice			
Young	0.4	0	0.5
Old NHL	1.7	0	0.9
Old HL	6.7	1.7	2.5
Patients NHL	0	0	2.1
Patients HL	15.8	7.4	4.3
Vowels			
	Different		Same
Young	1.6		0.6
Old NHL	1.5		2.2
Old HL	1.5		5.9
Patients NHL	1.9		3.5
Patients HL	10.7		2.1

HL = hearing loss
NHL = no hearing loss

The consequence of hearing loss should be to make discrimination of the "different" pairs more difficult (increasing the number of "misses"), but it should not increase error rates to "same" items (false alarms). This is indeed what we found. Miss rates were higher for the old controls and aphasic patients with poor hearing than for the young controls and for the old controls and patients with good hearing. The false-alarm (FA) rate is an indication of the extent to which the subject guesses the response. The false-alarm rates overall were very low, indicating that subjects were rarely guessing.

Correlations between hearing loss and miss rates for the old controls and the aphasic patients showed that there was a significant relationship between hearing loss and miss rate for both sets of subjects (old controls $r = 0.83$, $p < 0.005$, aphasic patients $r = 0.67$, $p < 0.05$). However, the correlations between hearing loss and false alarm rate for these two groups were not significant (Old controls $r = 0.32$, $p > 0.10$, aphasic patients $r = -0.4$, $p > 0.10$).

Overall, the discriminability of the contrasting phonemes was not influenced by the position in the word. Error rates were generally the same for word-initial and word-final contrasts, although there was a slight increase in word-initial errors for the voice contrasts for the hearing-impaired subjects.

For all of the subject groups, the place contrasts proved the most difficult set. This is most noticeable in the performance of the two groups with the poorest performance, the hearing-impaired old controls and the aphasic patients. For these two groups, misses on the place contrasts exceeded 20 percent in all types of contrast, whereas performance on voice contrasts and vowel contrasts showed a relatively small increase in miss rate compared to the hearing groups with good hearing. (Table 4.4 shows the distribution of the misses by manner of articulation.)

The difference in performance on the place and voice contrasts may be due to differences in the nature of the cues for these different classes of speech sounds. The perception of place contrasts depends on the extraction of such acoustic information as direction, rate, and extent of rapidly changing formant frequencies. In contrast, differences in voice are signaled primarily by the timing relations between the onset of the voicing relative to the release of the consonant (voice-onset time) and the extent of the cutback

Table 4.4
Percentage error rates for the place and voice contrasts by manner and word position

	Word-initial			Word-final		
	Plosive	Fricative	Nasal	Plosive	Fricative	Nasal
Place						
Young	0.3	0.0	17.0	0.3	0.0	3.3
Old NHL	1.7	2.2	40.0	0.0	22.2	6.7
Old HL	27.0	20.0	40.0	30.0	60.0	43.0
Patients NHL	0	5.6	33.3	0	5.6	0
Patients HL	30.6	43.2	66.6	31.5	44.5	72.2
Voice						
Young	0	0.7		0	0	
Old NHL	3.3	0.0		0	0	
Old HL	6.7	6.7		3.3	0	
Patients NHL	0	0		0	0	
Patients HL	13.0	18.5		5.6	9.2	

HL = hearing loss
NHL = no hearing loss

of the first formant relative to the higher formants. The duration of the preceding vowel is a further temporal cue to voicing. The temporal nature of the cue to the voice distinction may make it less vulnerable to hearing loss than the cue to place.

Both control subjects and patients have problems in identifying nasal contrasts, whether the contrast occurs word-initially or word-finally. Moreover, word-initial contrasts are even more difficult to discriminate than word-final contrasts.[1]

Looking at the data as a whole (tables 4.3 and 4.4), the main characteristic is that the aphasic patients with poor hearing show the highest error rates on those contrasts that are dependent on the ability to hear the higher frequencies. That is, the group data are consistent with what one would

Table 4.5
Percentage misses and false alarms by condition for aphasic subjects

	Misses					False alarms		
	Consonants				Vowels	Consonants		Vowels
	Word-initial		Word-final					
	Place	voice	Place	voice		Place	Voice	
Anomic								
PK(Y)	4	0	4	0	4	14	0	0
JA*	8	33	22	0	4	4	8	15
Nonfluent								
BN(Y)	8	0	0	0	0	6	4	7
VS(Y)	33	33	37	33	22	0	0	0
JG	8	0	37	0	7	6	0	0
CH*	58	0	74	0	19	0	0	0
GS*	25	0	26	0	0	10	13	0
JW*	58	42	70	25	33	0	0	0
DE(Y)	0	0	25	0	0	0	0	0
Fluent								
FB*	67	25	56	8	7	2	0	4
RH*	33	0	30	0	0	10	13	0
Global								
Geo S*	67	25	52	0	4	0	0	0
Patient group data								
HL	40	18	45	7	11	4	4	2
NHL	4	0	10	0	1	7	1	2

HL = hearing loss
NHL = no hearing loss
* = patient with significant hearing loss
Y = young patient (under 45 years when tested)

expect from subjects who show some degree of hearing loss. In fact, both the miss and false-alarm rates for the patients who have poor hearing (mean hearing loss 35.24 db) are very similar to the data from the old controls with poor hearing (mean loss 37.9 db). The miss rate for the old controls and patients were 18.7 percent and 23.7 percent, and the respective false alarm rates were 2.5 percent and 3.3 percent. The patients, like the old controls, had high error rates on the place contrasts, particularly the nasal and fricative contrasts, in both word initial and word nal position. They also had a high error rate on the short-vowel contrasts.

The data for each individual patient are summarized in table 4.5. The appropriate control group against which to compare PK, BN, VS, and DE is the young group. All other patients should be compared with the old-age controls. At the bottom of the table, we summarize the group data for the patients according to hearing loss.

Looking at the individual data in table 4.5, we can see that for all the aphasics (except VS) the predominant source of consonant errors was the place contrasts. Thus, these data do not support the claim that Wernicke patients find place contrasts more difficult than voice contrasts, whereas Broca patients perform equally well on both types of contrast (Blumstein et al. 1977). The two fluent patients, FB and RH, who conform to the Wernicke-type pattern on the BDAE, are not distinguishable from the rest of the group on the basis of differential performance on the place and voice contrasts.

Finally, we should note the performance of JG. He missed a large percentage of word-final place contrasts. This cannot be accounted for by hearing loss, since he shows only moderately impaired hearing (22 db). However, his poor performance here is consistent with his poor performance on the studies reported in chapters 12 and 15, where he was insensitive to violations at the ends of words.

Conclusions

This phoneme-discrimination test provides a practical way of testing a patient's ability to make a wide range of phonemic discriminations in different positions in naturally produced words. It includes place and voice contrasts for word-initial and word-final consonants, as well as a range of vowel contrasts. The test correlates well with degree of hearing impairment. The 214-item test can be easily administered in a single session of about 30 minutes.

It is important to test each aphasic patient's ability to discriminate naturally produced speech sounds in a test of this type. Unless we have this kind of information for each patient, we cannot be sure of attributing abnormal performance in various aspects of language comprehension to the correct underlying deficit. We need to know whether a patient has any problems in the initial phases of analyzing the sensory input before attributing his or her deficit to a later stage of the language-comprehension process.

Chapter 5

Recognizing Words from Fragments: Morphologically Simple Words

---

Overview

This study establishes whether aphasic patients are able to map the speech input onto representations of lexical form in the same way as normal listeners. To do this, we use the gating task, in which increasingly larger fragments of a word are presented to patients. After hearing each fragment they say which word they think they are hearing. In this way we can estimate the point in each word at which it is correctly identified and compare this to the point at which unimpaired listeners identify the word. We thus obtain a measure of the extent to which the speech input can be accurately mapped onto representations of lexical form.

Background

The process of identifying words lies at the heart of spoken-language comprehension. It is only when the speech input is mapped onto representations of lexical form that the syntactic and semantic properties of those words can become available and contribute to the construction of a meaningful interpretation of the utterance.

The gating task described here is designed to establish how effectively aphasic patients make use of the speech input to access representations of lexical form. Extensive research with normal listeners has shown that the sensory input is continuously projected onto representations of the form of a word. The speech signal activates a large set of word-candidates that share the same initial sound sequence (the "word-initial cohort") (Marslen-Wilson 1978, 1987; Warren and Marslen-Wilson 1987, 1988; Tyler and Wessels 1983, 1985). This set gradually diminishes in size as candidates fail to match the accumulating sensory input. A word is recognized at the point at which the speech input separates from all other words in the language sharing the same initial sound sequence. This is normally referred to as the "uniqueness point" (UP). This can occur well before the end of the word, especially in words with more than one syllable.

To determine whether listeners do indeed recognize a word at this uniqueness point, we need to use a task that allows us to measure when the word is recognized. One such task is the gating task (Grosjean 1980; Salasoo and Pisoni 1985; Tyler 1984; Tyler and Wessels 1983). In this task, subjects are presented with successively larger fragments of a word and, after each fragment, either say or write down the word they think they are hearing. We can thus determine the point in the speech stream at which a word is recognized. We can also build up a picture of how the sensory input is used over time by examining the candidate words (the members of the "cohort") that are produced in response to a particular fragment. Thus, we can chart both qualitatively and quantitatively the properties of the cohort at any point in time, and assess the response of the language-processing system to changes in the sensory input.

Although the standard version of the task does not require subjects to make a rapid response (they merely have to write down their word-choice and are not placed under time constraints), research has shown (Tyler and Wessels 1985) that the task is still on-line in the sense that listeners' responses can be directly related to specific stretches of the speech input. The gating task therefore provides a means of assessing how efficiently the sensory input is used as it accumulates over time. Clearly, this is one type of basic information we need to obtain in order to develop a processing profile of an aphasic subject.

We selected a set of words which varied in the point at which they could be uniquely identified. Some words became unique early in the word, while others became unique much later. By manipulating this uniqueness point, we were able to determine whether patients identified the word at the theoretically earliest point at which they could do so. The evidence from studies on nonimpaired listeners (Marslen-Wilson 1984; Tyler 1984) indicates that the point at which they correctly identify a word as measured in the gating task, known as the isolation point (IP), corresponds closely to the theoretical uniqueness point, established on the basis of a dictionary search.

Rather than simply test the patients on the type of word that they typically find easy to recognize, namely high-frequency concrete nouns, we tested them on a wider range of items, selecting both concrete and abstract words, and varying form class.

Design and Materials

We selected 24 polysyllabic words (a mixture of nouns, verbs, and adjectives). Twenty of these were test items and the remaining four were practice items. Half of the test words had early uniqueness points and half had late uniqueness points. These were determined first on the basis of a dictionary search and second by examining recordings of the words on an oscillo-scope. We used the same mixture of nouns, verbs, and adjectives in both groups. The mean frequency of the words in the early group was 31, in the late group 38 (Francis and Kucera 1982).

These words, pseudorandomly ordered, were recorded by a female na-tive speaker of English. They were digitized at a sampling rate of 20 kHz and segmented into fragments from word-onset, with each fragment in-creasing in duration by 50 msec. The first fragment consisted of the first 100 msec of the word, the second consisted of the first 150 msec, and so on, throughout the whole word. The total number of fragments for each word ranged from nine to 16. To avoid splicing artifacts at the end of each gated segment, we smoothed the end by imposing a Hamming window on the final 5 msec of each fragment.

The control subjects were tested in pairs in a quiet room. They were instructed to listen to the material carefully and to write down after each fragment the word they thought they were hearing. They were told to write down the first word they thought of, and urged to give a word response every time. Patients were tested individually, either at their homes or in the hospital where they received speech therapy. They gave their responses orally and the experimenter wrote them down. The number of words tested in each session depended on the ease with which the patient carried out the task.

Results

Scoring: General Information

1. The isolation point (IP) was calculated for each word. The isolation point for each group of subjects was defined as the mean gate on which 75 percent of the subjects gave the correct target item without subsequently changing their response.
2. We also examined the properties of the word-candidates produced by each subject in response to all the fragments of a particular word. To do this, we developed the following scoring procedure which we applied to each response:
(1a) Whether the subject produced a response at all
(1b) Whether or not the first phoneme was correct
(1c) Whether a patient's response was in the cohort of responses produced by the appropriately age-matched control group (this was just applied to the patient data).

On the basis of this scoring procedure, we calculated a number of statistics about the words produced by subjects.

(2a) The percentage of responses beginning with the correct first phoneme (CFP)

(2b) Mean gate (in msec) at which the correct first phoneme was first produced

(2c) The percentage of words given by the patient which were members of the cohort generated by the appropriately age-matched control group.

In general, most patients had no problem in performing the gating task and enjoyed participating. However, occasionally we needed to relax the scoring criteria slightly for the patients. For example, a patient might not produce a perfect repetition of the word because of articulatory problems. Sometimes a combination of gesture (e.g., mime) and verbal response (e.g., initial syllable) was accepted as signaling the correct word.

Analyses

The mean IPs and error rates for the two sets of words (early and late uniqueness points) for the different groups of subjects (patients and controls) are shown in table 5.1. Failure to recognize a word when all gates had been heard was counted as an error. We have also included the mean length of the sets of words with early and late UPs. This information can be compared with the IPs to provide an estimate of how early in the word it can be identified.

Table 5.1
Mean isolation points (IP), in milliseconds, and percentage errors (in brackets) for early and late uniqueness point (UP) words

	Early UP	Late UP	Mean
Young	195	395	295
Mid-age	230	415	325
Old NHL	240	405 (2.0)	320 (1.0)
Old HL	330 (10.0)	480 (18.0)	405 (14.0)
Patients NHL	275	460	395
Patients HL	350 (12.2)	465 (14.4)	408 (13.3)
Mean word length	590	710	650

NHL = no hearing loss
HL = hearing loss

Control Data

The data presented in table 5.1 show that all four groups of control subjects recognize words well before their offset. This is shown by comparing the IPs with the mean word length. On average, listeners are recognizing a word after they have heard about half of it. Listeners are not waiting for the end of the word, irrespective of whether the word has an early or late uniqueness point. The old controls with poor hearing tended to recognize the words later than their counterparts who had good hearing. The mean IP for the poor hearing group was 85 msec later than the mean IP of the good hearing group. This was particularly marked for the words with early UPs, where the subjects with poor hearing recognized the words 90 msec later than subjects with good hearing. There was less of a difference for the words with late UPs. Here the subjects with poor hearing recognized the words on average 60 msec later than subjects with good hearing. There were also more occasions on which the old people with poor hearing failed to recognize the word at all. This poorer performance of the old hearing-impaired controls is reflected in the strong correlation between hearing loss and mean IP ($r = 0.91$, $p < 0.0005$).

Items which caused particular difficulty for the old people with poor hearing were words which contained an initial fricative /f/. They tended to misperceive a word-initial /f/ as an /s/. This is why they failed to identify two of the test words (table 5.2).

We also analyzed the responses produced by subjects in the mid-age and both old-age control groups. We noted the first gate at which the first phoneme of a word was correctly identified (CFP in msec) and the percentage of words which included the correct initial phoneme (% CFP). These statistics are presented in table 5.2. We also listed the entire set of words produced by subjects in each of the three control groups (this is labeled as

Table 5.2
Control data: Means and ranges [ ]

Control group	Mean db loss	N correct (max = 20)	IP (msec)	CFP (msec)	% CFP
Mid-age	9.8	20	325 [300–375]	110	98.6
Old NHL	13.7	20	320 [305–370]	120	94
Old HL	37.9	18	405 [340–445]	160	87

CFP = gate at which the first phoneme was correctly identified
% CFP = percentage of words in which the first phoneme was correctly identified

Table 5.3
Patient data

Patient	db loss	N correct (max 20)	IP (msec)	CFP (msec)	% CFP	% cohort members
Anomic						
PK(Y)	12.9	20	335	125	96	86
JA*	30.8	20	395	240	72	93
Nonfluent						
BN(Y)	5.5	20	400	195	83	94
VS(Y)	21.7	16	390	150	79	74
CH*	55.9	13	475	240	50	51
JG	22.1	20	370	150	81	85
GS*	29.6	18	385	260	70	92
JW*	34.2	19	380	210	74	80
DE(Y)	7.0	20	300	110	96	96
Fluent						
FB*	37.9	13	470	235	57	68
RH*	30.0	19	420	255	91	94
Global						
Geo S*	28.3	18	375	155	89	76

CFP = mean point at which the first phoneme was correctly identified
% CFP = percentage of elicited words containing the correct first phoneme
% cohort members = percentage of responses which were members of the cohort of responses produced by the appropriate control group
* = patient with significant degree of hearing loss
Y = young patient (under 45 years when tested)

"% cohort members" in table 5.3). The major reason for calculating these statistics was to use them as a baseline against which to evaluate the responses a patient produced. The statistics for all three groups of subjects were very similar. They correctly identified the first phoneme of a word after they had heard between 110 and 160 msec of the speech input, and most of the candidates they produced were real words.

Patient Data

Taken as a group, the data from the patients show that they performed very well (tables 5.1 and 5.3). Even those patients suffering from major speech defects were able to recognize and produce words in response to fragments, as well as the old people with poor hearing. They recognized a word well before its offset (table 5.1). Error rates for the two patient groups were similar to the corresponding old-age control groups. Patients and controls with poor hearing produced more errors than subjects with good hearing (table 5.1).

Number of Words Correct   All but two patients (CH and FB) correctly identified most of the words by the time they had heard all of the word. Difficulty in recognizing the words was highly correlated with degree of hearing loss ($r = -0.716$, $p < 0.01$). The two patients with the greatest hearing loss (CH and FB) correctly recognized only 13/20 words.

Isolation Point   Hearing loss also correlates with mean IP for both early items ($r = 0.71$, $p < 0.01$) and for Late items ($r = 0.67$, $p < 0.01$). Subjects with poor hearing required more sensory information to recognize a word than subjects with no hearing deficit. In general, the patients with good hearing recognized the words at the same point as their age-matched controls.

Correct First Phoneme   The effect of hearing loss is also reflected in the correlation between loss and the mean gate at which subjects produced the correct initial phoneme (CFP) ($r = -0.84$, $p < 0.001$) and between loss and percentage of words containing the correct initial phoneme (%CFP: $r = 0.82$, $p < 0.001$). The patients with poor hearing needed more sensory input to identify the initial phoneme of the word correctly, and consequently produced a lower percentage of responses beginning with the correct phoneme.

Cohort Membership   The words each patient produced were compared to the set of words produced by the appropriate age-matched control group. This provides an estimate of the degree of correspondence between a patient's cohort and the cohort of the group. For most of the patients, over 72 percent of their word responses were in the cohort of the appropriate age-matched control group. The remaining word responses were almost always appropriate candidate words in that they were consistent with the sensory input—they had just not been given by the control group. The cases where the cohort percentage is low (only 51 percent of CH's words were cohort members), arose when the patient misperceived the initial segment of words. For example, as a result of misperceiving /f/ as /s/, CH gave many responses beginning with the wrong phoneme, which were therefore not cohort members.

The two anomic patients (PK and JA) had no special difficulty with this task. Although PK and JA suffer from severe word-finding difficulties in language production, this did not prevent them from producing word-candidates which were consistent with the sensory input, and from identifying words very close to the point at which they were identified by the controls. The fact that JA needs slightly more sensory input to identify a word than PK is undoubtedly due to his poorer hearing. This is born out by the fact that JA's mean IP is no different than the mean IP of the group of old subjects with poor hearing. His hearing loss also probably accounts for his difficulty in identifying some initial phonemes correctly. The results from these two anomic patients suggest that the word-initial fragments provided sufficient cues to enable these patients to access and produce members of the appropriate cohort.

Conclusions

These results show that the gating task provides a straightforward way of examining certain properties of the form-mapping process in a wide range of aphasic patients. It allows us to determine whether a patient is able to map the sensory input onto lexical representations of lexical form in the process of listening to a spoken word. The task is simple to administer and most patients have no difficulty in performing as well as normal listeners.

Chapter 6
Recognizing Words from Fragments: Suffixed Words

Overview

Most patients have no problems processing morphologically simple words. However, a number have particular difficulties with morphologically complex words. This type of word seems to be very vulnerable to brain damage in a large number of patients. In this study we use the gating task to determine, when a patient has difficulties with morphologically complex words, whether it is due to some abnormality in mapping the sensory input onto mental representations of its phonological form.

Background

Open-class words in English—including all nouns, verbs and adjectives—can have a morphological structure of greater or lesser complexity, due to the addition of one or more affixes. These affixes can be either derivational or inflectional. In English, derivational processes often cause changes to the semantic, syntactic, and phonological properties of the base-forms to which the derivational affixes are applied. For example, derivational suffixes can alter the syntactic form-class of base-forms, as in *nation/nationhood* and *trouble/troublesome*. In addition, these forms may become semantically opaque over time (as in *department*), and some classes of derivational suffixes change the phonological form of their stems (as in *chaste/chastity; decide/ decision*).

The inflectional morphology also causes syntactic and phonological changes to the stem but, unlike derivational processes, it does not cause semantic changes. Examples of the grammatical function of inflectional affixes are number on verbs (as in he *jumps/* they *jump*), the suffixes that mark plural on nouns (as in *dog/dogs*), and the comparative suffixes attached to adjectives (as in *dirty/dirtier/dirtiest*). In English the derivational morphology includes both prefixes (such as re-, ex-, and pre-) and suffixes (such as -ment, -ness, -ence), whereas the inflectional morphology is confined to suffixes (such as -ed, -s, -est).

Many aphasic patients have particular problems with morphologically complex words. Most investigations of these problems have focused on a patient's ability either to produce complex words (e.g., Miceli and Caramazza 1987) or to read them (e.g., Patterson 1979). Very little research has been devoted to examining patients' abilities to comprehend complex words when they are spoken. Patients may have difficulty in comprehending a spoken complex word either because they are unable to map the sensory input onto the appropriate form representation of the word in their mental lexicon or to access the semantic and syntactic properties of complex words and use them in the interpretation of an utterance.

To locate the basis for a patient's difficulties, we first have to determine whether there are any abnormalities in the process of mapping the sensory input of a complex word onto the appropriate representation of its phonological form in the mental lexicon. For words heard in isolation, this means establishing that complex words are recognized at the point at which they separate from all other words in the language, including other morphologically related words. A word like *management* should be recognized when the second /m/ is heard. This is the point at which the sequence *management* diverges from its morphological relatives, like *manager* and *manageable*, and from other members of its word-initial cohort.

We used the gating task to estimate the point at which suffixed words could be correctly identified. Because if has been claimed that some patients show differential impairment of derived and inflected words (Miceli and Caramazza 1987), we included a sample of both types of words. We also included a set of morphologically simple words as filler items.

Design and Materials

Because the gating task often takes a long time to administer to patients, we decided that the largest number of bisyllabic test words we could use was 18. Twelve of these were morphologically complex and six were simple. We included the simple words as filler items so that subjects did not hear only complex words (chapter 5 describes the test for access of simple words). All the morphologically complex words were suffixed and were selected from the test words used in our studies on recognizing morphologically complex words in sentences (chapter 12). Six consisted of a stem plus a derivational suffix (*child* + *ish*) and six of a stem plus an inflectional suffix (*paint* + *ed*). The median frequency of the three sets of words was similar—simple 9.5; derived 12; inflected 5 (Francis and Kucera 1982).

These stimuli were divided into two test blocks of nine words, each preceded by a single practice word. The inflected words contained the suffixes [-ed], [-ing], and [-es]. Each of these endings occurred once per block. A range of derivational suffixes was used. The morphologically simple words were a mixture of verbs and familiar, concrete nouns.

These words were pseudorandomly ordered and read by a female native speaker of English. They were digitized at a sampling rate of 20 kHz and segmented into fragments from word-onset, with each fragment increasing in duration by 50 msec. The first fragment consisted of the first 50 msec of the word. The second consisted of the first 100 msec, and so on throughout the whole word. The total number of fragments for each word ranged from nine to 15 (mean = 12). To avoid splicing artifacts at the end of each gated segment, we smoothed the end by imposing a Hamming window on the final 5 msec of each fragment.

The control subjects were tested in pairs in a quiet room. They were told to write down the first word they thought of after each fragment, and urged to give a word response every time.

Patients were tested individually, either in their home or at the hospital where they receive speech therapy. They gave their answers orally and the experimenter wrote them down. The number of words tested in each session depended on the ease with which they patient carried out the task.

Results

Scoring

First, we estimated the point at which listeners correctly identified the full form of each word. For a morphologically complex word, this meant that the listener had to produce the stem and its correct suffix (e.g., *manage + ment*). We did this by calculating the IP for the full form of each word. For control subjects, the IP was defined as the mean gate on which 75 percent of the subjects gave the correct target item without subsequently changing their response. IPs could not be calculated for those words which were not correctly recognized before their offset. For each patient, the IP was defined as the first gate at which the patient correctly identified the word and did not subsequently change his or her mind.

Second, we calculated the IP for the stem of each complex word (e.g., *manage*). This is potentially important in the case of patients who have difficulties with morphologically complex words. In such cases, we need to know whether they have difficulties with the stem and/or its affix.

Third, we calculated the percentage of responses which began with the correct first phoneme (% CFP), and the point at which subjects first correctly identified the initial phoneme of a word (CFP).

Table 6.1
Controls: Overall performance

Control group	Mean db loss	% correct	IP FF (msec)	CFP (msec)	% CFP
Mid-age	8.3	100	360	60	97.1
Old NHL	9.8	100	406	60	96
Old HL	35.7	73	425	70	84

NHL = hearing loss < 25db
HL = hearing loss > 25db
CFP (msec) = mean point at which subjects correctly identified the first phoneme of a word
% CFP = percentage of responses which began with the correct initial phoneme
IP FF = mean isolation point of the full form of all simple and complex words combined

Control Groups

Table 6.1 shows the mean IPs for the full form (FF) of the total set of words (simple and complex), the percentage of responses containing the correct initial phoneme, and the point at which the initial phoneme of a word was correctly identified for the three control groups.

Table 6.1 shows that the mean IPs for the two older groups of subjects are only slightly later than those for the mid-age group (mean mid-age: 360 msec; HL: 425 msec; NHL: 400 msec). The point at which the initial phoneme of a word is correctly identified is essentially the same for the mid-age group and the old people with good hearing, as is the percentage of responses containing the correct initial phoneme. Both groups of subjects identify the initial phoneme of a word very soon after word-onset, and their word-responses are constrained by this phoneme. This is consistent with the results from the simple gating study (chapter 5) and supports the claim that listeners make efficient use of the sensory input in the process of contacting form-based lexical representations.

The old people with poor hearing are only slightly less accurate than the other groups at producing responses which contain the correct initial phoneme. Where they do make errors, it is usually in identifying phonemes containing high-frequency information (/s/, /f/). Unlike some of the patients, these subjects never identified the stem of the word correctly but failed to attach the correct suffix. The only reason for failing to identify a word was because they were unable to discriminate word-initial phonemes containing high-frequency spectral cues. When this occurred, they were not able to activate the appropriate cohort and therefore never identified the word. Five of the words (2 derived, 2 inflected, and 1 simple) fell into this category and were never correctly identified by the old people with poor hearing.

As table 6.2 shows, for the mid-age controls, the IPs of both the stems and full forms of derived words were on average the same as the IPs of

Table 6.2
Control data

	IP derived words (msec)		IP inflected words (msec)	
	Full form	Stem	Full form	Stem
Mid-age	375	258	375	250
Old NHL	442	267	408	258
Old HL	438	300	388	230

Table 6.3
Summary of patient data

	% correct full forms	% correct stems	Full form IP (msec)	% CFP
Anomic				
PK(Y)	89	83	344	89
Nonfluent				
BN(Y)	83	100	322	85
VS(Y)	67	92	395	93
DE(Y)	83	100	377	86
JW*	78	92	400	89
GS*	78	78	403	78
JG	67	67	400	83
Fluent				
FB*	39	58	421	72
RH*	89	100	344	100

* = patient with poor hearing
Y = young patient (under 45 years of age when tested)

inflected words. For both groups of old controls, the stems and full forms of derived words were recognized slightly later than inflected words.

Patients

For the patients, we calculated the percentage of full forms correctly identified, the IP of the full form, and the percentage of words where the first phoneme was correctly identified. These data are shown in table 6.3.

Table 6.3 shows that all patients except FB correctly identified the entire form of most of the test items. Where patients fail to recognize a complex word, this is usually because they fail to produce the correct suffix. They invariably produce the correct stem. For example, BN fails to identify three words by word-offset. These are *fixes*, *sorted*, and *sicken*. He correctly identifies the stems of the two inflected words (*fixes* and *sorted*) at the point where the control subjects recognize them, but he fails to put the correct inflection on the stem. Instead he uses the inflection "-ing." He also produces the correct stem for the derived word *sicken* but instead of producing an alternate derived form, he then produces a different word altogether (*signal*).

Another patient, DE, similarly identifies the stems of the two inflected words which he never gets completely correct (*touches* and *fixes*) at the point at which the control subjects identify the stems. However, just like BN, he does not produce the correct inflection. In the case of *fixes* he finally produces the phrase *fix it* and for *touches* he produces *touching*. These two patients are typical of the kinds of changes patients make to the original complex word. They invariably produce the correct stem but add the wrong affix.

High levels of accuracy in identifying the correct stem are reflected in the accuracy with which patients correctly identify the first phoneme. It is usually when subjects fail to identify the first phoneme of a word correctly that they have problems identifying the word (e.g. JG). Table 6.3 shows that patients almost always correctly identify the first phoneme of the complex word.

Table 6.4 shows the IPs for the full forms and stems of derived and inflected words separately.

Table 6.4 shows that most patients recognize both the full form and the stem of derived and inflected words very close to the point at which the control subjects recognize them. This shows up in very similar IPs for both

Table 6.4
Mean IPs (msec) for the full form and stems of derived and inflected words

	Derived words		Inflected words	
	IP full form	IP stem	IP full form	IP stem
Anomic				
PK(Y)	350	180	390	170
Nonfluent				
VS(Y)	430	286	350	180
JW*	450	325	410	340
DE(Y)	390	200	402	250
BN(Y)	380	225	350	235
GS*	440	270	422	225
JG	430	300	417	250
Fluent				
FB*	450	400	417	175
RH*	500	233	317	150

patients and control groups. Moreover, as the table shows, this applies to both derived and inflected words. Thus, most patients can correctly recognize derived and inflected words on the basis of similar amounts of sensory input as control subjects. This, in turn, suggests that most patients are recognizing the phonological form of simple and complex words in the same way as control subjects.

The major exception to this description of patient performance is FB. He only correctly identifies 39 percent of the full forms of simple and complex words. Half of his errors consist of morphologically complex words made up of the correct stem but the wrong affix. The other half arise because he cannot correctly identify the first phoneme of the word and therefore does not activate the appropriate cohort. This is undoubtedly due to his severe hearing deficit and probably explains why he also performs poorly on the gating task with simple words (chapter 5).

FB's results in this experiment reveal the extent to which his hearing loss distorts his ability correctly to perceive speech sounds and makes it difficult for him to understand what he hears.

In summary, most patients show no major deficit in their ability to use the sensory input to access the phonological form of derived and inflected words. Although they occasionally fail to identify a word, they correctly recognize most of the derived and inflected words they hear and, moreover, recognize them at the same point as the control subjects. The results of this gating study, then, suggest that the problems which some of these patients have with morphologically complex words (see chapters 12–14) is not due to their inability to access their form representations on the basis of the sensory input.

Conclusions

This version of the gating task provides an effective way of determining whether a patient's difficulties with morphologically complex words are due to the early phases of the lexical-access process—namely, the processes involved in making contact with lexical representations of phonological form on the basis of the sensory input. Moreover, the task allows us to see whether a patient correctly identifies the stem of word even when he or she fails to recognize the fully derived or inflected form.

Chapter 7
Word/Non-Word Discrimination of Suffixed Words

Overview

This study complements the experiment reported in chapter 6, in that both examine the patient's ability to recognize the phonological form of a morphologically complex word. However, they reflect different aspects of the process. The gating study described in chapter 6 primarily taps into the continuous process of mapping the speech input onto representations of lexical form, whereas the lexical decision task used in this study taps into a later stage of the process.

In this study we use the auditory lexical-decision task and the same suffixed words as those used in the experiment described in chapter 12. This allows us to directly compare a subject's ability to process these words when they occur in isolation (the present experiment) and when they occur in a sentential context (chapter 12). In this way, we can determine whether a patient has difficulty accessing either the phonological form of a complex word (this study) or its syntactic and semantic content (chapter 12).

Background

We test the form-mapping process in the present study by seeing whether a patient can accurately distinguish between a morphologically complex real word and a non-word composed of an illegal combination of a real stem and suffix (e.g., *manage* + *ly*). If the patient can make this distinction, and if he or she can also identify a morphologically complex word at the point at which it separates from its morphological competitors (see chapter 6), then we can be confident that the patient's ability to map the sensory input onto the phonological form of a morphologically complex word is unimpaired. Only if the process of accessing the phonological form is unimpaired can we attribute a patient's problems in processing a morphologically complex word in context to an impairment in accessing its syntactic and semantic properties and integating them with the context.

This study uses an untimed version of the auditory lexical-decision task in which subjects are asked to indicate whether a spoken item is a real word or not. Subjects hear a combination of real suffixed words, morphologically simple words and non-words. The set of suffixed words includes both derived and inflected forms. There were two types of non-words: those created by illegally combining a real stem and a real suffix (morphologically complex non-words) and those created by changing the last syllable of a simple word to make it into a non-word (morphologically simple non-words). These latter items were the same as those used in the study reported in chapter 15.

Unimpaired listeners have no difficulty in accurately distinguishing between real words and non-words. Moreover, they are equally good at making the distinction for morphologically complex and simple words. If patients cannot contact the appropriate form representation, they will be more likely to confuse real words and non-words. If this problem is confined to morphologically complex words, then we should observe a difference in accuracy for simple and complex words Moreover, because the materials include derived and inflected words, we will also be able to tell whether a patient has greater difficulty with one type of complex word rather than another.

Design and Materials

The set of materials consisted of 45 suffixed real words, of which 21 were derived forms and 24 were inflected forms. In all cases, the stem and affix combination was both phonological and semantically transparent. That is, the suffix did not change the phonological form of the stem compared to when the stem occurred alone, and the meaning of the suffixed form was derived from the meaning of the stem and the meaning of the suffix. In other words, the meaning of the suffixed word was fully compositional. We also included 20 morphologically simple real words.

Each real word had a corresponding non-word. We created morphologically complex non-words by substituting each real word suffix with another suffix so that the resulting combination produced a non-word. For example, by changing the suffix on the real word *wasteful*, we created the non-word *wastely*. We turned morphologically simple words into non-words by changing the last syllable. So, for example, *nylon* became the non-word *nylup*.

We included 140 filler items, half of which were words and half non-words. The real-word filler items consisted of 25 complex words (both prefixed and suffixed words) and 45 simple words. Thus, the number of simple and complex words were fairly evenly balanced with the combination of test and filler items. The non-word fillers included simple words that had undergone phonetic changes in varying positions in the word as well as prefixed non-words.

So that each subject would only hear one member of a word/non-word pair at a single testing session, we created two versions of the materials. Each version contained half the test materials, with an even number of real words and non-words, and all the filler items. Only one member of a word/non-word pair occurred in each version.

Control subjects were tested in pairs in a quiet room. They listened to the sequence of words over headphones and wrote "word" or "non-word" on a response sheet. Patients were tested individually and gave their responses orally.

Results

Control Groups

The results of the old-age and mid-age control groups are shown in table 7.1. Subjects in all groups made very few errors in either correctly identifying a word or rejecting a non-word. There were no significant differences in the number of errors made for each of the three types of test item (simple, derived, inflected; F < 1). For the old-age controls, there was no correlation

Table 7.1
Old-age and Mid-age controls: Percentage of correct decisions and ranges [ ]

	Real words	Non-words
HL		
Simple	99 [100−95]	99 [100−98]
Derivations	99 [100−92]	98 [100−97]
Inflections	99 [100−96]	97 [100−95]
NHL		
Simple	99 [100−96]	100 [100−99]
Derivations	99 [100−94]	99 [100−97]
Inflections	100 [100−99]	99 [100−96]
Mid-age		
Simple	100	100
Derivations	97 [100−95]	100
Inflections	100	100

HL = old subject with > 25db hearing impairment
NHL = old subject with < 25db hearing impairment

between hearing loss and number of errors on either morphologically complex ($r = 0.4616$, $p = 0.25$) or morphologically simple words ($r = .557$, $p = 0.1412$).

The mean A's (cf. Linebarger, Schwartz, and Saffran 1983) for the two groups of old prople reflected the extent to which they were similarly sensitive to the three types of test items. The mean A's for the derived, inflected and simple words for the old people with good hearing were .98, .96, and .99, whereas for the old people with poor hearing they were .99, .99, and 1.0. The only difference between the two groups was in the ranges within the groups. The range was wider for the group with poor hearing (.87–1.0) than for the group with good hearing (.98–1.0).

Patients

The patient data are shown in table 7.2. The performance of all of the patients was well above chance, although a number of patients performed worse than the control group.

The major determinant of performance for most patients was degree of hearing loss. Three patients with poor hearing (FB, JW, and RH) all perform worse than the control group. The mean A' for each of these patients was: FB = .87; JW = .91; RH = .88. Although all three patients were less accurate than normal on all types of stimuli, they were somewhat better at discriminating simple words and non-words than suffixed words and non-words.[1]

Table 7.2
Patients: Percentage of correct decisions

	Real words			Non-words		
	Simple	Derived	Inflected	Simple	Derived	Inflected
Anomic						
PK(Y)	100	95	92	100	91	83
Nonfluent						
JG	81	90	87	93	52	37
JW*	86	86	87	86	76	75
BN(Y)	97	90	82	100	94	100
DE(Y)	86	82	91	100	100	100
Fluent						
RH*	87	90	92	93	64	60
FB*	89	90	71	83	70	75

* = patient with poor hearing
Y = young patient (under 45 years)

Three patients who did not have hearing problems (PK, BN, and DE) all performed well in this study. Their mean A's were all .97. Moreover, they were equally sensitive to the derived, inflected, and simple words.

Conclusions

This auditory lexical-decision task, in conjunction with the gating task described in chapter 6, provides a robust measure of whether a patient has any problems in accessing the phonological form of a complex word. Furthermore, since the complex words used in this study are the same test words that are used in the study described in chapter 12, we are able to compare a patient's ability to access the form and the content of the same set of complex words.

Chapter 8
Word/Non-Word Discrimination of Prefixed Words

Overview

Chapter 7 describes a study which uses the auditory lexical-decision task to determine whether patients can process the phonological form of a suffixed word. The present study describes a similar experiment. Once again, it uses the auditory lexical-decision task, but this time the stimuli are prefixed rather than suffixed words. The reason for testing prefixed words is to assess whether patients' problems with morphologically complex words are limited to suffixed words or whether they have a more widespread problem with morphologically complex words, which extends to prefixed words as well.

Background

Many studies in this book (chapters 6, 7, 12, 13, and 14) test whether a patient is able to process words containing either inflectional or derivational suffixes. If a patient has problems with suffixed words, we want to know whether this is confined specifically to suffixed words or whether it is part of a general problem with all types of morphologically complex words. As a first step toward making this assessment, we designed the study described in this chapter.

The class of English prefixed words is not a homogenous one. It includes words at various stages of lexicalization or opacity. Most simply, this refers to the extent to which the component morphemes of a prefixed word are semantically and phonologically independent. To take into account variations in the degree of opacity of prefixed words, we selected words that were representative of the two poles on the gradient of lexicalization of structures. We refer to items at these poles as either *opaque* or *transparent* forms. The more opaque the structure, the more integrated the affix has become with the stem and the closer the structure has come to be synchronically unanalyzable as two morphemes (e.g., *exile*) . The more transparent the structure, the less integrated the affix is with the stem and the more obviously bimorphemic it is (e.g., *misfit*). We assessed the degree to which each prefixed word was opaque or transparent with reference to the set of opacity criteria developed by Hall (1990). These criteria include productivity (the extent to which a prefix can be used to coin new terms), semantic analyticity (the degree to which each morpheme has an independent and recognizable semantic interpretation), phonological integrity (the degree to which prefix and stem have fused phonologically; the degree of allomorphy), and dependency (boundedness of the stem).

If patients cannot contact the appropriate form-based representation of a prefixed word in their mental lexicon, they will be more likely to confuse real words and non-words. If this problem is confined to prefixed words, then we should observe a difference in accuracy for simple and complex forms. Moreover, because the materials include prefixed words that vary in their degree of opacity, we will also be able to tell whether a patient has greater difficulty with one type of word over another.

Design and Materials

We selected 40 bisyllabic, prefixed real words. Half of these words were opaque and half transparent. Table 8.1 shows the criteria used to distinguish opaque from transparent forms.

Apart from the prefixed real words, there were 20 morphologically simple words. All three sets of words were matched as closely as possible for word frequency (Francis and Kucera 1982). The median frequencies of the three sets of test items were: opaque 7, transparent 1, and simple 5.

Table 8.1
Opacity/transparency criteria

	Opaque	Transparent
1. Productivity		
Affix: Status in current word formation rules	Low	High
Number of forms in the language	Few	Many
Stem: Frequency of occurrence	Rare	Frequent
2. Semantic analycity		
Affix: Separately semantically interpretable	No	Usually
Stem: Separately semantically interpretable	No	Yes
3. Phonological integrity		
Affix: Allomorphy	High	Low
4. Dependency		
Affix: Bound or free	Bound	Free
Stem: Bound or free	Bound	Free

To balance the number of simple and prefixed real words, we included 20 real-word filler items, all morphologically simple words. We also constructed 60 non-words. Twelve of these were "prefixed words" (*addure*) and 48 were "simple" words (*velvic*).

These items were pseudorandomly ordered into two blocks with an equal number of each type of item in each block. We created the two blocks (each of 70 items) so that we could test patients on two separate testing sessions. Each block was preceded by ten practice items.

Control subjects were tested in pairs in a quiet room. They listened to the sequence of stimuli over headphones and wrote down "word" or "non-word" on a response sheet. Patients were tested individually and gave their responses orally.

Results

Control groups

The results of the three sets of control groups are shown in table 8.2. The table shows that all groups of subjects had no difficulty in accurately judging that a prefixed word was a real word whether the relationship between the prefix and its stem was opaque or transparent (F < 1). For all three groups of subjects, prefixed words—whatever the relationship between the prefix and the stem—were discriminated as easily as simple words.

Table 8.2
Control groups: Percentage of correct decisions and range of percent correct ( )

	Misses (word errors)	False alarms (non-word errors)
Young controls		
Opaque prefix	97 (90–100)	Prefix 94 (83–100)
Transparent prefix	98 (95–100)	Simple 99 (98–100)
Simple	97 (85–100)	
Old HL		
Opaque prefix	97 (90–100)	Prefix 83 (67–100)
Transparent prefix	96 (90–100)	Simple 92 (81–98)
Simple	99 (95–100)	
Old NHL		
Opaque prefix	98 (95–100)	Prefix 92 (75–100)
Transparent prefix	99 (95–100)	Simple 95 (83–100)
Simple	99 (95–100)	

Subjects were not as consistently accurate in rejecting non-words as they were in accepting real words, although the mean percent correct was very high. One or two old people had difficulty with the simple non-words, tending to think that they were real words. This can be seen in the range of false-alarm errors produced in this category for both groups of old people (table 8.2). In spite of the larger number of errors on non-words, all control groups were on the whole very sensitive to the distinction between real words and non-words, as is shown in their A' scores. The young people's A's ranged from .96–1 (mean: .98). The mean A' was .96 for each of the three classes of items (range: .91–1.0) for the old people with hearing loss, and .98 for those with good hearing (range: .95–1.0).

Patients

The patient data are shown in table 8.3. The results for four of the patients show the normal pattern. GS, PK, FB, and BN are very accurate at deciding on the lexical status of both real words and non-words, and just as accurate for morphologically complex words as for simple words. This is true whether the prefixed form was opaque or transparent. Their A' scores reflect their high level of sensitivity to the lexical status of the stimuli. (Mean A's for GS, PK, FB, and BN were .95, .99, .97, and .98, respectively).

The sensitivity of three of the patients was outside the normal range for at least some of the conditions, although they were still quite accurate. In JG's case, for example, he was within the range for both types of prefixed words, but outside the range for simple words (A' = .92). This is consistent

Table 8.3
Patients: Percent correct decisions

| | Real words | | | Non-words | |
	Simple	Opaque	Transparent	Simple	Prefixed
Anomic					
PK(Y)	90	100	95	95	95
Nonfluent					
BN(Y)	100	95	85	100	100
DE(Y)	85	85	70	100	100
VS(Y)	95	76	85	95	95
JG	80	85	90	97	91
GS*	95	85	85	98	98
Fluents					
FB*	100	95	90	90	97

* = patient with poor hearing
Y = young patient

with his performance on simple words in the auditory lexical-decision task reported in the previous chapter.

In contrast, DE and VS were as sensitive as the control subjects on simple words (A': DE = .96; VS = .98) but they were outside the normal range for both opaque (A': DE = .90; VS = .90) and transparent (A': DE: .93; VS = .94) prefixed words. Comparing DE's performance in this study and in the previous one,[1] we see that he is less sensitive to the lexical status of a prefixed item than one which is suffixed. However, in both cases, although his performance is worse than that of the control group, it is still well above chance.

Finally, in contrast to the results of the auditory lexical decision task with suffixed words (chapter 7), degree of hearing loss did not affect a patient's ability to accurately discriminate real prefixed words from non-words.

Conclusion

This study tests whether a patient has difficulty accessing the phonological form of a prefixed word, and whether this is affected by the phonological opacity/transparency of the word. The results can be compared with the patient's auditory lexical-decision data on suffixed words (chapter 6) to determine whether he or she has a general problem with all types of complex words.

PART III

Accessing Lexical Content

Chapter 9
Verb-Argument Structures

Word-Monitoring Experiment

Overview

If a patient has no difficulty in mapping the sensory input onto representations of lexical form, the next question to ask is whether this mapping process makes available the syntactic and semantic properties of the word and whether these are appropriately used in the process of constructing a meaningful interpretation of an utterance.

Background

We ask these questions in the present study by focusing on the processing of verbs. Verbs are particularly useful in this context because part of their representation includes syntactic and semantic information. Moreover, both types of information constrain the possible arguments a verb can take. Still the most influential analysis of the properties of lexical representations is Chomsky's (1965) treatment of the co-occurrence constraints associated with a given verb. He distinguished two major types of constraint on verb-argument relations-strict subcategorization rules and selectional rules.

Strict subcategorization rules specify the categorical context in which verbs can occur. These specify, for example, that a verb like *grow* can be followed either by a noun phrase (NP), by an adjectival form, or by nothing (in its intransitive use). If this type of constraint is violated, as in the example "He slept the house," a syntactic structure cannot be constructed and the semantic relations between verb and noun are not semantically interpretable.

Selectional rules further subcategorize verbs in terms of the syntactic features of the words that can fill the categorical possibilities specified by the subcategorization rules. By syntactic features, Chomsky meant properties such as [+ Animate] or [+ Abstract], which in later treatments have usually been classified as semantic in nature (e.g., Jackendoff 1972). The sequence "He ate the house" would violate the semantic restrictions on the verb and its argument.

All subsequent analysis of the properties of lexical representations have preserved, in one form or another, this fundamental distinction between the categorial properties of the verb argument frame and the semantic and syntactic properties of the items that can fill these argument slots (Bresnan 1982; Chomsky 1981; van Riemsdijk and Williams 1986). Moreover, in all these formulations, the subcategorization properties of a lexical item are closely linked with its argument structure in a semantic interpretation. The argument frames associated with lexical items specify how these arguments might function not only in a purely syntactic representation of the utterance, but also in its semantic interpretation. Thus, the argument frames associated with verbs have consequences not simply for the linguistic analysis of an utterance, but also for the construction of an interpretation in the non-linguistic, pragmatic domain (Carlson and Tanenhaus 1986).

We can contrast subcategorization and selectional constraints, which we can assume to be lexically coded, with a different type of constraint on verb-argument structures—namely, pragmatic constraints. Pragmatic information is assumed to involve a process of interpreting information that is lexically represented with respect to real-world knowledge. In the sequence "He licked the house," the relationship between the verb and its argument is pragmatically implausible only with respect to our knowledge of real-world events. This division between what we can reasonably assume to be lexically represented (selection restrictions and subcategorization information) and what must be inferred (pragmatic information) provides an interesting set of contrasts for examining the ability of aphasic patients to access and use different types of information associated in different ways with lexical representations.

We have established in recent research (Marslen-Wilson, Brown and Tyler 1988) that the semantic, syntactic, and pragmatic implications of a verb are immediately used to constrain the verb-argument structures the listener constructs. We did this by having subjects monitor for target words occurring in materials of the type illustrated in table 9.1. The target word—the noun *guitar*—is the same in all cases. These sequences are identical except for variation in the verb and in the argument frames associated with the verb.

In sentence (1a) the relationship between the verb (*carried*) and the target (*guitar*) is fully acceptable on syntactic, semantic, and pragmatic grounds. The subcategorization requirements of the verb allow for a noun phrase as direct object; a guitar has the appropriate semantics for the action of carrying, and carrying a guitar is a perfectly reasonable activity in the

Table 9.1
Example of stimulus materials

1a. The crowd was waiting eagerly.
   John carried the *guitar....*

1b. The crowd was waiting eagerly.
   John buried the *guitar....*

1c. The crowd was waiting eagerly.
   John drank the *guitar....*

1d. The crowd was waiting eagerly.
   John slept the *guitar....*

---

context of a standard model of the world. Response-times to targets in normal contexts like (1a) formed the baseline condition.

Sentences (1b) and (1c) illustrate two grades of potential violation of the lexical representations evoked by the verb. In both cases the target NP (*guitar*) remains categorially appropriate; the verbs are transitive and accept a nounphrase as direct object. Sentence (1b), however, constitutes a pragmatic anomaly, and contrasts with (1c), which constitutes a semantic anomaly. This, in effect, is the distinction between the linguistic and the nonlinguistic aspects of the lexical representation of a verb. The anomaly, or the "oddness," of "John buried the guitar" cannot be part of the linguistic specification of the semantics of the lexical items involved. It is something that we have to infer, given our knowledge of the world, and given what we know about guitars, the likely effects of burying them, and so on.

The second type of violation, in (1c), is a violation of the selection restrictions on the semantic properties of the items that can fill the argument slots made available by the verb's subcategorization properties. The linguistic specification of drinking (that it involves liquids) and of guitars (that they are solid objects) is sufficient to make *guitar* anomalous following *drink* without having to invoke knowledge or operations outside the linguistic domain.

Finally, (1d) differs from the other two in violating the subcategorization frame associated with a given verb. A verb form like *sleep* is subcategorized as an intransitive verb and has no subcategorized argument slot into which a noun phrase like *guitar* can fit.

In the experiment, we found that subjects' latencies to respond to the target were slower compared to the baseline condition when a sentence contained any kind of verb-argument violation.

The effect for pragmatic anomalies means that the lexical representations associated with the verb must be being interpreted on-line, not only within a linguistic system of analysis, but also with respect to the listener's mental model of the utterance—that is, with respect to a level of representation that incorporates inferential processes operating on nonlinguistic as well as linguistic knowledge. This is consistent with a view of lexical processing that stresses the immediacy with which the thematic consequences of a given lexical argument frame can be projected onto nonlinguistic domains of interpretation.

The effects of semantic anomalies show that the semantic aspects of lexical representations are also immediately activated in on-line processing. Moreover, semantic anomalies tend to have a more disruptive effect on responses than pragmatic anomalies. This is probably because a semantic anomaly not only involves disruptions within the linguistic system; it also violates considerations of real-world plausibility. If it is unusual and implausible to bury a guitar, it is far more unusual to drink one.

Finally, categorical violations have the strongest effect on response time, with responses being significantly slower than to both the semantic anomalies and the same targets in undisrupted contexts. We expect these strong effects because this type of violation generates a structurally uninterpretable combination of words. The target noun is heard in the context of a verb subcategorization frame that contains no argument slot into which it can be attached. This means that the listener cannot construct the appropriate structure for semantic interpretation. Although a subcategory violation consists of an argument that is both syntactically and semantically inappropriate for the constraints imposed by the verb's specifications, it may well be the case that when the listener cannot construct the appropriate syntactic object, the semantic implications of the verb-argument structure are never evaluated. If this is indeed the case, then a subcategory violation is primarily a syntactic violation. For the purposes of the monitoring task, then, the listener can only have access to the monitoring target by treating it as a word heard in isolation.

These results show the immediate effects of the lexical information associated with a verb both at strictly linguistic levels of interpretation and at levels of interpretation and inference relevant to the listener's construction of a mental model of the current discourse. Given these results, we can use similar materials to determine whether a patient is able to use these different types of lexically associated information in the process of interpreting an utterance.

Design and Materials

Thirty-two common nouns were chosen as target words, and sentence-pairs were constructed for each of them (as shown in table 9.1). Each target occurred as the object noun in the second sentence of each pair. The first sentence provided a minimal, and not highly constraining, context for the interpretation of the second sentence. The second sentence always took the same form. A subject NP was followed by a verb which, in turn was followed by an object NP (the target word). The sentence continued with at least one other clause after the target. These 32 normal sentence-pairs (like 1a) constituted the baseline condition against which the other conditions could be evaluated. The other three conditions (1b–1d) were constructed by varying the relationship between the verb and the target noun. In the pragmatic violation condition (1b), the sentence became pragmatically implausible by replacing the verb preceding the target with another verb of the same frequency. For the selection restriction-violation condition (1c), verbs were selected so that their semantic properties were incompatible with the semantic properties of the noun. In the category-violation condition (1d) intransitive verbs were chosen that could not be followed by a noun in direct object position.

The mean frequency (Francis and Kucera 1982) of the verbs used in the four conditions was 27 (no violation), 19 (pragmatic violation), 24 (selection restriction violation), and 26 (categorical violation) per million. So that the subject would hear each target word only once per session, four versions of the materials were constructed. Each version contained one quarter of the targets in each of the four conditions. Items in the four conditions were pseudorandomly distributed across a version with 44 filler items interspersed between the test items. The filler items were designed to obscure the regularities in the test items. Thus, there were a total of 76 items in each version, preceded by nine practice items. See Appendix B for details of the word-monitoring task.

Results

Control Groups

Table 9.2 gives the mean monitoring RTs for the three groups of control subjects. All three groups show the same pattern of RTs. First of all, they

Table 9.2
Controls: Mean monitoring RTs in the four experimental conditions

	Normal	Pragmatic	Semantic	Categorial
Young	259	303	329	357
Old NHL	309	359	377	401
Old HL	322	380	399	411

NHL = no hearing loss
HL = hearing loss

Table 9.3
Controls: 95% confidence limits for the differences between the experimental
conditions (msec)

	Normal-pragmatic	Normal-semantic	Normal-categorial
Young controls	55–33	90–50	126–70
Old controls	69–39	93–53	107–67

all show significantly slower responses when sentences contain any type of violation [young: Min F'(3,155) = 12.41 p < 0.01; old-age with no hearing loss (NHL): Min F'(3,112) = 24.57, p < 0.01; old-age with poor hearing (HL): Min F'(3,79) = 26.51, p < 0.01).

A set of a posteriori comparisons (Newman-Keuls) for each group, using the error term derived from the Min F' analysis, showed that all three types of anomaly significantly increased RT compared to the undisrupted condition. Moreover, the presence of different kinds of anomaly had different effects on latency. Pragmatic violations had the smallest disruptive effect over normal. Semantic violations had a slightly larger effect[1] and violations of category membership had the largest effect.

When comparing each patient's data to that of the relevant control group, we are primarily interested in whether the patient's RTs are slower in the various disruption conditions compared to the undisrupted baseline condition. To establish this, we calculated the confidence limits for the differences between the various experimental conditions for the young controls and for the old controls. We combined the two groups of old controls for the purposes of calculating confidence limits, because both groups showed the same pattern across the various conditions. Analyses of Variance (ANOVAS) with hearing loss as a factor showed that the slightly longer RTs of subjects with poor hearing (378 msec) were not significantly longer than those with good hearing (361 msec) [Min F'(1,17) = 0.46, p > .05]. Moreover, hearing loss did not interact with the various experimental conditions (Min F' < 1).The confidence limits for the two groups are shown in table 9.3.

Patients

Each patient's data were cleaned according to the method described in Appendix 11. The data were then analysed by means of an ANOVA and post-hoc comparisons carried out on the differences between the experimental conditions. The mean RTs for each patient in each of the four experimental conditions are given in table 9.4.

Table 9.5 presents the differences between the baseline (undisrupted) condition and the three violation conditions. We have marked with * where

Table 9.4
Patients: Mean RTs in the four experimental conditions (msec)

	Undisrupted	Pragmatic	Semantic	Categorial
Anomic				
PK(Y)	512	560	620	599
Nonfluent				
BN(Y)	487	531	537	570
VS(Y)	448	533	549	599
JG	467	478	513	483
CH*	359	389	408	419
GS*	457	573	572	622
JW*	510	551	579	579
DE(Y)	227	329	280	316
Fluent				
FB*	436	477	534	497
RH*	367	436	443	406
WA*	391	431	444	497
Global				
Geo S*	419	441	450	470

Y = young patient (under 45 years of age when tested)
* = patient with poor hearing

Table 9.5
Patients: Difference scores (in msec)

	Normal-Pragmatic	Normal-Semantic	Normal-Categorial
Anomic			
PK	48*	108*	87*
Nonfluent			
BN	44*	50*	83*
VS	85*	101*	151*
JG	11	46*	16
CH	30*	49*	60*
GS	116*	115*	165*
JW	41^	69*	69*
DE	102*	53*	89*
Fluent			
FB	39*	96*	59*
RH	69*	76*	39*
WA	40*	53*	106*
Global			
Geo S	22	31	51*

the difference is statistically significant. A ^ indicates that a difference that is not significant is actually within the 95% confidence limits set by the appropriate control group. With only two exceptions—JG and Geo S—patients tended to produce longer latencies when the sentences contained disruptions compared with the undisrupted condition, as determined by the results of an ANOVA and post-hoc comparisons computed on each patient. These two exceptions showed minimal effects of the various types of violation, which was reflected in insignificant ANOVAs ($F < 1$). For JG, only the semantic anomalies significantly increased RT over the baseline condition ($p < .05$). But although the size of the difference was statistically significant, it was a weak effect, as can be seen by the fact that it is outside the confidence limits for the old-age control group. The second patient, Geo S, was only sensitive to violations of subcategory constraints. But once again, this effect was small and outside the old-age confidence limits.

JG is insensitive to most of the experimental manipulations in the word-monitoring experiments he has been tested on: global (chapter 10) and local (chapter 11) sources of processing information, word-endings experiment (chapter 15), and three morphology studies (chapters 12, 13, and 14). All these experiments test various aspects of the patient's ability to process words in context. Does JG's performance on the word-monitoring tasks simply indicate that he cannot perform the task? This seems unlikely, given his reasonably fast RTs and low error rate (he rarely misses a target word).

There are two other possibilities. The first is that he has such a severe comprehension defect that he can only carry out a word-level analysis of the speech input. This is supported by his relatively normal performance on the gating (chapter 6) and lexical-decision experiments (chapters 7 and 8). He may be unable to construct any form of higher-level respresentation.

However, data to be reported later in this chapter argue against this as an explanation of his deficit and suggest an alternative account. These are the judgment data, where he performs very accurately (80% accuracy on immediate judgments and 78% on delayed judgments). They suggest that JG's comprehension problems may be due to difficulties in *immediately* integrating the incoming speech input into the existing sentential representation. I will discuss this possibility in more detail at the end of this chapter.

Although all the other patients show sensitivity to some types of anomaly, five of them do not show the normal pattern. DE, the patient who conforms closely to the current conception of an "agrammatic" patient (see chapter 3 for details), deviates from normal in his response to sentences containing pragmatic anomalies. For normal listeners, pragmatic anomalies have the smallest disruptive effect, whereas for DE, they have the largest. For DE there was a difference of 102 msec between the undisrupted condition and the pragmatic anomaly condition ($t (31) = 6.051$, $p < .001$).

This compares with 44 msec for the appropriately age-matched (young) control group. This difference implies that DE is much more dependent upon pragmatic information in order to interpret the speech input than are unimpaired listeners. Because he is more dependent on it, he has more difficulty processing an utterance containing a pragmatic anomaly, and consequently his RTs increase more than those of the control group.

Finally, for four patients (JW, PK, FB, and RH) categorial violations do not significantly increase RTs over and above violations involving semantic selection restrictions. This suggests that, for these patients, what is critical is whether the syntactic relations between a verb and its argument are coherent. When they hear an utterance containing a subcategory violation, they cannot construct the appropriate syntactic representation and therefore do not even attempt to evaluate the semantic implications of the verb and the subsequent noun phrase. Thus, their RTs to the subcategory violation reflect their sensitivity to the syntactic properties of the verb and its argument.

Conclusions

This word-monitoring study tests a patient's ability to use different kinds of information to build verb-argument structures in the process of interpreting an utterance. As such, it focuses on the construction of "local" structures and thus complements the test described in chapter 10, which tests patients' abilities to develop representations spanning an entire utterance.

End-of-Sentence Judgment Task

Overview

The word-monitoring study described above taps the immediate processes involved in *constructing* a representation of the speech input. In this study and others described in this book we use a different task—the judgment task—to probe the nature of the *final* representation a listener constructs of the utterance. We use the term "acceptability" judgment because subjects make judgments on different kinds of utterances. Some of them contain purely grammatical violations, whereas in others the grammatical structure is normal and the violations involve aspects of meaning. By having patients perform both types of tasks on the same materials, we can determine whether their language-comprehension deficits are due to problems either in constructing representations of various types or in performing metalinguistic operations on the final representation that has been constructed.

Table 9.6
Old-age controls: Percentage of correct judgments in each condition

	Type of violation			
	None	Pragmatic	Semantic	Categorial
HL	86	76	98	98
NHL	91	95	97	97

Design and Materials

The same set of materials was used as in the monitoring study described above. Subjects heard the materials over headphones. They were asked to listen to each sentence normally and to indicate after the utterance had ended whether or not they thought it was an acceptable utterance of English. The instructions were not more specific than this because of the different types of anomaly in the sentences. Defining "acceptability" did not prove to be a problem for the control subjects, as is shown by the accuracy of their judgments. However, we could tell from the practice trials that some of the patients occasionally did not understand the task. When this occurred, the experimenter clarified the instructions until he or she was confident that the patient understood them. To help patients understand what we meant by the term "acceptability," we referred to sentences which were acceptable as "good" and those which were not as "bad."

We tested only two groups of old subjects on this task because we knew from other studies that young people were extremely accurate and rarely made errors.

Results

Controls

The results for the control subjects are given in table 9.6.

As the table shows, both groups of subjects made very few errors. Overall, the group with poor hearing made slightly more errors (11%) than the group with good hearing (5%).[2] In general, it was not difficult for the old controls to judge a sentence containing any of the three types of violation as an unacceptable sentence of English. Table 9.7 presents the range of errors produced by the two groups of old controls. This is important for assessing the error rate produced by the patients.

Patients

The percentage of correct judgments for each of the patients are shown in table 9.8, together with their mean A' score.

Table 9.7
Old-age controls: Range of (a) the percentage of correct judgements in each condition and (b) A′

	Type of violation			
	None	Pragmatic	Semantic	Categorial
HL				
Judgments	100−81	100−71	100−94	100−96
A′		1−.93	1−.95	1−.94
NHL				
Judgments	100−83	100−83	100−92	100−88
A′		1−.93	1−.96	1−.96

Table 9.8
Patients: Percentage correct judgments by condition

	Type of violation				
	None	Pragmatic	Semantic	Categorial	Mean A′
Anomic					
PK(Y)	94	88	84	94	.96
Nonfluent					
CH*	71	75	88	83	.89
BN(Y)	75	84	88	78	.87
DE(Y)	72	94	94	88	.89
JG	81	69	75	88	.87
VS(Y)	63	81	84	85	.85
GS*	96	75	79	71	.92
JW*	94	34	41	44	.80
Fluent					
FB*	69	94	75	94	.85
RH*	75	50	53	49	.73
Global					
Geo S*	67	71	83	79	.81

* = patient with poor hearing

The first point to note is that almost all patients worse than the control subjects. Only one patient—PK (Mean A′ = .96)—was within the A′ confidence limits for the controls (A′ confidence limits: HL: .98−.95; NHL: .97−.96). The A′ scores of all the other patients were outsde the confidence limits. However, some patients (e.g., BN, DE, JG, GS, FB, and VS) while not producing normal performances were still reasonably accurate in their judgments. The A′ scores for these patients ranged from .85−.92. The performance of two patients (RH: A′ = .73; and JW: A′ = .80) was clearly abnormal. These patients find it difficult to discriminate between a sentence containing an anomaly and one that does not. This, in turn, suggests that they are insensitive to the types of violation which we introduced in the stimuli.

In general, patients responded with a similar degree of accuracy to all three types of anomaly. The A′ for RH, for example, ranged from 76−.71, and for JW they ranged from .78−.81. This was true for all the other patients. The A′s for the three conditions were always very similar.[3]

For most of the patients, there were no major discrepancies between the monitoring and judgment data. Two exceptions to this were RH and JW. Their performance on the judgment task contrasted sharply with their performance on the monitoring task. In the monitoring task, their performance indicated that they were sensitive to all three types of anomaly. Their RTs were longer in the anomaly conditions compared to the undisrupted baseline condition. The fact that RTs increase in the presence of an anomaly means that the patient must be trying to establish an appropriate relationship between the verb and its argument and finding, for different reasons, that this is not possible. Thus, the processes involved in constructing a representation of the speech input are sensitive to the presence of an anomaly. But as soon as the relationship between the verb and its argument has to be explicitly evaluated for the purpose of making a decision about the relationship, the performance of these patients is no better than chance.

If we had tested comprehension only by using the acceptability task we would have concluded that these patients had severe comprehension problems. Similarly, if we had used only the word-monitoring task, we would have concluded that their comprehension was comparatively normal. It is only by comparing data from the two types of tasks that we can gain proper insight into the nature of these patients' comprehension problems. The two types of data together suggest that these patients have problems with some particular types of comprehension processes and not with others. The comprehension processes that seem to be intact are those involved in constructing representations of the speech input—at least, those representations that are necessary to interpret the types of verb-argument relations we manipulated in this study. From the results of other studies reported in this book we know that this contrast between on-line and off-line performance is consistent for RH. He shows essentially normal performance on all on-line tasks, and yet performs at chance on off-line tasks. JW, on the other hand, does not always show the normal pattern of performance on on-line tasks, although he is always very poor at off-line tasks.

JG is another patient who shows a contrast between performance on monitoring and judgment tasks. However, in contrast to RH and JW, he performs reasonably well on the judgment task, although he showed only the most minimal sensitivity to verb-argument violations in the monitoring study. One possible explanation for this is that he integrates the speech input into the developing sentential representation more slowly than normal. He is able to build a structural representation of an utterance, but the effect of brain damage has been to slow down this process. When we use an on-line task that reflects the immediate integration of the speech input (such as word monitoring), he looks impaired. But when a task probes at a later point in time, after he has had more time to process the input, he looks relatively normal.

Anomaly Detection Task

Overview

In this task, the subject presses a response key as soon as he or she detects an anomaly. Timing pulses placed at the onset of the point of the anomaly (the onset of the target word) allow us to measure the time it takes the listener to detect different kinds of anomalies in the sentences.

In this task and the judgment task described above, where the listener has to wait until the end of the utterance before making a judgment, we are tapping aspects of the listener's conscious knowledge about the representation he or she has constructed of the utterance. However, the two tasks differ in that the immediate detection task places no burden on the listener's short-term memory, whereas the delayed judgment task may do so. Because many aphasic patients suffer from various types of memory deficits, it is necessary to use both types of task. Moreover, by using the verb-argument materials we are able to compare a patient's performance directly on the same materials with three different tasks:

1. The word-monitoring task, which requires a fast response to a particular target word but does not depend on any awareness of the relationship between the target and the prior verb.
2. The end-of-sentence acceptability judgment, which requires awareness of the structural relationships within an utterance.

3. The anomaly-detection task, which requires both an immediate response and an awareness of the structural relationship between verb and target.

If a patient has particular problems operating on the representations he or she constructs of the speech input, then performance should be just as poor on the anomaly detection task as on the end-of-sentence judgment task, because in both cases the listener has to become aware of the linguistic representation for an appropriate response to be made.

Design and Materials

We used exactly the same materials as in the word-monitoring and end-of-sentence judgment studies. Subjects were asked to listen to each sentence and to press a response key as soon as they detected anything wrong with the sentence. We stressed the point that they should press the response key as soon as they detected an anomaly.

Results

Control Groups

We obtained two measures in this study. The less important measure was the time it took subjects to detect the anomalies. We were able to collect these anomaly detection RTs because there were timing pulses at the onset of each target word, the point at which the utterance becomes anomalous. These give us a general idea of the speed with which subjects responded to the anomalies.[4] For the young controls, the mean detection RT was 682 msec, and for the two groups of old controls the mean RT was 878 msec. There were no significant differences between RTs for the three types of anomaly ($F^1 < 1$; $F^2 < 1$).

Table 9.9
Control subjects: Mean percent of correct anomaly detections and ranges [ ]

	Type of anomaly			
	None	Pragmatic	Semantic	Categorial
Young	97	98	98	98
Old HL	86	88	89	86
	[100−75]	[100−81]	[100−69]	[94−75]
Old NHL	84	98	99	94
	[94−75]	[100−94]	[100−94]	[100−88]

* The range is not included for the young group because each subject made so few errors.

The more informative aspect of the data is the percent detection of anomalies in the three anomaly conditions. These are presented in table 9.9.

The table shows that all three groups of subjects were very accurate at detecting anomalies in the three conditions. The worst performance was from the old-age controls with poor hearing, who detected an average of 87 percent of the anomalies.[5] The old-age controls with good hearing were more accurate with an overall detection rate of 94 percent.[6] We also tabulated the percentage of correct "no" responses (when subjects did not press the response key) for sentences that did not contain an anomaly. All subjects were very accurate here. The mean correct nondetection rate for the young subjects was 97 percent, for the old group with poor hearing 86 percent, and for the subjects with good hearing 84 percent.

Table 9.10 presents the data from the anomaly detection and delayed judgment tasks for the two groups of old people.

As the table shows, the control subjects are very accurate at judging whether an utterance contains any type of anomaly, irrespective of whether they make the judgment immediately (anomaly detection) or wait until the end of the sentence. However, the range of performance is much larger for the immediate anomaly detection than for the delayed judgment. The subjects with poor hearing are slightly worse when they have to make an immediate decision compared to when the decision is delayed, but they are still very accurate since they average 87 percent correct judgments.

Patients

The data from the patients are shown in table 9.11.

Two patients perform particularly poorly on this task—RH, and JG. Their A' scores were well outside (below .8) the confidence limits of the control group's (A' confidence limits: HL: .94–.9; NHL: .96–.94). All other patients perform reasonably well (A' = .89 and above). Table 9.12 shows both the anomaly detection and delayed judgment data for comparison.

Table 9.10
Old-age controls: Comparison between anomaly detection and delayed judgment tasks by percentage of correct judgments

| | Type of violation | | | | |
	None	Pragmatic	Semantic	Categorial	Mean
Old HL					
Anomaly detection	86	88	89	86	87
Judgment	86	76	98	98	90
Old NHL					
Anomaly detection	84	98	99	94	94
Judgment	91	95	97	97	95

Table 9.11
Patients: Percentage of correct detections

	Type of violation			
	Pragmatic	Semantic	Categorial	Mean
Anomic				
PK(Y)	91	81	88	87
Nonfluent				
BN(Y)	88	78	88	84
JW	84	97	84	88
JG	100	81	84	88
DE(Y)	94	94	88	93
Fluent				
RH	59	56	53	56
FB	75	78	81	78

Most patients perform consistently on both the delayed judgment and immediate anomaly detection tasks. The major exception to this is JG, who is much better at making delayed acceptability judgments than at immediately detecting anomalies. His performance on anomaly detection is consistent with his monitoring data on the same materials. In the monitoring study, he showed essentially no sensitivity to the appropriateness of the verb and its argument. In contrast, his delayed judgments were relatively normal. On the basis of these seemingly disparate results, I argued that JG is able to construct the appropriate verb-argument structures (hence his accurate end-of-sentence judgments), but that the processes involved were slowed down in some way (hence no effects in the word-monitoring tasks). The anomaly detection data support this analysis. His performance on anomaly detection was very poor and similar to the monitoring data. Thus, when the task requires a relatively close relationship between stimulus (the verb-argument violation) and response (word monitoring or immediate anomaly detection), it reflects the fact that the verb-argument structure has not yet been constructed. But when the response is made at the end of the sentence, we can see that he has eventually attempted to construct the appropriate representations.

RH is the single patient who has difficulty detecting anomalies, whether he does this immediately or waits until the end of the sentence. His performance on the judgment tasks stands in sharp contrast to his performance in the monitoring study. Here he showed the normal pattern of performance—his RTs increased when he encountered any type of linguistic violation. The results of the three different versions of the verb-argument studies suggest that for RH the obligatory mental processes required

Table 9.12
Patients: Comparison between anomaly detection and delayed judgment tasks by percentage correct

	Type of violation			
	Pragmatic	Semantic	Categorial	Mean
Anomic				
PK				
Anomaly detection	91	81	88	97
Judgment	88	84	94	89
Nonfluent				
BN				
Anomaly detection	88	78	88	85
Judgment	84	88	78	83
JG				
Anomaly detection	100	81	84	88
Judgment	69	75	88	77
JW				
Anomaly detection	84	97	84	88
Judgment	34	41	44	39
DE				
Anomaly detection	91	88	91	93
Judgment	94	94	88	89
Fluent				
RH				
Anomaly detection	59	56	53	56
Judgment	50	53	49	51
FB				
Anomaly detection	75	78	81	78
Judgment	94	75	94	88

to interpret the speech input (as reflected in the monitoring data) remain relatively unimpaired, while at least some of the processes that require conscious awareness (as reflected in the judgment tasks) no longer function normally. It appears that, although he can develop a normal representation of an utterance, he has difficulty gaining access to it for the purposes of making explicit decisions about it.

Conclusions

The three versions of the verb-anomalies study enable us to see whether a patient can access the semantic and syntactic content of verbs and integrate them into the developing sentential representation, and to what extent the processes involved in constructing representations and those involved in gaining conscious access to those representations are differentially impaired following brain damage.

PART IV

Constructing Higher-Level Representations

Chapter 10
Global Sources of Processing Information

Overview

In the process of understanding spoken language, listeners construct an interpretation of each utterance they hear. Research on neurologically unimpaired listeners shows that this interpretation is constructed word by word as the utterance is heard, and that both syntactic and semantic information is used in its development. This chapter describes a study designed to test whether patients build a representation of an utterance in the same way, using the same kinds of processing information as normal listeners.

Background

The study described here was based on an earlier experiment with unimpaired listeners (Marslen-Wilson and Tyler 1975, 1980), which tracked the availability of syntactic and semantic information as it accumulated over time as the utterance was heard. The experiments used the word-monitoring task, and asked listeners to monitor for target words occurring at various word-positions across three different kinds of prose materials—normal sentences, anomalous sentences (where the syntactic structure was intact but the material was meaningless), and scrambled strings of words (where there was neither syntactic nor semantic structure). These variations in the word-position of the target and in the presence or absence of syntactic and semantic structure allowed us to track the availability of different kinds of processing information across an entire utterance.

Overall, word-monitoring latencies to targets occurring in normal prose were consistently faster than those in anomalous prose which, in turn, were consistently faster than those in scrambled strings. More importantly, we found that latencies became progressively faster in both normal and anomalous prose utterances, but not in scrambled strings. We argued that this was because the semantic and/or syntactic (and prosodic) structure in normal and anomalous prose develops across the sentence and increasingly facilitates word identification.

We adapted this experiment for use with patients because it provides us with a general picture of a patient's ability to take advantage of the global syntactic and semantic structure of a spoken utterance. If a patient cannot take advantage of these properties of an utterance, then this should be reflected in monitoring performance. For example, an inability to use syntactic information in the process of interpreting an utterance should result in no facilitation of word-monitoring RTs, that is, no "word-position effect", across an utterance that can only be interpreted syntactically (anomalous prose).

Design and Materials

We constructed 54 pairs of normal prose sentences, each of which contained a target word in the second sentence of each pair. The first sentence provided a minimal context for the interpretation of the second sentence. The targets were all names of common objects. Forty-one of the targets were monosyllabic, ten were bisyllabic, and three were trisyllabic. The serial position of the target varied, with targets appearing either early, middle or late in the sentence. The early category covered word-positions 2−4, the middle category covered positions 6−8, and the late group covered positions 10−14.

Anomalous prose versions of the normal prose sentences were made by replacing each content word (except the target) with another word of the same form-class and frequency, so that the sentences, although semantically anomalous, were still grammatical. Scrambled strings were made by pseudo-randomly mixing the words in the normal prose sentences so that the resulting strings had no semantic or syntactic structure. We scrambled normal prose as opposed to anomalous prose sentences to ensure that any word-position effects in normal prose could not simply be due to the accumulation of lexical semantic information. The position of the target word was unchanged throughout these manipulations. Examples of the three types of prose, with target emphasised, are:

(1)   Normal prose: Everyone was outraged when they heard. Apparently, in the middle of the night some thieves broke into the *church* and stole a golden crucifix.

(2)   Anomalous prose: Everyone was exposed when they ate. Apparently, at the distance of the wind some ants pushed around the *church* and forced a new item.

(3)   Scrambled Strings: They everyone when outraged heard was. Of middle apparently the some the into the broke night in thieves *church* and crucifix stole a golden.

Three versions of the material were made so that every target word could appear in each of the three types of prose without being repeated in a single session. Each version contained one occurrence of each of the 54 targets, with 18 targets in each of the three types of material. To distribute any effects due to learning, each version was divided into two parts, each containing half of the targets. Targets were blocked according to type of material in order to reduce the possibility of confusing the patient by constantly changing from one type of material to another. Within each part there were nine normal prose sentences, followed by nine anomalous prose items and nine sets of scrambled strings. This order of presentation ensured that any decrease in latency due to practice would not disproportionately benefit the normal prose materials. Four practice sentences preceded each block of nine test sentences.

Each version was recorded in the order described and timing pulses were placed at the onset of each target word. See Appendix B for additional details on the word-monitoring task.

Because we had the original Marslen-Wilson and Tyler (1975, 1980) results from young subjects tested on a set of similar materials, we tested only our two groups of old-age subjects.

Results

Old-Age Controls

Table 10.1 shows the mean monitoring RTs for each group of old-age controls plotted separately. We computed two ANOVAs, both with hearing loss, prose type, and target position as the main factors.

Although the subjects with poor hearing were generally slower (mean RT = 428 msec) than those with good hearing (mean RT = 401 msec), this difference was not significant (Min F' < 1), nor did hearing loss interact with any other variable. Therefore, we ignore hearing loss in further discussion of the results.

Just as we found for young people, these older subjects were faster to monitor for targets occurring in normal prose than anomalous prose, and RTs in anomalous prose were faster than those in scrambled strings (Min F'(2, 133) = 70.43, p < .01).

Table 10.1 shows that subjects were also faster to monitor for a target the later it occurred in a sentence—but only for targets occurring in normal and anomalous prose. For targets in scrambled strings, RTs were not

Table 10.1
Old-age controls: Word-position effects in each type of prose (means (msec) and standard devivations)

Prose type	Word position			
	Early	Middle	Late	Mean
No hearing loss				
Normal	386 (59)	332 (49)	314 (38)*	344 (57)
Anomalous	439 (60)	394 (56)	367 (72)*	400 (69)
Scrambled	477 (60)	444 (57)	454 (48)	458 (56)
Hearing loss				
Normal	416 (58)	347 (49)	314 (44)*	359 (66)
Anomalous	482 (73)	423 (53)	402 (45)*	436 (67)
Scrambled	503 (59)	481 (58)	484 (38)	489 (53)

* = significant word-position effect

affected by the serial position of the target word in the sequence. The ANOVAs showed a significant effect of target position [Min F′ (2, 74) = 11.54, p < .01]. Although the prose × position interaction did not reach significance on a Min F′ [Min F′(4, 126) = 2.37, p > .05], it was significant on both the subjects [F^1(4, 64) = 21.596, p < .001] and items [F^2(4, 102) = 2.656, p < .05] analyses. This distinction between the pattern of RTs in normal and anomalous prose, compared to scrambled strings, supports the claim that increasingly faster RTs are due to the developing syntactic and/or semantic representation listeners construct as the utterance unfolds over time. Since the words in scrambled strings are unstructured, there is no basis for RTs to be facilitated as more of the sequence is heard.

Patients

The mean RTs for each patient by prose type are summarised in table 10.2. A two-factor (prose type × target position) ANOVA was performed on each patient's data. As table 10.2 shows, all patients showed a significant effect of prose type. In all cases, latencies were faster in normal prose than anomalous prose, and these in turn were faster than RTs in scrambled prose. In this respect, then, all the patients show the same pattern as normal listeners.

However, not all patients are able to develop normal syntactic and semantic representations across the entire course of a sentence, as the pattern of word-position effects shows in table 10.3.

Scrambled Prose
We will first consider the results for scrambled prose since this is the baseline condition. RTs need to stay constant across word positions in this

Table 10.2
Patient data: Mean RTs (msec) by prose type

	Prose type			Differences			Prose effect (p value)
	Normal	Anomalous	Scrambled	N-A	A-S	N-S	
Anomic							
PK(Y)	430	531	583	−99	−52	−153	<.001
JA	485	620	700	−135	−80	−215	<.001
Nonfluent							
BN(Y)	559	589	647	−30	−58	−88	<.001
VS(Y)	487	566	621	−79	−55	−134	<.001
JG	371	450	500	−79	−50	−129	<.001
CH	432	489	542	−57	−53	−110	<.001
GS	437	571	647	−134	−76	−210	<.001
DE(Y)	258	358	409	−110	−41	−151	<.001
JW	483	580	617	−97	−37	−134	<.001
Fluent							
FB	465	513	569	−48	−56	−104	<.001
RH	473	523	595	−50	−72	−122	<.001
WA	388	499	571	−111	−72	−183	<.001
Global							
Geo S	477	551	593	−74	−42	−116	<.001

condition so that we can interpret any facilitation across word positions in the other two prose conditions as being due to the development of syntactic and/or semantic representations, rather than serial-position (expectancy) effects.

Only one patient, CH, shows a significant word-position effect in scrambled prose. However, the size of the word-position effect (as measured by the decrease in RTs from early to late positions) in scrambled prose is only one third the size of the word-position effect in normal and anomalous prose. Therefore, it is unlikely that the word-position effects in normal and anomalous prose can be accounted for in terms of the same simple serial-position effect as in scrambled prose.

Six other patients (JA, JG, GS, JW, FB, and Geo S) show a nonsignificant trend toward RTs decreasing across scrambled prose. Since a word-position effect in scrambled prose cannot be due to the presence of any structural representation, we have to entertain the possibility that the word-position effect these patients show for other types of prose may also reflect a simple serial-position effect rather than the development of structural representations. This could certainly be the explanation for their trend towards a word-position effect in anomalous prose. For these patients, the size of the difference between RTs in the early and late conditions in anomalous prose

Table 10.3
Patients: Word-position effects in each type of prose

	Normal prose			Anomalous prose			Scrambled prose		
	Early	Middle	Late	Early	Middle	Late	Early	Middle	Late
Anomic									
PK(Y)	491	411	382*	525	528	539	586	564	596
JA	564	435	454*	642	612	605	706	718	675
Nonfluent									
BN(Y)	636	512	530*	638	543	585*	644	650	649
VS(Y)	563	440	459*	584	583	530	581	647	635
JG	441	331	342*	472	431	448	495	536	468
CH	531	388	378*	559	479	429*	571	521	533*
GS	523	383	405*	589	581	543	665	651	626
JW	549	511	390*	580	587	574	614	641	593
DE(Y)	305	265	205*	355	379	370	388	427	412
Fluent									
FB	510	448	439*	542	512	485	585	574	548
RH	524	519	377*	571	538	459*	550	600	634
WA	421	386	357*	531	481	485	566	559	589
Global									
Geo S	520	453	459*	580	544	530	632	576	570

* = latencies significantly faster across word-positions

was very similar to the size of the difference in scrambled prose. Therefore, the word-position effect for both types of prose are probably due to a simple serial position effect.

However, the serial-position account is unlikely to be the correct explanation for the word-position effects in normal prose shown by five of these patients—JA, JG, GS, FB, and JW—because the effect is twice the size in normal prose as in either anomalous or scrambled prose. Therefore, the word-position effect in normal prose for these four patients probably reflects their ability to develop an interpretative representation of an utterance as they hear it. The absence of a true word-position effect in anomalous prose suggests that they are unable to use syntactic information appropriately in the development of this representation.

For the sixth patient—Geo S—the size of the word-position effect is very similar in all three types of prose, suggesting that he is merely anticipating the occurrence of the target word and not building structural representations.

All the other patients, like the control subjects, produce latencies in the scrambled condition that do not get faster across word-positions. This means that we can attribute any word-position effects in normal and anomalous prose to the development of syntactic and/or semantic representations across the entire course of the sentence.

Normal Prose
Table 10.3 shows that all patients produce significantly faster latencies to targets occurring later in a normal prose sentence compared to those which occur early. All patients (except perhaps Geo S whose normal prose data may just reflect a serial-position effect) appear to be able to use semantic information in the on-line interpretation of an utterance. This semantic information is used to construct a pragmatically coherent representation of the utterance. This conclusion is supported by the contrast between normal and scrambled prose. The word-position effect in normal prose must be due to pragmatically interpreted semantic information rather than merely lexical semantic information, since when the same words appear in an unstructured list (scrambled prose) patients do not show any word-position effects.

Anomalous Prose
Turning to the word-position effects in anomalous prose, we see again that a number of patients show the normal pattern. Although only three patients (BN, CH, RH) show a significant word-position effect, two other patients (VS and WA) show a trend in the right direction and a larger difference between RTs in the early and late word-positions in anomalous prose compared to scrambled prose. There are four patients (PK, JW, JG, and DE) whose latencies do not appreciably decrease as more of an anomalous prose sentence is heard. This suggests that these patients are unable to use syntactic structural and prosodic information to construct a representation of a grammatical but meaningless sentence.

As mentioned at the beginning of this chapter, this study provides a general picture of whether a patient can use syntactic and semantic information in the on-line interpretation of an utterance. Other studies in this book look in more detail at patient's ability to use particular types of syntactic and semantic information (e.g., chapters 9, 11, and 13). The data from these studies, in conjunction with the data from the present experiment, help to build a picture of which aspects of syntactic and semantic information patients have problems with and which are unimpaired. So, for example, the results of the present study suggest that DE has problems with syntax since he does not show the normal word-position effect in anomalous prose. To try to locate the source of his problem, we also tested him on the experiments reported in chapters 9, 11, and 13. We found that he had no difficulty accessing syntactic (subcategory) information when it was part of the lexical representation of verbs and using this information to build verb-arguments structures. He did have problems when the correct interpretation of an utterance depended on his being able to process the syntactic implications of inflectional markers (chapter 13). He was unable to use this information to constrain the interpretation of an utterance. Moreover, this problem was confined only to the syntactic implications of inflections. He had no difficulty in using inflectional markers when they played a semantic role in utterances. The results of all these studies together help to locate his problems with syntax, which were first shown by the absence of a word-position effect in anomalous prose, to difficulties in exploiting the syntactic implications of the inflectional morphology. Whether this is his only difficulty remains to be determined by further experimentation.

Conclusions

The prose-monitoring task is sensitive to a patient's ability to use different kinds of structural information in the process of interpreting an utterance. It is, therefore, a useful gauge of a patient's general sensitivity to these different types of structural information. Subsequent tests in this book probe more specific aspects of the processes involved in sentence interpretation.

Chapter 11
Local Sources of Processing Information

Overview

From the previous study we saw that a number of patients are unable to develop a normal representation of a spoken utterance. In particular, these patients do not show the normal word-position effect in anomalous prose, indicating that they are not developing a syntactic representation of the entire utterance. And yet these same patients produce faster responses to anomalous prose than to scrambled prose. This facilitation for anomalous prose, in the absence of a word-position effect, may be due to their residual ability to construct local phrases using the syntactic and prosodic information which is available in anomalous prose. The present study was designed to assess this possibility.

Background

The previous chapter describes a study which tracks the availability of different kinds of processing information—syntactic and semantic—as they become available to the listener. In it, we use the word monitoring task and ask listeners to monitor for target words occurring in three types of prose contexts: *normal prose*, which is grammatically well-formed and meaningful; *anomalous prose*, which is grammatical but meaningless; and *scrambled strings* of words, which have no structure at all. Examples of each type of prose (with target word in italics) are:

(1a) Normal prose: Apparently, in the middle of the night some thieves broke into the *church* and . . . .

(1b) Anomalous prose: Apparently, at the distance of the wind some ants pushed around the *church* and . . . .

(1c) Scrambled strings: Of middle apparently the some the into the broke night in thieves *church* . . . .

Apart from varying the type of prose context, we also manipulated the position of the target word in the sentence. In this way, we were able to track the ways in which listeners use different sources of processing information as they become available over time.

For unimpaired listeners, monitoring latencies to targets in scrambled strings remain constant across the sentence. This is because there is no structural information of any kind available to the listener to facilitate monitoring latencies. In contrast, latencies get progressively faster across the course of both normal and anomalous prose sentences, indicating that listeners are using semantic and syntactic information to develop a higher-level representation of the utterance.

We saw how some patients differed from unimpaired listeners in their response to anomalous-prose utterances. Instead of RTs getting progressively faster throughout an anomalous prose utterance (referred to as the "word-position effect"), as they do for unimpaired listeners, the monitoring RTs of these patients remained stable across the entire sentence. We interpreted faster RTs across the course of an anomalous prose utterance as evidence that the unimpaired listener is using syntactic information in the process of developing a representation. When a patient doesn't show this pattern, we take this to mean that he or she is unable to use syntactic information appropriately in the process of comprehending an anomalous prose utterance.

However, these patients were not completely insensitive to all aspects of syntactic information. We found that their overall monitoring RTs (collapsed across word positions) in anomalous prose were faster than when the same words occurred scrambled in an unstructured list. This raised the following question: If these patients are unable to use syntactic information (as the lack of facilitation across the course of an anomalous-prose utterance suggests), why are their overall RTs in anomalous prose faster than those in scrambled lists of words? This is an important question because if a patient has an across-the-board syntactic deficit, then he or she should be unable to use any kind of syntactic information. Being able to determine what kinds of syntactic information patients are still able to use in the process of comprehending an utterance, tells us about the limits of their syntactic deficit.

In recent research (Tyler and Warren 1987) we have shown that when unimpaired listeners process anomalous prose utterances, they organize the speech input into local phrases which have both syntactic and prosodic integrity. These local phrases are integrated into larger units by means of the overall prosodic structure spanning the utterance. This produces the word-position effect in anomalous prose. The question is whether patients who do not show a word-position effect in anomalous prose can combine words into local phrases using the same types of information as unimpaired listeners. If they can, then this would account for their faster overall monitoring latencies in anomalous prose compared to scrambled strings. Their failure to show a word-position effect in anomalous prose could then be argued to stem from their inability to combine these local phrases into a global representation.

To determine whether these patients structure the speech input into local phrases as they process an anomalous prose utterance, we developed a study based on Tyler and Warren 1987. The experiment used sentences which were structured into local units defined in terms of "phonological phrases" (Gee and Grosjean 1983; Nespor and Vogel 1982; Selkirk 1980). We chose the phonological phrase as our unit of local structure because it has prosodic as well as syntactic coherence, and prosodic structure is clearly important in spoken (as opposed to written) language comprehension.

Phonological phrases are defined as groups of adjacent words that form syntactic, prosodic, and semantic units. They are intermediate in size between the word and the syntactic phrase. There are two defining properties of phonological phrases. First, each one has a "head". The head is the main word around which the phrase is organized; for example, the head of a verb phrase is the main verb. All the other words in the phrase are dependent elements of the head and serve to modify, complement, or specify it in some way. The second property of the phonological phrase is that each has one major stress, and this stress is on the head (in the unmarked case). An example sentence, with phonological phrases marked off by slashed lines, is:

(2)   An orange dream/ was loudly watching/ the house/ during smelly lights/ because within these signs/ a slow *kitchen*/ snored/ with crashing leaves.

Each sentence contained a critical phonological phrase. In example (2) this was *a slow kitchen*. The word which the patient had to monitor for was the head (*kitchen*) of the critical phonological phrase. This constituted the baseline condition against which we could evaluate the effect of the various experimental manipulations. The first of these was the *prosodic disruption condition*. Here we introduced a local prosodic disruption within the critical phonological phrase. This consisted of a pause with accompanying prosodic closure effects (Warren 1985) immediately before the target word. This break is denoted by "//" in (3) following.

(3)   An orange dream/ was loudly watching/ the house/ during smelly lights/ because within these signs// *kitchen* in mist/ snored/ with crashing leaves.

This way of disrupting the local prosodic structure reduced the possibility of inadvertently introducing phonetic distortions.[1] There was a danger with this phonological restructuring that the target word might be spoken as part of the following phonological phrase, in which case it might have lost both its status as head and its associated phrasal stress. A change in stress might have made the target less salient. To reduce this possibility, the target word was followed by new material, as in (3), attached to it as sister elements, thus preserving the headhood of the target. The monitoring latencies of normal listeners are significantly disrupted (over the baseline condition) when they hear the target word in the phonologically disrupted phrase, confirming that this is one type of information which they use to structure the speech input.

We also included a *syntactic disruption condition* where we violated constraints on word order within the critical phonological phrase. To maintain the serial position of the target word, we removed the first word of the phrase and inserted an adverb between the adjective and the target noun, creating a syntactically illegal sequence (adjective + adverb + noun), as in (4) below:

(4)   An orange dream/ was loudly watching/ the house/ during smelly lights/ because within these signs/ slow very *kitchen*/ snored/ with crashing leaves.

This manipulation leaves local prosody intact and thus allows us to measure the effect of disrupting local syntactic structure. The question is whether a patient's latencies will increase, as normal listeners do (Tyler and Warren 1987), when he or she encounters this type of syntactic violation.

The fourth condition was a control condition in which the critical phonological phrase occurred early in the sentence, as in (5):

(5)   A slow *kitchen*/ was loudly watching/ the house/ because an orange dream/ snored/ with crashing leaves.

This is in contrast to the position of the critical phonological phrase in the other three conditions, where it occurred toward the end of the sentence. Our purpose here was to have each patient monitor for the same target word when it occurred early and when it occurred toward the end of a sentence, in order to replicate the lack of a word-position effect in anomalous prose, which we found in our earlier study. We expected that latencies to the target word would not decrease when it occurred in the late condition compared to the early condition (unlike normal listeners, who do show faster monitoring RTs when a target occurs later in an anomalous prose sentence).

Finally, we included a fifth condition (the scrambled condition) in which the phonological phrases within each sentence were reordered before recording, creating (6) out of (2).

(6)   Because within these signs/ during smelly lights/ was loudly watching/ the house/ an orange dream/ a slow *kitchen*/ snored/ with crashing leaves.

We included this condition because it was in the original study with normal listeners (Tyler and Warren 1987), and we wanted to maintain comparability with that study. Normal listeners show no sensitivity to this condition. Their latencies do not increase over the baseline condition, suggesting that they do not construct a hierarchical syntactic representation of a grammatical but meaningless utterance. There is no reason to suppose that patients will do so either.

Design and Materials

We used the 25 test sentences in the Tyler and Warren study (1987). These sentences had been analyzed into phonological phrases according to the definitions of metrical phonology (cf. Selkirk 1980). One phonological phrase in each sentence had been selected as the test phrase. This was either a noun phrase (with the structure: determiner + adjective + noun) or a prepositional phrase (preposition + adjective + noun). The target word was always the head noun and therefore the last word in the phrase.

These sentences were used in the five conditions described earlier—early, late, scrambled, phonological disruption, and syntactic disruption. The test phrase containing the same word target was used in all five conditions, and occurred in the same serial position in the sentence in all but the early condition. A sample set of sentences is given in table 11.1.

Table 11.1
Example set of materials

(a)   Early: A SLOW KITCHEN/ was loudly watching/ the house/ because an orange dream/ snored/ with crashing leaves.

(b)   Late: An orange dream/ was loudly watching/ the house/ during smelly lights/ because within these signs/ A SLOW KITCHEN/ snored/ with crashing leaves.

(c)   Scrambled: Because within these signs/ during smelly lights/ was loudly watching/ the house/ an orange dream/ A SLOW KITCHEN/ snored/ with crashing leaves.

(d)   Syntactic disruption: An orange dream/ was loudly watching/ the house/ during smelly lights/ because within these signs/ SLOW VERY KITCHEN/ snored/ with crashing leaves.

(e)   Phonological disruption: An orange dream/ was loudly watching/ the house/ during smelly lights/ because within these signs/ A SLOW// KITCHEN IN MIST/ snored/ with crashing leaves.

Five versions of the 25 test sentences were constructed as described earlier, so that the same 25 test words appeared in each of the five conditions. There were also 60 filler items which were similar in structure to the test items. Ten filler items were anomalous prose and 50 were normal prose. The position of the target word in the fillers was varied relative to the position of targets in the test items to reduce anticipation effects. Filler targets were a mixture of verbs, adjectives, and nouns. Test and filler items were pseudorandomly ordered, and this sequence of fillers and test items was constant across all five versions. Each version was preceded by a set of eight practice items. Five tapes were prepared, each with five test items for each of the five experimental conditions. These materials were recorded by a female native speaker of English at a normal conversational rate. See Appendix B for additional details on the word-monitoring task.

We selected as our control subjects 15 of the 30 subjects who had been tested in the original Tyler and Warren (1987) study. They were aged between 24 and 37 years. We tested three patients (DE, JG, and GS) who had shown no word-position effect in anomalous prose in the previous study.

Since we were taking the absence of a word-position effect in anomalous prose as being diagnostic of a patient's inability to construct a global syntactic representation, it was important to ensure that the anomalous prose materials in the present study were comparable to those used in the previous study. Therefore, we also tested CH, who had shown a word-position effect in anomalous prose, as a type of patient control. We wanted to make sure that he showed the same word-position effect for the current set of anomalous prose materials as he had shown in the previous study.

Results

Control Subjects

The mean monitoring latencies in the various experimental conditions are shown in table 11.2.

There was a significant main effect of condition (F^1 [4, 56] = 9.163, $P < 0.001$) showing that the experimental manipulations had different effects on RTs (see table 10.2). Newman-Keuls post-hoc tests established

Table 11.2
Controls: Mean monitoring latencies (msec)

Early	Late	Scrambled	Phonological	Syntactic
449	361	392	462	440

that RTs in the early condition (449 msec) were significantly slower (p < .01) than those in the late condition (361 msec). Thus, normal listeners' responses to monitoring targets are facilitated when the target occurs later in an utterance.[2]

The position of the target word in the sentence was the same in the late, scrambled, phonological disruption, and syntactic disruption conditions. Therefore the late condition (in which the target occurs in an undisrupted context) constitutes the baseline against which the effects of the three types of linguistic violations can be evaluated.

RTs to targets in scrambled phonological phrase materials (392 msec) were also significantly faster (p < 0.05) than RTs in the early condition (449 msec). However, the difference between RTs in the late condition and those in the Scrambled scondition (31 msec) was not significant on either a t-test or the Scheffe test for differences (p > 0.05). This suggests that listeners do not process anomalous prose sentences by constructing hierarchical syntactic structures spanning the entire utterance.

The remaining two conditions examined the role of local syntactic and prosodic information in spoken-language comprehension. The use of local syntactic structure is tested by comparing syntactically and prosodically well-formed late sentences with versions of the same items containing a local syntactic disruption. The disruption was achieved by using an illegal word order combination. This manipulation significantly increased RTs over the baseline condition by 79 msec (p < 0.01), suggesting that local syntactic organization is a source of information that listeners use in the process of developing a representation of an anomalous prose utterance.

The phonological phrase was selected as the unit of local structure in these studies because it is a unit not only of syntactic structure but also of prosodic organization. In the last condition of the experiment, the prosodic continuity within a phonological phrase was disrupted by inserting a short pause immediately prior to the target word. Local syntactic structure is preserved. This disruption increased latencies over the late condition by 101 msec (p < 0.01). The effect occurs despite any predictive consequences of having the test word occur immediately after such a phonological disruption.

Both these types of local disruption had similar effects on latencies. The difference between them of 22 msec was not significant (p > 0.05). These results suggest, then, that when normal listeners process a meaningless but grammatical utterance, they structure the input into local phrases, defined both prosodically and syntactically, as were the local phrases used in the present study. The confidence limits for the differences between the relevant conditions are shown in table 11.3.

Table 11.3
95% Confidence limits in msec

Early–Late	Late–Scrambled	Late–Phonological	Late–Syntactic
127–49	54–6	129–71	123–34

Table 11.4
Patient data: Mean RTs (msec) in the five conditions

	Early	Late	Scrambled	Phonological disruption	Syntactic disruption
Nonfluent					
GS*	691	660	675	750	692
JG	597	550	576	584	563
DE(Y)	511	496	482	484	549
CH*	527	474	486	684	563

* = patient with hearing loss

Patients

For each patient we ran an ANOVA with the five experimental conditions as the main factor. We then carried out a series of Newman-Keuls post-hoc comparisons on the differences between various conditions for each patient. There was a significant main effect of condition for DE, CH, and GS, but not for JG. The mean RTs for each patient in each condition are shown in table 11.4.

We will first of all consider the data from our "patient control," CH. In the previous study, he showed a word-position effect in anomalous prose, and he does so again here. The difference of 53 msec between monitoring RTs in the early and late conditions was significant ($p < .05$). His responses in the other three conditions followed the normal pattern. Scrambling phonological phrases did not significantly affect his reaction times, but they were considerably slowed down by the presence of both syntactic and prosodic violations.

In the previous study GS, JG, and DE showed no word-position effect in anomalous prose. The first thing we need to establish is whether they also fail to show it in this study. To do this, we compare RTs in the early and the late conditions. For unimpaired subjects, RTs are significantly faster in the late compared to the early condition, the basis of the word-position effect. All three subjects fail to show this pattern. This can be seen in table 11.5, which shows the difference scores between the relevant conditions.

The difference between the early and late conditions was not significant for any of the patients, and the size of the difference was outside the confidence limits established by the control subjects. This finding replicates

Table 11.5
Patient data: Difference scores (msec) between the relevant conditions

	Early−late	Late−scrambled	Late−phonological disruption	Late−syntactic disruption
Nonfluent				
GS	−31	15	90*	32
JG	−47	26	34	13
DE	−15	−14	−12	53*
CH	−53*	12	210*	89*

* = significant at the .05 level or above on the Newman-Keuls statistic

the lack of a word-position effect in anomalous prose for these patients, as we found in the previous experiment. All three patients also show no effect of scrambling phonological phrases (the differences between late-scrambled in table 11.5), but in this respect they do not differ from normal.

The next question is whether the patients are sensitive to violations of local prosodic and/or syntactic coherence. To answer this question we need to compare latencies in the various disruption conditions with those in the late, rather than the early, undisrupted condition. This is because targets occur in the same position in the late sentences and in the disruption conditions.

For GS, latencies only increase over the undisrupted baseline condition (late) for the phonological disruption. The difference between the late and phonological disruption conditions of 90 msec was significant on the Newman-Keuls statistic ($p < .01$) and the size of the difference was within the normal confidence limits. This suggests that she is as sensitive as unimpaired listeners to the presence of a local prosodic disruption.

In contrast, GS shows a small and insignificant effect of local syntactic disruptions (see table 11.5), suggesting that she is insensitive to the type of word-order violation involved here. We cannot, however, draw the conclusion that she is insensitive to all kinds of syntactic information. In the verb-argument study (chapter 10), for example, her word-monitoring latencies were significantly slowed down when the target word violated subcategory constraints.

This pattern suggests that GS was faster to monitor for a word in anomalous prose compared to scrambled strings in the study described in chapter 10 because she was able to use prosodic, rather than syntactic, information to structure the speech input into phonologically coherent phrases. These phrases have major stress on the head of the phrase. Because the head is also the target word, its prosodic prominence within the phrase facilitates its identification.

So we can conclude from the results of this and the previous study that GS is unable to use global syntactic information spanning an entire utterance. Although she is able to use some types of local syntactic information as she constructs a representation of an utterance (e.g., subcategory information), she is unable to use the type of local word-order information we manipulated in the present study. However, she can use local prosodic information to structure the speech input into phonological phrases, and this helps her to identify the most salient word in the phrase, its head.

DE's pattern of RTs to the two types of local violations was the opposite of that just described for GS. Like normal subjects, DE's latencies to local syntactic disruptions were significantly slower than in the late condition (see table 11.5), suggesting that he is sensitive to violations of syntactic organization within a phonological phrase. However, unlike unimpaired listeners, his RTs were not slowed down by the presence of a phonological disruption. In fact, his RTs in the phonological disruption condition were 12 msec faster than in the late condition.

This pattern of RTs suggests that DE primarily relies on local syntactic information to process an anomalous prose utterance. When the syntactic structure within a phonological phrase is disrupted by producing illegal word-order sequences, his RTs increase significantly. This type of local structural information seems to be of primary importance to him for when it remains intact and local prosodic structure is distorted, his processing is not disrupted. This suggests that he builds a representation of an anomalous prose utterance by constructing local phrases based solely on syntactic information and without regard to prosodic structure. It is because he is able to build these local syntactic structures that his latencies were faster in anomalous prose than in scrambled prose (chapter 10).

In contrast to the other patients, JG shows no effect of any of the experimental manipulations. This does not mean that he cannot do the word monitoring task, for the following reasons. First, in other word monitoring studies his monitoring latencies are affected by various types of linguistic manipulations (chapters 9 and 10). Second, his performance on various word monitoring studies is matched by his performance on off-line tasks on the same materials. So, for example, when he shows no effect of the contextual appropriateness of a morphologically complex word (chapter 12) as measured by monitoring latencies, he shows exactly the same pattern of results when he is asked to make an off-line decision about the acceptability of the sentence.

JG's insensitivity to violations involving various aspects of syntax shown in the present study is consistent with his results reported in chapter 9, where he was insensitive to violations of subcategory constraints. In addition, he also seems to have particular problems with morphologically complex words. In chapters 12 to 14 his monitering latencies did not increase when a morphologically complex word was contextually inappropriate. Where JG does show some sensitivity to linguistic manipulations in the word monitoring task is when these involve violations of meaning. JG is able to construct some kind of meaningful representation of an utterance, based on the meaning of individual words. However, it is unlikely that this representation is the same as that which an unimpaired listener constructs since he seems unable to use a variety of different types of syntactic information in the process of interpreting an utterance.

Conclusions

This study complements the study described in chapter 10 that tests whether a patient can build global representations spanning an entire utterance. It tests whether patients are able to use prosodic and syntactic information to contruct local structures in the process of interpreting an utterance.

PART V

Processing Morphologically Complex Words in Utterances

In this section, I describe four experiments designed to test whether a patient has problems processing different aspects of morphologically complex words when they occur in utterances. These studies complement those described in chapters 5, 6, and 7, which examine processing of complex words when they occur in isolation. This contrast between the two sets of studies enables us to determine whether a patient has problems accessing either the form or the content of a complex word.

It is common to encounter aphasic patients who have problems with members of what is known as "the closed class." This consists of the affixes attached to morphologically complex words (bound morphemes) and freestanding grammatical morphemes (such as *the, and, but*). A patient may have problems either producing or comprehending this type of morpheme. English-speaking patients rarely produce either morphologically complex words or freestanding grammatical morphemes. In languages such as Italian and Hebrew, where an uninflected root is a non-word in the language, such patients do produce inflected words, but they tend to be inappropriate for the context (Grodzinsky 1984).

Some patients have been reported as having analagous problems in comprehension (Zurif et al. 1972; Heilman and Scholes 1976; Goodenough et al. 1977; Bradley et al. 1980; Swinney et al. 1980; Friederici 1985; Grossman et al. 1986; Patterson 1980; Miceli and Caramazza 1987). The general claim is that this is part of a more widespread syntactic deficit. The patient cannot access the syntactic functional properties of closed class morphemes and thus has "no knowledge of the structural roles played by grammatical morphemes and .... (is) thereby unable to use these items as markers of phrasal constituents—that is, as syntactic place holders" (Cooper and Zurif 1983). Moreover, because the inflectional morphology is assumed to be more relevant to the development of syntactic representations than the derivational morphology (e.g., Anderson 1982), patients have more trouble with the inflectional than the derivational morphology (Miceli and Caramazza 1987).[1]

The major problem with this account is that it has not been directly tested. To determine whether a patient can exploit the syntactic properties of a closed-class morpheme, that morpheme has to appear in a context which allows the functional significance of those properties to have an effect. This means that the morpheme should not appear in isolation but must appear in an appropriate context. Unfortunately, only the comprehension of freestanding grammatical morphemes has been tested in this way (e.g., Goodenough et al. 1977; Grossman et al. 1986). Tests of a patient's ability to exploit the syntactic properties of the bound grammatical morphemes has always involved presenting isolated words (e.g., Patterson 1979; Coltheart 1980). Few attempts have been made to study the comprehension of bound morphemes in a context where they can actually function as syntactic markers (Shankweiler, Crain, Gorrell, and Tuller 1989).

A second problem is that the inflectional and derivational morphology are rarely systematically distinguished in current research (but see Miceli and Caramazza 1987), even though there are grounds for thinking that they should be. According to a number of linguistic theories (Aronoff 1976; Scalise 1984), derivations and inflections fall into relatively distinct classes. The major difference between them is assumed to be in the syntactic and semantic roles they fulfill. English derivational morphemes change the meaning and form-class of their stems. Inflectional morphemes, on the other hand, primarily have a syntactic function, in that they are bound up with the syntactic organization of the utterance in which they appear.

I would argue, however, that the role of inflectional morphemes is more complex than the foregoing would suggest. Depending on the nature of the utterance, inflectional morphemes appear to function in two different ways. First, when they occur in particular syntactic contexts, they can determine the syntactic structure of an utterance. Second, because the inflectional morphology marks tense, aspect, and number, it can serve an anaphoric role. That is, it can maintain time and reference within a discourse (Reichenbach 1947; Webber 1988). Since these are very different functions, we need to determine whether a patient has problems with inflectional markers when they serve one role or another.

Chapter 12
Processing Derived and Inflected Words in Context

Overview

The studies described in chapters 6, 7, and 8 test whether problems with morphologically complex words are due to a patient's inability to access the phonological form of such words. If we establish that this process is unimpaired, then we need to ask whether the patient is unable to access the semantic and syntactic properties of complex words and integrate them into the sentential representation. The study described in this chapter provides a general test of a patient's abilities to process derived and inflected words when they occur in sentential contexts.

a) Word-Monitoring Study

Background

The starting point for the research was the finding (Tyler and Marslen-Wilson 1986) that normal listeners use the prior context to help in their identification of a morphologically complex word. If a word like *corresponding* is heard in a sentential context which makes the inflection *-ing* the only appropriate suffix ("Peter and Janet were old friends. For many years they had been regularly corresponding . . .") then listeners identify *corresponding* much earlier than when the word occurs in a non-constraining context where different suffixes (e.g., *correspondence*) are permissible ("Alice was getting worried. The only news she had received was through corresponding . . .").

   We interpreted this finding in terms of the cohort model of spoken-word recognition (Marslen-Wilson and Welsh 1978; Tyler and Wessells 1983; Marslen-Wilson 1987), which claims that the process of recognizing a spoken word involves the gradual reduction of a set of word-candidates defined on the basis of the initial sensory input. The set is reduced as its members fail to match the accumulating sensory input and when they are contextually inappropriate. For a word spoken in a context which constrains the form of the suffix, all its derivational and inflectional variants will initially be activated, but only those which meet contextual specifications will continue to be activated. In the case of the word *corresponding* this means that although other variants of the stem will be initially activated, their activation levels will rapidly decrease because only the *-ing* form is contextually appropriate.

The present study exploited this earlier finding in order to examine the processing of derived and inflected words in context. The materials consisted of sentences that contained a derived or inflected test word. This word was either contextually appropriate or inappropriate. Example (1) illustrates the general structure of the sentences we used (with test word emphasized):

> (1)   The technique was very new. They claimed that it would *soften* tissue by a chemical reaction.

Given the prior context, only certain morphological variants of the stem *soft* are contextually appropriate. In this particular case, the derivational forms *soften* and *softly* are permissible, whereas the form *softness* is not. Given the earlier Tyler and Marslen-Wilson (1986) result, we expect normal listeners rapidly to integrate an appropriate form (*soften*) into the context, and to be disrupted when they encounter an inappropriate form (*softness*).

We also included a condition in which the test word consisted of a real stem and a real suffix which produced a non-word when combined (e.g., *soft + ive*). We included this condition in case there was no difference between the appropriate and inappropriate conditions. In this event, we would not be able to tell whether the task was insensitive to the experimental manipulations or whether listeners were insensitive to suffixes. If RTs in the non-word condition are significantly slower than in the appropriate condition, then we can be sure that the task is sensitive and that listeners are processing the suffixed forms.

To test our predictions, we had subjects press a response key when they heard a particular target word. This word always immediately followed the morphologically complex test word. In the example above, the word to be monitored was for *tissue*.

We found that for normal listeners monitoring latencies are fastest when the target is preceded by an appropriately suffixed word. When the suffixed word is contextually inappropriate, monitoring latencies to the following word are delayed as listeners try, unsuccessfully, to integrate the suffixial form into the prior context. When the suffixed form is a non-word, processing is disrupted both because the component morphemes do not fit together to form a word and because the resulting word-form is not contextually appropriate. This results in significantly delayed monitoring

RTs for the following word. RTs in the non-word condition were also significantly longer than in the inappropriate condition. However, this difference was smaller than the difference between the inappropriate and appropriate conditions, suggesting that the nature of the violation in the inappropriate and non-word conditions was of secondary importance to the fact that these suffixed forms were contextually inappropriate.

This overall pattern of latencies held for both the derivational and inflectional items. Listeners were fastest in the appropriate condition for both derivations and inflections, with both the inappropriate and non-word conditions being significantly slower than the appropriate condition, but not differing significantly from each other. This suggests that, for normal listeners, the relationship between the prior context and the form of a suffixed word is similar for both derived and inflected words.

This study, then, provides the kinds of contrasts between different types of morphologically complex words and their contextual appropriateness that we need in order to determine whether a patient has difficulty interpreting derived or inflected words in contexts.

Design and Materials

The test materials consisted of a set of 45 sentence-pairs, each containing a target word which the subject had to monitor for. Each target word was preceded by a test word.

The test words were always morphologically complex word-forms consisting of a base and a suffix. There were two sets of test words—those taking derivational suffixes and those taking inflectional suffixes. The base forms were chosen so that, depending on the suffix, the resulting word-form would be appropriate for the prior context, inappropriate for the prior context, or a non-word (*mixly, washness*) formed by using the derivational suffixes used in the appropriate or inappropriate conditions. The frequency of the appropriate and inappropriate test words were matched as closely as possible. The median frequency of the sets of appropriate and inappropriate inflections was 14 and 11, respectively, and the median frequency of the appropriate and inappropriate derivations was 11 and 6, respectively (Francis and Kucera 1982).

The test-target combinations always occurred in the second sentence of each sentence-pair. An example of a derivational set and an inflectional set, illustrating the three experimental conditions, with target word emphasized is:

(2)   Derivation

Context: Sarah could not understand why John used so much butter.

Continuation:

(a)   Appropriate: He was the most *wasteful* cook she had ever met.

(b)   Inappropriate: He was the most *wastage* cook she had ever met.

(c)   Non-word: He was the most *wastely* cook she had ever met.

(3)   Inflection

Context: I have to be careful when eating ice cream.

Continuation:

(a)   Appropriate: It often *causes* pain in my loose filling.

(b)   Inappropriate: It often *causing* pain in my loose filling.

(c)   Non-word: It often *causely* pain in my loose filling.

The choice of suffixes was constrained by several factors. First the target words had to be either nouns or adjectives, because patients usually have no difficulty in monitoring for these word classes (cf. Tyler 1985, 1988). Since the test words had to immediately precede the target word, this limited the set of suffixed forms that could legitimately be used. Second, in order to ensure that there were no difficulties in perceiving the suffixes, they all had to be syllabic.[1] Third, as far as possible we only used suffixes that could occur in all three experimental conditions in order to reduce any confounding effects due to different suffixes occurring in different conditions.

In the appropriate condition, the suffixed form was semantically and syntactically appropriate in both the preceding and the following context. The prior syntactic structure restricted the set of suffixes that could be legitimately combined with the base form to a small set.[2] Out of this subset, only one suffixed form (the appropriate form) was compatible with the pragmatic context.

In the inappropriate condition, the left context up to and including the base was contextually appropriate, but the suffix made the resulting word form inappropriate. In example (2b) above, it is only when the listener hears the suffix [-age] in the inappropriate condition that the word form does not fit the context. Up to that point it is no different from the appropriate condition.

The relationship of the inappropriate suffix to the appropriate suffix was different in the derivational and the inflectional sets, both syntactically and semantically. In the derivational set, the form class of the inappropriately suffixed word was different to the form class of the appropriately suffixed word. Furthermore, although derivational suffixes do change meaning, we explicitly avoided derivations resulting in major meaning changes (help*ful* vs help*less*). The derivations we did use had a minor effect in changing the meaning of the stem. In contrast, the inappropriately suffixed inflections were of the same form class as the appropriately suffixed inflections, and they differed minimally in meaning.

In the non-word condition, it is only when the suffix is processed that the violation can be detected—the verb stem is perfectly appropriate for the prior context.

Target Words

The target words were all common nouns or adjectives, such as *potatoes*, *toys*, and *quiet*. Their median frequency was 41.

Pre-tests

To obtain the 45 test items described above, we ran two pre-tests on an initial set of 81 items. These pre-tests established that the context, up to and including the base form of the test item, was consistent with the appropriate suffix and inconsistent with the inappropriate suffix. On the basis of the results from the two pre-tests, 45 items were selected for the monitoring experiment. These items were subjected to a third pre-test to establish that the acoustic realizations of the suffixes in the inappropriate and non-word conditions were distinguishable from the suffix in the appropriate condition.

Pre-test 1   evaluated the extent to which the appropriate test item fit the context. Ten subjects were presented with the written form of the sentence-pair up to the test word, with the base form of the test item printed below. For example:

> (4)   Mr. Wilson went to see the doctor about his back. He hurt it yesterday when he was ... PUSH

The 81 test items were interspersed with 74 filler items designed to obscure the regularities of the test items. Subjects were asked to continue the incomplete sequence with an appropriate word, using the base form provided. They were also asked to rate the appropriateness of their choice on a scale of 1–5, where 5 was very appropriate and 1 was very inappropriate.

Pre-test 2   measured the extent to which the inappropriate test items did not fit into the prior context. Nine subjects who had not participated in pre-test 1 were presented with a written version of the sentence-pair up to and including the inappropriate form of the test item. For example:

> (5)   Mr. Wilson went to see the doctor about his back. He hurt it yesterday when he was PUSHES ...

Subjects were asked to judge how well the test word fit in with the text that preceded it, using a scale of 1–10, where 10 indicated that the word fit in with the context extremely well and 1 indicated that it fit the context extremely badly.

Only those items that satisfied the following criteria were subsequently tested in pre-test 3. For each item, the appropriate form of the suffix had to be rated higher than 3.5 on pre-test 1, and the inappropriate form had to be rated less than 3.0 in pre-test 2. A total of 45 items satisfied these criteria. Of these, 21 were derivationally suffixed items and 24 were inflectionally suffixed. The mean rating of the appropriate suffixes (on a scale of 1−5) was 4.4 for the derivational set and 4.5 for the inflectional set. The mean rating for the inappropriate items was 1.6 for the derivational set (on a scale of 1−10) and 1.5 for the inflectional set.

These items were tested in pre-test 3 to ensure that the suffixes in all three conditions (appropriate, inappropriate, and non-word) could be perceived as being different from each other when presented in a spoken utterance. In this pre-test, subjects listened to the sentence-pairs over headphones and, at the same time, read a written version of the sentence-pair they were listening to. The written version always contained the correctly suffixed form. As subjects listened, they marked down any differences between what they heard and what they saw.

For this pre-test, three versions of the materials were recorded, each containing an equal number of items in each of the appropriate, inappropriate, and non-word conditions, together with 43 filler items. Fillers were pseudorandomly dispersed among the test items. Six practice items preceded the test materials. The three versions were recorded by a female native speaker of English at a normal conversational rate. Six new subjects were tested on each version of the materials, ensuring that each subject heard only one form of a test item.

The results indicated that the inappropriate and non-word versions of all 45 test items were easily distinguishable from the appropriate word-forms. The mean successful detection rate of the inappropriate forms was 99.3 percent and of the non-word forms was 100 percent.

Those recordings of the materials which were used for pre-test 3 were also used for the monitoring experiment. See Appendix B for additional details on the word-monitoring task.

Results

Control Groups

Young Controls
Subjects had no difficulty performing the task. Their RTs were fast and they made very few errors (overall error rate = 2.6%). The raw data were trimmed in the usual way (see Appendix B for details). Means were calcu-

Table 12.1
Young controls: Mean monitoring latencies (msec)

	Appropriate (A)	Inappropriate (I)	Non-word (N)	Differences		
				A-I	I-N	A-N
Derivations	218	286	319	68	33	101
Inflections	231	295	322	64	27	91
Mean	224	290	321	66	30	97

lated on the trimmed data, both by items and by subjects and these were entered into two ANOVAs. Table 12.1 shows the means for each condition.

There was essentially no difference between the overall RTs to the derivational and inflectional items. The mean latency to targets occurring after derived words (274 msec) was only 9 msec faster than those occurring after inflected words (283 msec).

The differences between the three conditions was significant (Min F' $(2,112) = 36.7, p < 0.001$). A set of Newman-Keuls comparisons, using the Min F' error term, indicated that targets in the appropriate condition (228 msec) were responded to faster than in both the inappropriate (292 msec) and non-word (319 msec) conditions ($p < 0.01$), and targets in the inappropriate condition were faster than in the non-word condition ($p < 0.05$).

The derived and inflected sets were also analyzed separately. There was a main effect of condition for the derivations (Min F' $(2,82) = 12.53$, $p < 0.001$), with post-hoc comparisons indicating that all three conditions produced significantly different RTs ($p < 0.01$). Similarly for the set of inflected words, there was a significant main effect of condition (Min F' $(2,24) = 28.86, p < 0.001$), with all three conditions differing significantly from each other ($p < 0.01$).

These results show that subjects were sensitive to the experimental manipulations. On-line processing, as measured by word monitoring RTs, was disrupted when the suffixed word did not fit the context or when it was a non-word composed of two real morphemes.

Since the young subjects act as controls for our young aphasic patients, we also calculated the confidence limits on the differences between the three conditions for the derivations and inflections. These are given in table 12.2.

Old-Age Controls
Turning to the two groups of old-age controls, we find essentially the same pattern of results. These are shown in table 12.3. Each subject's data were trimmed individually (see Appendix B for details), and entered into two ANOVAs.

Table 12.2
Young controls: 95 percent confidence limits on the differences (msec) between conditions

	A-I	I-N	A-N
Derivations	90−46	65−1	138−64
Inflections	82−46	39−15	111−71

Table 12.3
Old-age controls: Mean latencies (msec)

	Appropriate (A)	Inappropriate (I)	Non-word (N)	Differences		
				A-I	I-N	A-N
NHL (subject with good hearing)						
Derivations	290	348	378	58	30	88
Inflections	304	334	387	30	53	83
HL (subject with poor hearing)						
Derivations	292	360	388	68	28	96
Inflections	315	351	397	36	46	82

Hearing loss had no significant effect on performance. The mean RT for the group with poor hearing was 351 msec, and for the group with good hearing it was 340 msec (Min F' < 1). More importantly, degree of hearing loss did not interact with either the type of suffix (derivational or inflectional; Min F' < 1) or with the appropriateness of the suffix (Min F' < 1). For both groups of subjects there was a significant effect of the nature of the suffix (Min F' (2,134) = 35.02, p < .01.) RTs to targets following suffixed words that were contextually inappropriate were significantly slower than when the targets followed contextually appropriate suffixed words (HL: 355 msec cf 304 msec; NHL: 341 msec cf 297 msec). RTs in the non-word condition were significantly slower than RTs in the other two conditions (HL: 393 msec; NHL: 382 msec). This pattern held for both the inflections and the derivations. There was no significant difference between them (Min F' < 1), nor did this variable interact with any other.

Comparing the old-age controls with the young subjects, we see that the overall pattern is the same. Although the old people are generally slower to make a monitoring response, all subjects produce significantly faster RTs when the sentence contains a contextually appropriate suffixed word.

Finally, we calculated the confidence limits for the differences between the various conditions and these are given in table 12.4. For this analysis we combined the two groups of old-age controls since our analyses showed them to be no different from each other (Min F' < 1).

Table 12.4
Old-age controls: 95 percent confidence limits on the differences between condition.
(msec)

	A-I	I-N	A-N
Derivations	73−53	39−19	101−81
Inflections	45−21	64−34	100−63

Table 12.5
Patients: Mean RTs (msec) in the three conditions for the derivations

	Appropriate (A)	Inappropriate (I)	Non-word (N)	A-I	I-N	A-N
Anomic						
PK(Y)	483	506	576	23	70*	93*
Nonfluent						
BN(Y)	545	489	526	−56*	37*	−19
VS(Y)	556	529	601	−27	72*	45
JG	374	357	363	−17	6	−11
CH	373	424	417	51*	−7	44*
GS	507	475	544	−32	69*	37
JW	380	385	368	5	−17	−12
DE(Y)	247	254	262	7	8^	15
Fluent						
FB	430	459	460	29	1	30*
RH	379	450	415	71*	−35	36
WA	422	444	490	22	46	68*
Global						
Geo S	466	487	477	21	−10	11

Patients

Each patient's data were analyzed individually (see Appendix B for details).
The results for each patient on the set of derivational and inflectional items
are shown in tables 12.5 and 12.6. We have tabulated the means for each
condition and the differences between the means. For convenience, we have
noted on the tables whether the differences between the various conditions
are significant on post-hoc tests (*). We also note with a ^ when the
difference between two conditions is within the confidence limits set by the
appropriate control group, even though the difference is not significant.

Only two of the patients, CH and RH, show the most important aspect
of the normal pattern for the derivations and inflections; their RTs are

Table 12.6
Patients: Mean RTs (msec) in the three conditions for the inflections

	Appropriate (A)	Inappropriate (I)	Non-word (N)	A-I	I-N	A-N
Anomic						
PK(Y)	486	531	525	45*	−6	39*
Nonfluent						
BN(Y)	434	458	471	24	13	37*
VS(Y)	506	537	547	31	10	41*
JG	332	353	369	21	6	37
CH	372	434	416	62*	−18	44*
GS	482	542	553	60*	9	71*
JW	356	417	419	62^	2	63
DE(Y)	223	225	257	2	32^	34*
Fluent						
FB	420	430	461	10	31*	41*
RH	345	394	426	49*	32	81*
WA	347	351	408	4	57	61*
Global						
Geo S	404	434	475	30^	41*	71*

significantly faster when a derived or inflected word is contextually appropriate compared to when it is contextually inappropriate.

JG is the only patient who shows no significant effects at all. Latencies to targets following derived or inflected words that are contextually appropriate are not significantly faster than latencies to targets in the inappropriate and non-word conditions. JG's problems in this study may be due to a selective deficit for morphologically complex words, or to more general problems with the ends of any kind of word, whether morphologically simple or complex. If he shows a similar insensitivity to deviations at the end of simple words as he does to morphologically complex words, then we can assume that he has a general problem with word-endings. If, on the other hand, he is disrupted by deviations at the ends of morphologically simple words, then we can argue that his problems with word-endings are confined to morphologically complex words.

JW, PK, and GS have particular problems with derived words. They show no effect of the contextual appropriateness of derived words, suggesting that they cannot integrate them into the prior sentential context. They do, however, show the normal pattern for inflected words. Although the differences between conditions in the inflectional set are not significant in the case of JW, they are within the control-group confidence limits.

The remaining patients—BN, FB, WA, VS, Geo S, and DE—all have difficulty processing both derived and inflected words. None of these patients were sensitive to the contextual appropriateness of a derived or inflected word.[3] All patients were sensitive to the non-words in the inflected set of materials, but only FB and WA were sensitive to derived non-words. It may be the case that the non-words in the inflected set were more non-word-like than those in the derived set, because they were created by combining a verbal stem (which can only be legally combined with an inflectional suffix) with a derivational suffix. In contrast, the stem in the derived set was combined with a derivational suffix, but the two did not form a legal combination.

The question that arises for these patients is whether their problems with complex words stems from their inability to process their syntactic or semantic/referential aspects. We can answer these questions by testing the patients on the studies described in chapters 13 and 14.

It is important to note that the abnormal monitoring performance of these patients does not extend to all other monitoring tasks. There is ample evidence from the results of other studies described in this book that much of their on-line language comprehension is unimpaired. Only a few aspects of the comprehension process—such as the ability to process some aspects of morphologically complex words—do not function normally.

Conclusions

The results of this study give a general indication of the range and variety of problems which patients have with morphologically complex words. The pattern of results indicate where particular problems lie, and suggest where we should look further to determine the underlying basis for the deficit. The other experiments in this section are designed to investigate more specific aspects of the relationship between context and derived and inflected words.

Finally, the results of this study show that it is clearly not the case that a patient's problems in processing morphologically complex words can be predicted by his or her diagnostic category. Indeed, it seems clear from these data that most patients, whatever their diagnostic label, have problems with morphologically complex words in context. The inflectional and derivational morphology seems to be particularly vulnerable to brain damage. FB, for example, is classed as a fluent patient and yet he shows a similar insensitivity to the contextual appropriateness of derived and inflected words as BN or DE, who would be diagnosed as agrammatic on standard aphasia tests. Many of our patients showed some abnormalities in their ability to process complex words even when this was not accompanied by problems with any other aspects of syntax (e.g., BN).

b) End-of-Sentence Judgment Task

Overview

The word-monitoring study described above taps the immediate processes involved in constructing a representation of the speech input. In this study we use the acceptability judgment task to probe the nature of the final representation a listener constructs of the utterance. The contrast in performance on these tasks enables us to determine whether language comprehension deficits are due to problems in constructing representations of various types or in performing metalinguistic operations on the final representation that has been constructed.

Design and Materials

The same set of materials was used as in the monitoring study described above. Subjects heard the materials over headphones. They were asked to listen to each utterance and to indicate after the sentence had ended whether or not it was an acceptable sentence of English. To help patients understand what we meant by the term "acceptability," we referred to sentences which were acceptable as "good" and those which were not as "bad."

Results

Controls

The results for the control subjects are given in table 12.7.

The mid-age controls were very accurate in their decisions and rarely made an error. The old controls made slightly more errors, but they were still very accurate. Their average error rate was 5 percent.[4] The range of errors for each group of controls are given in table 12.8.

Patients

The percentage of correct responses for each patient is given in table 12.9.

All of the patients (with the exception of PK) perform poorly on this task. Their A's range from .59 — .79. Patients vary with respect to the relationship between the judgment data and the word-monitoring data. For BN, VS, and DE the judgment (BN A' = .67; DE A' = .79; VS A' — .68) and monitoring data are consistent. Both measures show that these patients have difficulty processing utterances containing morphologically complex words. However, without testing these patients on simple words that are

Table 12.7
Control subjects: Percentage of correct judgments in each condition

	Appropriate	Inappropriate	Non-word
Derivations			
Mid-age	99	99	99
Old HL	98	91	94
Old NHL	97	88	95
Inflections			
Mid-age	98	100	99
Old HL	97	90	98
Old NHL	98	93	93

Table 12.8
Controls: Range of correct responses (%)

	Appropriate	Inappropriate	Non-word
Derivations			
Mid-age	100−99	100−99	100−99
HL	100−95	95−81	99−89
NHL	100−99	95−71	100−81
Inflections			
Mid-age	100−99	100−99	100−99
HL	100−88	100−67	100−96
NHL	100−92	100−75	100−80

appropriate or inappropriate by virtue of their non-morphological word-endings (chapter 15), we cannot determine whether they have problems with suffixes per se or with any type of word-ending.

Leaving this issue aside for the time being, it is clear that there is something about suffixes (or perhaps about word-endings more generally) that these patients find particularly problematical, for they are able to evaluate the contextual appropriateness of stems without any difficulties (chapter 9).

Two other patients, FB and WA, are also poor at judging the acceptability of the sentences, even when they contained non-words (FB $A' = .64$; WA $A' = .62$). However, in their case, this is only partially consistent with the monitoring data. Although their monitoring RTs showed them to be insensitive to the contextual appropriateness of derived or inflected words, their RTs increased when the target followed a non-word.

RH is the only patient who showed a complete contrast between the monitoring and the judgment data. His ability to judge the appropriateness of the sentences was very poor ($A' = .59$), whereas his monitoring perfor-

Table 12.9
Patients: Percentage of correct judgments in each condition

	Appropriate	Inappropriate	Non-word
Derivations			
Anomic			
PK(Y)	86	86	90
Nonfluent			
BN(Y)	76	33	38
VS(Y)	71	57	29
JG	86	29	38
JW*	86	53	43
DE(Y)	71	62	76
Fluent			
FB*	91	38	52
RH*	93	57	36
WA	81	43	33
Inflections			
Anomic			
PK(Y)	83	92	100
Nonfluent			
BN(Y)	88	21	54
VS(Y)	88	31	25
JG	67	29	46
JW*	92	21	42
DE(Y)	79	67	71
Fluent			
FB*	71	17	50
RH*	75	25	13
WA	71	17	29

Y = young patient (under 45 years when tested)
* = patient with poor hearing

mance was normal. For RH, this contrast between his normal monitoring performance and his abnormal acceptability-judgment data is consistent with the result of the studies reported in chapter 9, where he performed the same two tasks on materials containing verb-argument violations of various types. We found the same essentially normal performance on the monitoring task accompanied by very poor performance on the acceptability-judgment task. We accounted for those results in terms of a distinction between the processes involved in constructing representations of the speech input (which remain relatively intact in RH) and those involved in reflecting on those representations for the purposes of making metalinguistic decisions about them (which are severely impaired in RH). The two sets of data reported in this chapter support that explanation.

JW's judgments were poor for both the derived and inflected sets (A' derived = .77; A' inflected = .73). This is consistent with his monitoring performance for derived words, where he showed no sensitivity either to the contextual appropriateness of a derived word or to the presence of a non-word. However, his judgment data for the inflected set were not entirely consistent with the monitoring data. He was poor at judging the acceptability of sentences containing either an inappropriately inflected word (A' = .68) or a non-word (.79), whereas in the monitoring study he was sensitive to the presence of a non-word although not to a contextually inappropriate inflected word. Although some other aspects of JW's ability to construct on-line representations of the speech input are also impaired (see chapter 10), his main difficulty appears to be with those aspects of comprehension involving metalinguistic awareness. In this respect he is similar to RH, WA, and FB. All four patients consistently perform poorly on tasks involving awareness of the linguistic representations that have been constructed.

JG showed no appreciation of the appropriateness of a complex word, whether measured by the judgment (A' = .62) or monitoring task. In addition, he seems to have a language comprehension deficit that extends beyond the processing of morphologically complex words. He is largely unaffected by the syntactic violations we introduced in our studies, suggesting that he is unable to use syntactic information in the process of interpreting an utterance.

Conclusions

This study is a first step toward establishing whether a patient has difficulties processing derived and/or inflected words in sentential contexts. The two following chapters probe the nature of the problem in more detail to determine whether a patient is unable to access either the semantic or the syntactic properties of complex words.

Chapter 13
Inflectional Morphemes as Syntactic Structural Devices

Overview

This study examines the role of inflectional suffixes as they relate to the syntactic structure of an utterance. It enables us to determine whether a patient has problems in processing inflections when they serve a purely syntactic role, in this case by constraining the structural organization of an utterance.

Background

As I explained in the introduction to this section, it has been claimed that when a patient has problems with inflected words it is because he or she is unable to exploit their syntactic properties. It is impossible to evaluate this claim without separating the syntactic and semantic implications of inflected words and seeing whether patients have difficulties only when they have to process the syntactic implications of the inflection. In the present study we do this by having the inflection alone determine the syntactic structure of the utterance. The type of materials we used are illustrated in 1(a) and 1(b), where a context sentence is followed by one or other of two continuation sentences.

(1a) Eric spent long hours sitting by his easel. He was *painting boats* down by the riverside.

All of our test materials had the structure: NP + Aux + [V + inflection] + NP. The second noun was the target word the subject had to monitor for (*boats* in the example above). The nature of the inflection on the verb determined whether the verb was transitive or intransitive, and this in turn set up a structural preference for either a NP or a PP to follow the verb. When the suffix is [-ing], the verb is transitive and an NP is the preferred continuation. When the suffix is [-ed], as in 1(b), the sentence is in the passive voice, the verb is intransitive and a PP is the preferred continuation.[1]

(1b)   Eric spent hours sitting by his easel. He was *painted boats* down by the riverside.

If a patient can access the syntactic properties of the inflected verb and integrate them into the sentence representation, RTs to targets following transitive verbs should be faster than to those following intransitive verbs.

The test sentence was either heard in isolation or preceded by a context sentence. We introduced this manipulation to see whether the presence or absence of a prior context affects a patient's ability to use the syntactic properties of the suffix.

To evaluate the role of the suffix alone in determining the syntactic structure of the utterance, we have to consider another variable. We have to take into account potential structural preferences introduced by the other words in the sentence (cf. Bresnan 1982; Caramazza, Grober, and Garvey 1977), in particular the number, gender, and animacy of the first NP in the test sentence as well as the syntactic and semantic properties of the verb stem. These alone (without the suffix) provide biases toward the active or passive reading and thus interact with the role of the suffix. To examine these biases, we have three types of sentence: where the combined biases of the initial NP and verb stem are toward the active reading; where they are toward the passive reading; where they are neutral. This enables us to determine whether the syntactic effect of the inflection is modulated at all by biases generated by the previous words in the continuation sentence.

For unimpaired listeners, we find that monitoring latencies to the target word are faster when it follows a transitive verb ([-ing]) as opposed to an intransitive verb ([-ed]). This means that the inflectional suffix functions immediately to constrain the syntactic structure of the utterance; this is reflected in the appropriateness of the following noun. When the noun is appropriate to the syntactic structure generated by the inflected form, RTs are faster than when it is inappropriate. This is not affected by the presence or absence of a context sentence. The only effect which the discourse context has is generally to make it easier to identify the target word. Moreover, the biases generated by the first NP and the verb stem have no effect on RTs. These are always faster to the target noun if it is consistent with the syntactic structure of the sentence, as determined by the inflectional suffix.

The contrasts in this experiment enable us to evaluate the extent to which a patient can process inflectional markers when they have primarily a syntactic role in an utterance.

Design and Materials

The test sentences are composed of an initial NP followed by an inflected verb (the test word). This in turn is followed by a target word which the subject has to monitor for. In one condition—the consistent condition—the verb is inflected with a present-progressive suffix [-ing]. This makes the verb transitive, and therefore the following phrase should be a NP. Since the target word is always a noun, it is always syntactically appropriate in this condition.

In a second condition—the inconsistent condition—the verb is inflected for the past tense and thus ensures that it is an intransitive verb. Thus, the following phrase cannot be a NP; it can be a PP. In this case the noun target is syntactically inappropriate. All past-tense inflections are regular and syllabic, and both inflected forms appropriate for the prior context. The form-class of the target word following the inflected verb creates a syntactically legal or illegal continuation.

These two types of test sentence are either presented in isolation or are preceded by a prior context sentence. This produces four experimental conditions.

The test sentences were pre-tested in a series of two written tests. Pre-test 1 determined whether past-tense verbs used in the inconsistent condition would be given a valid interpretation if the verb was parsed as an adjective ("They were baked potatoes . . . "). The possibility of subjects interpreting the verb as an adjective had to be excluded; otherwise items in the inconsistent condition would not necessarily be interpreted by the listener as being incorrect.

In this pre-test, subjects were presented with the test sentence (without its context sentence) up to and including the target word. They rated the sentences for their "naturalness" on a scale of 1–5, where 1 was very unnatural and 5 was very natural. The [-ing] and [-ed] forms of the verb were tested in separate versions, so that no subject saw both versions of an item. In order to be included in our final set of test materials, an item had to receive a mean naturalness rating of 3.5 or above.

Pre-test 2 tested the strength of biases in the no-context condition. The number and animacy of the first NP of the test sentence, combined with the semantic features of the verb itself, may combine to provide a bias towards either a progressive or a passive reading, or they may be neutral and provide no specific bias. For example, the fragment "She was decorate . . . " is biased toward an active reading and therefore requires the verb to take the progressive inflection (*decorating*). In contrast, "They had been roast . . . " is biased toward the passive form and the past tense inflection (*roasted*). The sequence "They were parade . . . " generates no biases. Active and passive readings are equally preferred.

This pre-test consisted of a cloze task using the no-context versions of the materials, excluding the prior context sentence. After each sentence, the base form of the verb was provided. Subjects were asked to use the verb to provide an appropriate continuation for the fragment. They also rated their choice for its appropriateness on a scale of 1–5, where 1 was very inappropriate and 5 was very appropriate. We selected items that received a mean naturalness rating of 3.5 or above. These items were categorized into one of the three bias categories according to subjects' responses.

Thirty-six of our original items satisfied the pre-tests. These were used in the monitoring study. For these 36 test items, the median frequency of the inflected verbs in the consistent and inconsistent conditions was 3 and 8.5, respectively. The median frequency of the target nouns was 27.

There were four versions of the 36 test items, such that each test item appeared on each version in each of the four conditions. In each version, the test items were interspersed with 56 filler items designed to counteract the regularities of the test items. The sequence of test items and fillers was constant across the four versions. They were preceded by ten practice items on each version. See Appendix B for details on the word-monitoring task.

Results

Young Subjects

There was a significant effect of the prior context sentence (Min F' $(1,49)$ = 17.91, p < 0.01). Latencies were faster when the test sentence was preceded by a context sentence (242 msec) compared to when the test sentence was heard in isolation (281 msec).

Subjects were also sensitive to the consistency of the target word (Min F'$(1,55)$ = 15.13, p < 0.01). Latencies were significantly faster when the target noun followed an inflected verb in the active voice (246 msec) compared to when the verb was in the passive voice and, consequently, a noun was an inappropriate continuation (278 msec).

The consistency of the target noun did not interact with the presence or absence of a prior context sentence (Min F' < 1). Noun targets following verbs inflected for the active voice were always responded to faster (context: 227 msec; no-context: 264 msec) than following past tense verbs (context: 257 msec; no-context: 298 msec).

Subjects also showed a main effect of bias (Min F' $(1,47)$ = 4.09, p < .001). This was because latencies were faster in the no-bias condition (232 msec) than in either the active or passive bias conditions (active: 270 msec; passive: 276 msec). Since different target words occur in these three groups, subjects' variation in responding to different targets undoubtedly accounts for the differences between groups. The presence of a prior context and the consistency of the target did not interact with bias (Min F' < 1). Irrespective of bias, targets were responded to faster when they were consistent with the utterance and when they were preceded by a context sentence (bias x suffix: F^2 (2,33) = 0.170, p = 0.846; F^1 (2,70) = 0.077, p = 0.926). The results for the three categories of bias (collapsed across context) are shown in table 13.1.

These results show that if there are structural variables generated by other words in the sentence, they do not interact with the role which the suffix plays in determining syntactic organization. We can therefore disregard this variable in our discussion of the results.

Our next step was to select a subset of the materials for presentation to patients. This was necessary since the original set was too long for patients. We therefore selected 20 of the test items[2] and 30 fillers from the original set. The old-age controls and patients were tested on this reduced set of materials.

We ran ANOVAs on the subset, and these showed the same pattern as the full set of items. The mean RTs are shown in table 13.2. There was a significant effect of context (Min F' (1,27) = 4.57, p < 0.05), due to faster RTs when the test sentence was preceded by a prior context (261 msec) compared to when it occurred in isolation (292 msec.). RTs were also faster when the suffix was consistent (242 msec) compared to when it was inconsistent (293 msec) (Min F' (1,41) = 25.0, p < .01). There was no interaction between the presence or absence of a context sentence and the consistency of the target (Min F' < 1).

Using this subset of items, we established confidence limits against which to evaluate the performance of patients of similar age to these young controls. Because we are concerned with whether patients are sensitive to the syntactic appropriateness of the suffixed word, confidence limits were calculated for the differences between consistent and inconsistent targets in

Table 13.1
Young controls: Mean RTs in the three bias conditions (msec)

Bias	Consistent	Inconsistent	Difference
Active	251	284	33*
Passive	264	296	32*
Neutral	222	252	30*

* = signufucant difference

Table 13.2
Young controls: Mean monitoring RTs (msec)

	Consistent	Inconsistent	Difference
Context	228	282	53*
No-context	255	322	67*

* = significant difference

Table 13.3
Old controls: Mean monitoring RTs (msec)

	Consistent	Inconsistent	Difference
Context	289	311	22*
No-context	388	402	14*

* = significant difference

both the context and no-context conditions. In the no-context condition, the confidence limits were 40−94 msec, and in the context condition they were 87−23 msec.

Old Controls

Although subjects with poor hearing produced slower mean latencies (366 msec) than those with good hearing (328 msec) this difference was not significant on the Min F' analysis or the F^1 analysis [$F^1(1,14) = 1.29$, $p = 0.28$], although it was significant on the items analysis [$F^2(1,19) = 62.84$, $p < .001$]. More important, however, was the fact that hearing loss did not interact with any other variable (Min F' < 1). Therefore, we will not consider it further in our discussion of the data.

Just like the young controls, older subjects were faster to respond to targets when they occurred in sentences preceded by a context sentence (300 msec) compared to when they occurred without (366 msec) one [Min F' (1,30) = 50.05, $p < .01$]. Subjects' monitoring RTs were also faster when the target word was consistent with the structure determined by the suffixed word (338 msec) compared to when it was inconsistent (356 msec). Although this difference just failed to reach significance on the Min F' [(1,29) = 3.81, $p > .05$], it was significant on both the subjects [$F^1(1,14) = 15.8$, $p < .001$] and items analyses [$F^2(1,19) = 5.023$, $p < .05$]. The presence or absence of a prior context sentence did not interact with the appropriateness of the suffix (Min F' < 1). The mean RTs for the older subjects are shown in table 13.3.

We also computed the confidence limits for the difference between the consistent and inconsistent RTs for the context and no-context conditions. The 95 percent confidence limits for the difference scores in the context condition were 33−11, and those for the difference scores in the no-context conditions were 27−1.

Patients

The patient data are shown in table 13.4. We have reported the mean RTs for each of the four experimental conditions together with the difference

Table 13.4
Mean RTs in the four conditions and difference scores (msec)

	Context			No-context		
	Consistent	Inconsistent	Difference	Consistent	Inconsistent	Difference
Anomic						
PK(Y)	414	445	31^	469	483	14
Nonfluent						
BN(Y)	374	378	4	382	387	5
VS(Y)	486	528	42^	574	605	31
DE(Y)	257	260	3	334	333	−1
JG	324	339	15^	428	419	−9
Fluent						
FB	407	453	46*	475	458	−17

Y = young patient (under 45 years when tested)

scores between the correct and incorrect RTs for the context and no-context items. A * denotes that the difference is significant on a t-test at the 5 percent level or beyond; a ^ denotes that the difference, although not significant, is within the confidence limits, for the appropriate age-matched control group. The appropriate control group against which to compare DE, VS, PK, and BN's performances is the young group. All other patients should be compared with the old-age controls.

Table 13.4 shows that most of the patients had difficulty exploiting the syntactic implications of inflected verbs, especially when there was no prior context sentence. For BN, PK, VS, DE, and JG, the differences between the consistent and inconsistent conditions were small and not statistically significant. Even though some of these differences were occasionally within the confidence limits established by the control groups, they are clearly marginal effects.

For BN, VS, and DE this result is consistent with the data from chapter 12, where monitoring RTs did not significantly increase when the target word followed a contextually inappropriate suffixed word. The present data elaborates on the earlier result by establishing that these patients have problems accessing the syntactic content of complex words and integrating it with the context. What we now need to know is whether they also have problems processing inflected words when they play a semantic role in utterances. This is the question we will address in the next chapter.

JG shows no effect of the syntactic implications of inflected words. At first glance, we might want to attribute this to a specific deficit in processing morphologically complex words in context, because he shows the same kind of insensitivity to the contextual appropriateness of both derived and inflected words in chapter 12. However, there are other aspects of his data which argue against this interpretation. First, he is also insensitive to distortions at the ends of morphologically simple words (see chapter 15). This suggests that whatever problem he has is not just confined to derivational or inflectional morphemes, but rather extends to all word endings. Second, the results of the verb-argument and prose-monitoring experiments (chapters 9 and 10) suggest that his comprehension deficit is far more extensive than ends of words. In these two studies, he shows no effect of any of the experimental manipulations, indicating either that he cannot construct the appropriate higher-level representations on-line as he hears the speech input or that he is slow to build these representations. Given that his performance is above chance when tested on the same materials using the acceptability-judgment task, the latter interpretation is more likely to be correct.

In contrast to his problems constructing higher-level representations, he processes single words essentially normally. In the gating studies described in chapters 5 and 6 he recognized simple and complex words at the point at which they were recognized by unimpaired listeners. He differed from normal in that he failed to recognize some of the complex words (33 percent) even by the last gate. This was because he did not access the appropriate cohort to start with. For example, he heard "touches" as "purchase," "sorted" as "forted," and "tunnel" as "camel." His performance was also essentially normal in the auditory lexical-decision studies reported in chapters 7 and 8, averaging 87 percent correct decisions.

In chapter 12, PK's monitoring data for inflected words was normal. His latencies increased both when an inflected word was contextually inappropriate and when the sentence contained a non-word. What we see in the present experiment is that he does not process inflected words by exploiting their syntactic implications. Like many of the other patients, his latencies increased only slightly when the utterance contained a syntactically inappropriate inflected form.

FB showed a significant effect of the syntactic appropriateness of inflected words and the presence of a non-word. This contrasts with his monitoring performance in chapters 12 and 14. These results are not inconsistent. The materials used in chapter 12 were not constructed so that the inflected verbs were contextually appropriate by virtue of their syntactic properties. And in chapter 14 it is the semantic, rather than syntactic, properties of the inflected verbs that determines their contextual appropriateness. The monitoring data from all three experiments suggest that FB can process inflected verbs when it is their syntactic, rather than semantic, implications that have consequences for the developing representation.

Conclusions

We can tell from the results of this study whether a patient has selective problems with inflected words when they play a syntactic role in utterances. These results can be compared with the same patient's data in the study described in the next chapter, which examines the patient's ability to process inflected words when they play a semantic role in utterance interpretation.

Chapter 14
Inflectional Morphemes as Anaphoric Devices

Overview

In evaluating the reason for a patient's problems with inflected words, we have to consider the possibility that he or she may have difficulty processing either the syntactic implications of inflected words or their semantic properties (or both). If patients have problems processing inflected words because they have a syntactic deficit that includes the inability to exploit the syntactic implications of inflected words, then these patients should process inflected words normally when they play a semantic rather than a syntactic role in language comprehension. The previous study examines the processing of inflected words when the inflection plays a syntactic role in utterances. In this study, we describe an experiment that tests the processing of inflections when they play a semantic/pragmatic role in utterance interpretation.

Background

In English, the inflectional morphology functions in at least two ways in sentences. First, in particular syntactic contexts, it can determine the syntactic structure of an utterance. We see an example of the inflectional morphology functioning in this way in chapter 13. However, the inflectional morphology, by virtue of the fact that it marks tense, number, and aspect, also serves an anaphoric or deictic role (Reichenbach 1947; Webber 1988). That is, inflectional morphemes maintain time and reference within a discourse. For example, the present-tense morpheme can either maintain the tense of the discourse or signal a change of time. In this way, inflectional morphemes serve a semantic/pragmatic function in sentences.

We exploited this fact to test for selective deficits with inflectional morphemes when they serve this anaphoric function. We used test materials consisting of a context sentence followed by a continuation sentence. The context sentences were constructed so that they set up the present tense. The continuation sentence contained a verb either in the present or past tense. When the verb was in the present tense, verb tense and context tense were consistent. But when the verb was in the past tense, the verb tense was inconsistent with the tense set up by the context sentence. A noun functioning as a target word immediately followed the tensed verb. For unimpaired listeners, a mismatch between context tense and verb tense disrupts processing, which is reflected in longer monitoring latencies when the verb tense is inconsistent with the context tense. This is presumably because the context sentence does not provide the appropriate semantic context within which the pragmatic implications of the inflected verb can be integrated. If a patient is insensitive to the semantic implications of inflectional morphemes marking tense, then monitoring latencies will be unaffected by the mismatch between context and verb tense.

Design and Materials

The test materials consisted of a context sentence followed by a continuation sentence. The context sentence was constructed so that it set up the present tense. The continuation sentence contained a verb either in the present or past tense. When the verb was in the present tense, verb tense and context tense were consistent (1a). But when the verb was in the past tense, then the verb tense was inconsistent with the tense set up in the context sentence, as in example 1b below where the tensed verb is underlined and the target word is in italics:

> (1a)   Consistent tense: Alison isn't frightened of many things. These days she only hates *bees* and wasps if they crawl into her food.

> (1b)   Inconsistent tense: Alison isn't frightened of many things. These days she only hated *bees* and wasps if they crawl into her food.

To ensure that the test verb in its present tense form was appropriate for the tense established by the prior context whereas the past tense form was not, we carried out two types of pre-test. In the first, we used a cloze task to establish that subjects selected the appropriately tensed verb. Subjects were presented with written versions of the context and test sentence up to the test verb. The stem of the verb was given in parentheses and subjects were asked to provide a form of the verb that would fit the context. They also rated the appropriateness of the form they supplied on a scale of 1–5, where 1 was very inappropriate and 5 very appropriate.

In the second pre-test we established that the inappropriately inflected verbs (the past tense forms) were judged to be inappropriate by subjects by presenting them with the context and test sentence up to and including the past-tense form of the verb (which was underlined). Subjects rated the underlined word for how well it fit into the prior context. They used a scale of 1–5, where 1 indicated that the word fit very badly and 5 indicated that it fit very well.

The test items were pre-tested in the ways described above and modified where necessary until 20 of them satisfied our criteria for inclusion in the study. That is, in the first type of pre-test, subjects had to produce the correctly inflected form and give an appropriateness rating of 4 or more. In the second type of pre-test, subjects had to give a rating of 2 or less to the past tense verb.

The test items were counterbalanced for the syllabicity of the inflections, in case patients had special problems perceiving nonsyllabic inflections. Half the test verbs had syllabic present-tense forms (consistent items) and their corresponding past-tense forms (inconsistent items) were nonsyllabic. For the other ten verbs, the present tense forms were nonsyllabic and the past tense forms were syllabic.

There were 20 test items. The median frequency of the targets in these items was 18. Each test item appeared in two conditions: where the context and verb tense were consistent and where they were inconsistent. Two versions of the materials were constructed so that each subject would hear each test item in only one condition. In each version the test items were pseudorandomly interspersed with 60 filler sentences. Half of these contained no inconsistency and half contained an error (e.g., a number error). These filler sentences served to obscure the regularities of the test sentences. See Appendix B for details on the word-monitoring task.

Results

Young Controls

The results for the young control subjects are given in table 14.1. Latencies were significantly slower when the verb tense was inconsistent with the context tense, but only when the inflection was syllabic. When the inflection was not a full syllable, then RTs were not affected by the consistency of verb and context tense. This is shown in the significant interaction

Table 14.1
Young controls: Mean RTs by condition (msec)

	Consistent	Inconsistent	Difference
Syllabic	213	265	52*
Nonsyllabic	223	234	11

* = significant difference

between syllabicity and consistency of the suffix:[1] $F^1(1,39) = 24.87$, $p < 0.001$.

The lack of a consistency effect for the nonsyllabic inflections may be due to the specificity of the bottom-up input. A nonsyllabic inflection is a more impoverished acoustic-phonetic stimulus than an inflection that is a full syllable, and the context may compensate for this minimal stimulus. There is ample evidence that listeners modulate their use of various kinds of information as the situation demands it. For example, less acoustic-phonetic information needs to be provided by a speaker for the correct identification of a word when an appropriately constraining context is available (e.g., Marslen-Wilson and Tyler 1980; Grosjean 1980). Such data suggest that the normal language processing system is organized to allow the cooperative integration of different types of processing information with respect to the primary goal of interpreting an utterance within its discourse context. The fact that we don't see a consistency effect for nonsyllabic inflections may be another example of this general process. Supporting this hypothesis is the fact that RTs for both the consistent (223 msec) and inconsistent (234 msec) nonsyllabic inflections are more similar to RTs for the consistent syllabic inflections (213 msec) than to RTs for the inconsistent syllabic inflections (265 msec). This suggests that the tense of both the consistent and inconsistent nonsyllabic inflections is being interpreted as consistent with the tense of the context.

Finally, we calculated the confidence limits for the young controls. Because we were interested in determining whether a patient is sensitive to the consistency of the tense of the inflected test words with respect to the tense established by the prior context, we calculated 5 percent confidence limits on the differences between RTs in the consistent and inconsistent conditions. These limits were: syllabic inflections, 40–64 msec; nonsyllabic inflections, 22–1 msec.

Old-Age Controls

The mean RTs for the two groups of old-age controls are given in table 14.2.

Table 14.2
Old controls: Mean RTs (msec)

	Syllabic			Nonsyllabic		
	Consistent	Inconsistent	Difference	Consistent	Inconsistent	Difference
HL	229	264	35*	262	257	−5
NHL	261	283	22*	265	293	27*

Both sets of old controls behaved like the young subjects on the syllabic verbal inflections. Their RTs were significantly slower when the tensed verb did not match the tense of the context compared to when it was consistent with the tense of the context. Where the two groups of old people differed from each other was in their sensitivity to the nonsyllabic inflections. The old subjects with poor hearing were like the young subjects. They showed no effect of the consistency of the tense of the verb when the inflection was nonsyllabic. This is revealed in a significant consistency by syllabicity interaction for both the subjects and items analysis ($F^1(1,36) = 3.95$, p = .05; $F^2 (1,6) = 12.034$, p < .01) which just failed to reach significance on the Min F' statistic (Min F' (1,39) = 2.97, p > .05).

Old people with poor hearing may show no effect for the nonsyllabic inflections for the same reason as young subjects. Alternately, they may have difficulty hearing verbal inflections when they are not full syllables.

For the old people with good hearing, there was a significant effect of the consistency of the inflection (Min F'(1,38) = 5.39, p < 0.05), but no interaction between syllabicity and correctness. This can be seen in table 14.2 where the difference between the consistent and inconsistent inflections was essentially the same for both syllabic and nonsyllabic inflections.

Although performance is variable on the nonsyllabic items, all three sets of control groups show the same pattern of results for the syllabic inflections. Therefore, this is the most important set against which to compare the performance of the patients.

We calculated the confidence limits on the differences between the consistent and nonconsistent items for the syllabic and nonsyllabic sets separately. These are given in table 14.3.

Patients

The data for the patients are presented in table 14.4. We present both the syllabic and nonsyllabic data for direct comparison with the control data. However, because the data for the nonsyllabic inflections were not reliable for the controls, we ignore this set of items in our discussion and concentrate upon the syllabic inflections (all three of the control groups showed a significant effect for the syllabic inflections).

Table 14.3
Old controls: 95 percent confidence limits for the syllabic and nonsyllabic sets

	Syllabic	Nonsyllabic
HL	55–15	11–3
NHL	35–9	43–11

Table 14.4
Patients: Mean monitoring RTs (msec)

	Syllabic			Nonsyllabic		
	Consistent	Inconsistent	Difference	Consistent	Inconsistent	Difference
Anomic						
PK(Y)	362	415	53*	341	394	53*
Nonfluent						
BN(Y)	358	282	−76*	375	370	−5
VS(Y)	403	463	60^	423	467	44^
JW	334	322	−12	340	379	39
DE(Y)	239	235	−4	202	237	35
GS	366	418	52*	378	499	119*
JG	371	296	−75 ^	308	341	33^
Fluent						
FB	408	394	−14	408	405	−3

Y = young patient (under 45 years)
* = size of difference is significant
^ = size of difference is within confidence limits

VS showed only a very small effect of the contextual consistency of inflected verbs. The difference of 60 msec between the consistent and inconsistent items was not significant because of the extreme variability of her RTs resulting in large standard deviations. So, although the difference appears to be a respectable size and is within the appropriate confidence limits, it does not represent a robust effect.

The remaining patients, BN, JW,[2] JG, FB, and DE, all show non-significant effects of the consistency of the tensed verb with the context. For BN, JW, and JG this is compatible with the data from the two earlier studies (chapters 12 and 13) where they also showed no sensitivity to inflected words. These three studies taken together show that these patients are unable to appreciate either the syntactic or semantic implications of inflected words. In the following chapter we will see whether they are similarly insensitive to non-morphological word-endings. If they are, I will argue that their apparent difficulty in processing morphologically complex words is in fact part of a more widespread problem with any type of word-ending.

FB presents a slightly different case. He, too, is not sensitive to the referential implications of the inflected words. However, unlike the other patients, he does show some sensitivity to the syntactic functional role of inflectional morphemes (chapter 13).

GS and PK are the only two patients who produce significantly slower RTs to inconsistent inflected words. Both patients also show a significant effect of the contextual appropriateness of inflected words in chapter 12. The data from these experiments suggest that GS can exploit the referential aspects of inflected words. Given that PK is insensitive to the syntactic implications of inflections, this may be the only property of inflected words that he can access as he processes an utterance.

Conclusions

The results from this and the previous study test the claim that patients who have problems comprehending inflected words do so because of a general syntactic deficit that surfaces in their inability to exploit the syntactic properties of inflected words. Patients who have problems processing inflected words when they play a semantic/discourse role in utterance interpretation (as in the present study), such as BN, VS, JW, and DE, clearly cannot be said to have only a syntactic processing deficit. What is notable from these three studies (chapters 12, 13, and 14) is the extent to which patients with a variety of comprehension and production deficits have particular difficulty comprehending morphologically complex words in sentential contexts. Our data do not support the widespread view that it is only Broca-type patients, or patients with specific syntactic deficits, who have problems with morphology.

Chapter 15
Distortions at the End of Morphologically Simple Words

Overview

This experiment complements those described in chapters 12, 13, and 14, which examine various aspects of the relationship between morphologically complex words in contexts. In these studies, some patients (BN, JG and Geo S) show no sensitivity to the contextual appropriateness of various types of derived and inflected words and no effect of the morphological legality of some types of non-word. This could be due either to a selective impairment for morphological suffixes or to a general insensitivity to the ends of words. In this study, we test whether the patient has problems with word-endings that are not morphological affixes.

Background

To determine whether a patient was difficulty processing the ends of words irrespective of their morphological status, we developed a set of materials consisting of sentences containing morphologically simple words (*syrup*) that were either intact or became non-words by changing the final syllable (*syruff*). This manipulation is comparable to the way in which morphologically complex non-words were created in chapter 12, except that here the non-words are derived from monomorphemic real words. Following each test word (*nylon/nylup* in the examples below) was a target word (*tie* in the examples), which the subject was asked to monitor for. An example of the materials is given in (1).

> (1a)   No deviation: John always got the most hideous presents from Aunty Mary. This year it was a *nylon tie* which he knew he'd never wear.

> (1b)   Word-ending deviation: John always got the most hideous presents from Aunt Mary. This year it was a *nylup tie* which he knew he'd never wear.

For unimpaired listeners, monitoring latencies are slower when the target follows a deviant word compared to an undisrupted word. This shows that listeners are immediately sensitive to the deviation in the final syllable of the test word. If a patient shows a similar increase in monitoring latencies when the test word is deviant, but shows no sensitivity to the various manipulations in the series of experiments using morphologically complex words, then we can be confident that the patient does not suffer from a general inability to process the ends of words. Rather, he or she must have a selective deficit for processing suffixed words in context.

Design and Materials

We generated a set of 34 sentence-pairs in which a test word immediately preceded a target word. There were two forms of each test word, the correct form and the non-word form. The non-word was a phonotactically valid string, produced by changing the final syllable of the correct form (e.g., the final syllable of *shadow* was changed to produce the non-word *shadit*).

The non-words were produced in the following way. A set of unambiguously monomorphemic bisyllabic and trisyllabic verbs, adjectives, and nouns were selected. The set excluded all affixed and pseudoaffixed words, productive bound stems (e.g., [-ject] in the final syllable), and pseudostems in the first syllable. Theoretical uniqueness points were then calculated for these items by reference to a dictionary. The theoretical uniqueness point is the point in a word at which it separates from all its competitors in the language (see chapter 2). Items where the theoretical uniqueness point was on the final phoneme were discarded. The remaining items were then given alternative endings, after the uniqueness point, according to a number of general criteria:

- At least one other real word had to have the same ending as the non-word, so that the non-word could be considered to be a blend of two real words.
- The new ending had to differ from the original ending in place and manner of articulation.
- The change should only involve the final syllable.
- Word endings had to be unambiguously nonsuffixal.
- Non-word endings were matched in segmental structure to the original.

To obtain some variety in the materials, we alternated the combination of the form classes of the test-target pair. The form-class of the test item was a noun, verb, or adjective, whereas the form-class of the target word was a verb or noun. This produced three sets of test-target combinations:

noun-verb, verb-noun and adjective-noun. The verb-noun pairs provide a condition directly comparable to the set of inflectional items in chapter 12, where the test item was an inflected verb preceding a noun target. These three subsets differed structurally. In the adjective set the target was the head of a NP containing the test item and target, whereas in other two sets the test item and the target were not within the same phrase, and did not belong to same phonological phrase. Within the three subgroups, the syntactic relationship and environment of the test-target pair was kept consistent. All the verb test items were infinitives, modifying a single noun object target. All the adjectives attributively modified the following noun target. The nouns were all subjects of following past-tense verb targets.

The set of 34 items were tested in a *perceptibility pre-test*. This established that the differences between the word/non-word versions of each test word were perceptually distinguishable. Two versions of the materials were produced for the pre-test. The two versions of each of the test items were distributed equally across the two versions, such that only one member of each pair occurred in a version. In each version, the test items were pseudorandomly mixed with 38 filler items designed to disguise the regularities in the test materials.

Subjects listened to one of these versions, and at the same time read a written version of the materials in which only the correct form of each test word appeared. They were asked to listen to the materials presented through headphones, and mark the text at any point where the auditory and visual presentations differed. They were told that the difference may be a whole word, or part of a word. Eleven subjects performed the pre-test, five on version 1 and six on version 2.

On the basis of the results, we dropped five of the test items from the set. Of the 29 remaining items, the detection rate was 99 percent for the non-words.

Two versions of the materials were prepared, with word/non-word items balanced across versions and including the 38 fillers used in the pre-test. The correct and non-word versions of each test item were presented in separate versions, such that each subject heard only one member of each word/non-word pair. A set of ten practice items preceded the test items in each version. See Appendix B for details on the word-monitoring task.

Results

Control Groups

The mean monitoring RTs for the mid-age group are shown in table 15.1.

Subjects were significantly slower to monitor for a target word following a disrupted word (Min $F'(1,30) = 29.93$, $p < 0.001$). There was also a significant effect of the form-class of the test-target pairs (Min $F'(2,34) =$

Table 15.1
Mid-age group: Mean monitoring RTs (msec)

Form-class of test/target pair	Correct	Non-word	Difference
Noun-verb	241	283	−42*
Adjective-noun	209	264	−55*
Verb-noun	254	296	−42*
Mean	235	281	−46*

* = significant difference

3.54, $p < 0.05$). Latencies were faster when the test-target combination was an adjective followed by a noun target. Since different test-target combinations occur in the three groups, we cannot draw any conclusions from the fact that overall RTs differ between the groups. The most important result is that that subjects were seriously disrupted by the presence of a mispronounced word, regardless of its form-class, or the form-class of the preceding word. The form-class of the test-target pair did not interact with the word/non-word manipulation ($F < 1$). The 95 percent confidence limits for the difference scores between the correct and incorrect conditions (collapsed across form-class) were 57–36 msec.

Old-Age Controls

The data from the two old-age groups are given in table 15.2. There was no significant effect of hearing loss ($F(1,8) = 4.206$, $p < 0.07$), and both groups of old subjects showed exactly the same pattern as the mid-controls.

For both groups of old subjects, latencies to targets following a real word were faster than to those following a non-word (poor hearing (Min F′ $(1,10) = 6.69$, $p < 0.05$; good hearing: Min F′$(1,30) = 18.09$, $p < 0.01$). The form-class of the test-target pair was not significant for either group (poor hearing: (Min F′$(2,31) = 2.27$, $p > 0.1$; good hearing: Min F′$(2,34) = 0.59$, $p > 0.1$), nor did it interact with the word/non-word manipulation. The confidence limits (95 percent) for the difference scores between the correct and non-word conditions (collapsed across form-class) were 67–37 msec.

In summary, all three sets of control subjects show the same pattern. Their monitoring latencies are significantly slowed down when the target follows a non-word.

Patients

Four patients—Geo S, BN, JG, and DE—who failed to show normal sensitivity to the contextual appropriateness of morphologically complex words (chapter 12) were tested in this experiment. Because of the small

Table 15.2
Old controls: Mean monitoring RTs (msec)

Form-class of test/target pair	Correct	Non-word	Difference
No hearing loss			
Noun-verb	283	322	−39*
Adjective-noun	244	314	−70*
Verb-noun	264	322	−58*
Mean	266	319	−53*

Form-class of test/target pair	Correct	Non-word	Difference
Hearing loss			
Noun-verb	346	376	−30*
Adjective-noun	272	346	−74*
Verb-noun	342	406	−63*
Mean	320	376	−56*

* = significant difference

Table 15.3
Patients: Mean RTs (msec) and error rates

	Correct	Non-word	Difference
Nonfluent			
BN	464 (10%)	490 (7%)	26 ns
JG	351 (3%)	386 (17%)	35 ns
DE	287 (3%)	347 (3%)	60*
Global			
Geo S	418 (0)	446 (10%)	28 ns

* = significant difference

number of items within each form-class category, the analyses for the patients are collapsed across form-class. The mean RTs for the correct and non-word conditions are given in table 15.3.

DE is clearly sensitive to deviations at the ends of morphologically simple non-words. His RTs increased by 60 msec when the target word was preceded by a morphologically simple non-word ($t(26) = 3.08$, $p < 0.004$). Moreover, the differences between the correct and non-word forms for all three types of form-class were within the mid-age group's confidence limits. This result, in conjunction with his sensitivity to some of the non-words in the experiment reported in chapter 12, suggests that DE is sensitive to deviations at the ends of words, when the deviation creates a non-word. Other research, which is not reported in this book (Ostrin and Tyler, in prep.), shows that DE is not sensitive to word-end deviations when the deviation creates a contextually inappropriate real word. So, for example, when he hears sentences such as:

Sam ran into the college building to register for the course.

and monitors for the word *building*, his RTs are no slower than when he monitors for *cage* in the sentence:

Sam ran into the collar building to register for the course.

The pair of words *collar* and *college* are members of the same word-initial cohort and deviate in their final syllable. Unlike DE, unimpaired listeners are sensitive to the deviation. Our results suggest that DE does not have a deficit that is specific to the processing of bound morphemes. They imply, instead, that his deficit involves word-endings in general, irrespective of their morphemic status. The only time he shows any sensitivity to word-endings is when they constitute a non-word.

In contrast, BN does not appear to be sensitive to word-endings that create non-words. In the present experiment and in the derivational set of materials in chapter 12, his RTs did not significantly increase in the non-word conditions. His latencies did significantly increase to non-words in the inflectional set, but the effect was small and outside the confidence limits for the control group. He shows similar insensitivity to the ends of real words—whether they are morphologically complex or simple (as in the *collar/college* case described above). Taken together, his data suggest that, like DE, he does not have specific problems with morphological endings but with word-endings per se.

Although Geo S has not been tested as extensively as BN, the weight of evidence suggests that he, too, has problems with word-endings rather than morphological affixes.

Finally, JG also shows no sensitivity to violations of word-endings, whether they occur at the ends of morphologically simple or complex words. However, in JG's case, this is not a problem that is specific to word-endings, as he is insensitive to all of the linguistic manipulations we have introduced in the entire series of experiments.

Conclusions

This test, in conjunction with the tests described in chapters 12–14, enable us to determine whether a patient has specific problems in processing morphologically complex words when they occur in context, or whether the deficit is a more general one involving any kind of word ending. The results of the patients we have tested so far demonstrate that these tests, taken together, allow us to evaluate these two possibilities.

PART VI

Conclusions

Chapter 16
Examples of Processing Profiles

In the introduction, I explained that the purpose of the tests described in this book was to develop processing profiles for individual aphasic patients. The processing profile provides a detailed picture of a patient's ability to carry out the appropriate on-line analyses of the speech input, from the initial phases of interpreting the speech signal with respect to lexical representations to developing a pragmatically coherent representation of each utterance. In addition to providing data on these on-line processes of interpretation, it also provides data on the nature of the final representations the patient constructs of an utterance.

Needless to say, the tests described in this book do not exhaust the set of tests that need to be done to provide a comprehensive assessment of a patient's poken-language comprehension abilities. Nevertheless, they constitute the beginnings of a comprehensive assessment in that they probe many of the major analysis processes involved in understanding spoken language.

I illustrate the ways in which the tests described in the book constitute a processing profile with detailed examples of processing profiles from two patients (RH and BN) who have very different kinds of language disorders. RH is a patient who conforms to the traditional category of a Wernicke aphasic. That is, he produces fluent, meaningless speech and appears to have a severe comprehension deficit. BN, on the other hand, is a patient who, according to standard criteria, would be classified as a Broca-type agrammatic patient. He produces nonfluent, hesitant speech and does not appear, on standard tests, to have a very marked comprehension deficit.

The processing profiles of these two patients show how tests of the type described here, which provide a detailed picture of where a patient performs normally and where performance is disrupted, enable us to pinpoint the source(s) of a patient's language disorder, and how the traditional diagnostic categories provide inadequate descriptions of the nature of a patient's comprehension deficits.

I also present summaries of the processing profiles for the other patients (PK, GS, VS, CH, JG, JW, FB, and DE) who have been tested on most of the studies described in the book. Where a patient has only been tested on a few studies (JA, Geo S, and WA), I have not drawn a processing profile.

For each processing profile, I have summarized the patient's data for each experiment alongside the data from the appropriate control group. I have also included confidence limits, where these have been calculated, and I have indicated which effects are statistically significant by an asterisk. In this way, I have collected all of the data for each patient in one place to make it easy for the reader to see how a single patient performs across the range of experiments. In contrast, by reading each of the experimental chapters (chapters 4–15), the reader can see how all of the patients perform in any individual study. By presenting the patient's performance in these two ways, I hope that the differences and similarities between patients become very clear.

Detailed Processing Profiles

Profile 1:   RH

General Details
RH is a male patient who was born in 1920 and had a left hemisphere CVA in 1977. He has a significant degree of hearing loss (30db) and is right hand dominant. His speech is fluent, containing relatively few content words, but many stereotypical phrases, as well as occasional verbal paraphasias.

On standard aphasia tests, such as the BDAE and the Token test, he is diagnosed as having a severe comprehension deficit. On the Boston exam, administered in 1979, RH was classified as a Wernicke with a poor auditory comprehension (z score = $-.5$). His comprehension was also poor when measured by the Token test (De Renzi and Vignolo 1962). His score of 7/36 indicated that he has a severe aphasia. This diagnosis is confirmed in informal interaction, in which he appears to have a severe comprehension deficit. This impression is, no doubt, partly due to his profound difficulty in producing coherent language.

His digit span (as measured on the BDAE) was only 3. However, he was able to match four digits with 100 percent accuracy on a digit-matching task, and five digits with 66 percent accuracy, suggesting that he does not have a severe STM deficit for digits. He completed the trailmaking test in 205 sec, indicating that he has severe brain damage, but his general intellectual abilities are above average as measured by the Ravens Progressive Matrices.

When we first saw RH he had been tested on this range of standard tests and had been diagnosed as a typical "Wernicke" with a severe comprehension deficit. However, nothing further was known about the nature of this deficit or whether it was attributable either to problems in the on-line processes involved in constructing representations or to problems with off-line processes.

We ran RH through our battery of tests and found that on many of the tests of on-line processing his performance was essentially normal. I will describe his performance on these tests in some detail.

Accessing Lexical Form

RH had few problems with lexical processing. Whatever difficulties he did have were probably attributable to his profound hearing loss.

In three studies we found that the processes involved in contacting form representations of real words were essentially unimpaired for both simple and morphologically complex words. In the first study—the phoneme-discrimination study involving real words (chapter 4)—he could accurately discriminate speech sounds occuring in real words. The only problem he had was with voiceless fricatives and plosives. He was very accurate in discriminating words containing voiced plosives and fricatives, presumably because of the extra low-frequency information these speech sounds contain. In general, then, his error pattern was consistent with his degree of hearing impairment (30 db). In two further studies using the gating task, he recognized words at the theoretically optimal point, irrespective of whether the words were morphologically simple (chapter 5) or complex (chapter 6). In an auditory lexical-decision experiment with suffixed words (chapter 7), he was less sensitive (A' = .88) than normal controls (A' = .99) to the lexical status of a stimulus, as were all the other patients who had a similar degree of hearing loss.

Results

Phoneme discrimination

	Percentage of errors
Controls	10 [range: 1–22%]
RH	11

Simple words/gating task

	Mean hearing loss (db)	N correct (max = 20)	Mean isolation point (mesc)	% cohort membership
Controls	37.9 db [range: 26–48]	18	405 [range: 340–445]	
RH	30 db	19	420	94

IP = isolation point (see chapter 4).

Simple words/auditory lexical decision

| | % correct and range [ ] | |
	Real words	Non-words
Controls	99 [100−98]	99 [100−98]
RH	87	93

Complex words/gating task

	% correct full-forms	% correct stems	Mean isolation point/ derivation full-forms (msec)	Mean isolation point/ derivation stems (msec)	Mean isolation point/ inflection full-forms (msec)	Mean isolation point/inflection stems (msec)
Controls	73	73	438	300	388	230
RH	89	100	500	233	317	150

Suffixed words/Auditory lexical decision:

| | % correct and range [ ] | | | |
| | Real words | | Non-words | |
	Controls	RH	Controls	RH
Simple	99 [100−95]	87	99 [100−98]	93
Derived	99 [100−92]	90	98 [100−97]	64
Inflected	99 [100−96]	92	97 [100−95]	60

Accessing Lexical Content
RH had no difficulty accessing lexically associated representations (syntactic, semantic, and pragmatic) and using them immediately to construct
structural representations of the speech input. This was shown in the
word-monitoring experiment described in chapter 9. In this study, we had
utterances containing a test verb followed by a target noun. The verb was
either appropriate for the context and for its argument (the following noun
target word), or it was inappropriate syntactically (it violated subcategory
restrictions between the verb and its argument), semantically (it violated
selection restrictions between verb and argument) or pragmatically. For RH,
just as for unimpaired listeners, monitoring latencies to the target words
were longer for all three types of verb-argument violation compared to the
appropriate condition. This shows that RH accesses the content of the verb
as soon as he hears it and uses this information to constrain permissible
verb-argument structures. The only way in which RH differed from normal

was his failure to show longer RTs to the subcategory violation compared to the semantic violation. This suggests that he may have slightly more difficulty than normal listeners in using the syntactic constraints on building verb-argument structures. But there is no doubt that he can use them, because his RTs in the subcategory violation condition were significantly longer than those in the baseline condition.

Results

Verb-argument study/word monitoring

| | | Mean monitoring RTs (msec) | | |
	Normal	Pragmatic violation	Semantic violation	Syntactic violation
Controls	322	380	399	411
RH	367	436	443	406
		Differences between conditions (msec)		
		Control group mean	95% confidence limits	RH
Normal-pragmatic		58*	69–39	69*
Normal-semantic		77*	93–53	76*
Normal-syntactic		89*	107–67	39*

* = significant difference.

Constructing Higher-Level Representations
RH was able to develop the appropriate type of syntactic and semantic global representations spanning an utterance, as was shown by the pattern of his word-monitoring latencies on the study described in chapter 10. In that study, we presented RH with three types of sentences (normal prose, anomalous prose, and scrambled strings). We placed target words at different word positions in each type of material in order to chart the processing of syntactic and semantic information as they become available over time. We found that RH performed just the same as unimpaired listeners. His latencies in normal prose were faster than those in anomalous prose, and these in turn were faster than those in scrambled strings. More important, latencies got progressively faster across both normal and anomalous prose utterances, indicating that RH (as well as unimpaired listeners) is able to develop both syntactic and semantic representations spanning an entire utterance. His ability to construct global representations across an utterance seems to be intact.

Results

Global sources of processing information

	Mean monitoring RTs (msec)		
	Normal prose	Anomalous prose	Scrambled prose
Controls	359	436	489
RH	473	523	595
	Controls: Mean RTs across word-positions (msec)		
	Early	Middle	Late
Normal prose	416	347	314*
Anomalous prose	482	423	402*
Scrambled prose	503	481	484
	RH: Mean RTs across word-positions (msec)		
	Early	Middle	Late
Normal prose	524	519	377*
Anomalous prose	571	538	459*
Scrambled prose	550	600	634

* = significant word-position effect.

Processing Morphologically Complex Words

RH was also as sensitive as unimpaired listeners to the contextual appropriateness of inflected and derived words (chapter 12). In this experiment, we used the word-monitoring task to gauge whether listeners are able to access the syntactic and semantic properties of derived and inflected words and integrate them into the prior sentential context. RH performed as normal in this study. When either the inflected or the derived word was contextually appropriate his monitoring latencies were significantly faster than when they were inappropriate. This suggested that whether the word was derived or inflected, he could access its syntactic and semantic properties and immediately integrate them into the context.

Results

Derived and inflected words in context

	Mean monitoring RTs (msec)		
	Appropriate	Inappropriate	Non-word
Controls (HL)			
Derived	292	360	388
Inflected	315	351	397
RH			
Derived	379	450	415
Inflected	345	394	426
	Differences between conditions and 95% confidence limits [ ]		
	Appropriate-Inappropriate	Inappropriate-Non-word	Appropriate-Non-word
Controls (HL + NHL)			
Derived	63* [73−53]	28* [39−19]	91* [101−81]
Inflected	33* [45−21]	49* [64−34]	82* [101−63]
RH			
Derived	71*	−35	36
Inflected	49*	32	81*

* = significant difference.

Interim Summary
From these studies alone we would have concluded that there was no evidence that RH had a discernible comprehension deficit. But this confronted us with an apparent paradox. All the standard tests of aphasia suggested that he had a severe comprehension deficit, whereas the results of our tests of immediate language comprehension suggested that his language comprehension processes were intact.

It was difficult to resolve this anomaly without further testing, in that the materials and tasks were so different in the two sets of experiments. One important way in which the two sets of studies differed was that the standard tests did not probe the immediate processing of the speech input, whereas this was the explicit purpose of the word-monitoring tasks we had tested him on. To try to resolve this anomaly, we retested RH on the same materials we had used in the various word-monitoring studies, using the acceptability-judgment task. This does not measure immediate processing and is typically used in the standard tests of aphasic deficits. In this task, RH listened to a sentence and then, either immediately or at the end of the sentence, judged whether it was an acceptable sentence of English.

The Relationship between On-Line and Off-Line Tasks
In contrast to his performance in the monitoring studies, his performance on tasks requiring acceptability judgments (whether immediate or delayed) was extremely poor, usually at chance levels. This held for the acceptability-judgment version of the verb-argument study (chapter 9) and the study involving morphologically complex words (chapter 12) using the same materials for which he had shown essentially normal patterns of performance in the monitoring task.

Results

Verb-argument study/judgments

	% correct judgments and range [ ]			
	Normal	Pragmatic	Semantic	Syntactic
1. End of sentence				
Controls	86 [100–81]	76 [100–71]	98 [100–94]	98 [100–96]
RH	75	50	53	49
2. Immediate				
Controls		88 [100–81]	89 [100–69]	86 [94–75]
RH		59	56	53

Derived and inflected words in context/end-of-sentence judgments

	% correct responses and range [ ]		
	Appropriate	Inappropriate	Non-word
Controls			
Derived	98 [100–95]	91 [95–81]	94 [99–89]
Inflected	97 [100–95]	90 [100–67]	98 [100–96]
RH			
Derived	93	57	36
Inflected	75	25	13

Summary
The initial possibility we entertained was that a short-term memory deficit was the underlying cause of his poor performance on the judgment tasks. We thought this unlikely for two reasons. First, we had tested his STM by means of digit-span and digit-matching tasks, and found that it was relatively unimpaired. Second, and perhaps more convincing, was the fact that he also performed at chance when he made his acceptability judgment immediately, rather than wait until the end of the sentence (chapter 9). This

eliminated memory load as a possible factor affecting his acceptability judgments.

What are the implications of this dissociation between relatively normal performance on tests of "on-line" language processing and significantly impaired performance on "off-line" tests using tasks such as grammaticality judgments and sentence–picture matching (see chapter 3)?

First, it raises important questions about the nature of language comprehension and how it is tested in aphasia assessment. If, in keeping with most other research in this area, we had tested RH's comprehension only by using standard off-line tasks, we would have concluded that he had the severe comprehension deficit typical of Wernicke patients. A comparison of the on-line and off-line data shows that the picture is more complex than this. It suggests that RH has problems with some aspects of the comprehension process but not with others. The comprehension processes that appear to be intact are those that are involved in constructing representations of the speech input.

Language comprehension involves more than just the processes involved in constructing linguistic representations. These representations, once constructed, form the output of the language-processing system. They have to be made available to conscious awareness so that, for example, listeners can act in response to an utterance they hear or carry out tasks that require some kind of metalinguistic decision. These are tasks requiring the listener to pay attention to particular aspects of the linguistic output. For example, listeners need to be aware of different aspects of the representation they have constructed, depending on whether they are performing a sentence–picture matching task or a grammaticality-judgment task.

In RH's case, it appears that the nonconscious processes involved in constructing representations remain unimpaired, while at least some of the processes involving conscious awareness no longer function normally. I would argue that RH can construct the appropriate representations of an utterance; his problem lies in being unable to gain access to them for the purpose of making explicit decisions about them.

Finally, the dissociation we see in RH between the processes involved in constructing intermediate representations and those involved in making explicit decisions about the final representation throws into question the standard methods of aphasia assessment. To assess accurately a patient's specific language deficit, RH's data clearly show that we must complement the standard tests with tests of on-line performance.

Almost all aphasia testing involves some form of off-line task, and claims about the nature of deficits and their relation to normal processing systems are based almost exclusively on these kinds of data. The results for RH challenge the validity of these claims and force us to examine closely the assumptions and theoretical implications underlying the use of different paradigms in aphasia.

Profile 2:   BN

General Details

BN is a male native speaker of English who was born in 1944. In 1984 he suffered a left hemisphere CVA. He is right-hand dominant with no appreciable hearing loss (mean loss of 6 db). After his stroke, he was left with a right-side weakness and a nonfluent aphasia, as assessed by the BDAE.

We first tested BN one year after his stroke. His speech output was effortful and primarily consisted of an unstructured string of short noun phrases and the occasional verb. Most of the words he produced were morphologically simple. He rarely produced an affixed word, whether inflected, derived, suffixed, or prefixed.

His memory capacity as measured by digit span and digit matching was slightly below normal. He could accurately recall or match only up to four digits. However, we would not necessarily expect this shortened digit span to have an effect on his ability to comprehend spoken language. There seems to be no clear correlation between language disorders and memory impairments, as assessed by digit span tasks (Butterworth, Campbell and Howard 1986).

BN was tested on various standard tests to determine whether his comprehension was normal. On tests of spoken-language comprehension, such as the auditory-comprehension subtests of the BDAE, BN's performance suggested that he only had a slight comprehension deficit. He made almost no errors on the word discrimination and body-part identification subtests, and on the commands and complex ideational material subtests, he scored 75 percent accuracy.

On the TROG (Bishop 1983), a sentence/word-picture matching task, he made no errors in matching a spoken word to a picture. He was also very accurate on the sentence materials. With NP-V-NP and NP-V-PP constructions, he only made one error in ten trials. He made no errors at all with passive sentences or with comparatives. Where he did make errors were on sentences containing modifier phrases such as "The pencil that is on the book is yellow." He also had some problems with sentences of the form NP-be-PP, but this may have been due to his inability to interpret particular words correctly. For example, he had no difficulty in matching sentences like "The cup is in the box" to the appropriate picture, but he could not match sentences of the same structure where the preposition was either "above" or "below." The results of the TROG and the BDAE, then, suggest that he does not have a severe syntactic-comprehension deficit. He is able correctly to match sentences consisting of a variety of syntactic constructions to the appropriate picture. Perhaps of most interest, given the nature of his speech and his obvious diagnosis as a nonfluent patient, is that he appears to have no difficulty judging the grammaticality of passive sentences (Linebarger et al. 1983).

He does, however, perform poorly on the Token test (De Renzi and Faglioni 1978). Only 31 percent of the items were correct, which indicates that he has severely impaired comprehension. The difficulty in judging the severity of comprehension deficits on the basis of the Token test is that it involves much more than merely the ability to comprehend spoken language. It is as much a problem-solving test as a test of language comprehension. When a patient performs poorly on the test it may be for reasons other than difficulties in comprehending spoken language (cf. Caplan 1987).

Accessing Lexical Form
A series of studies established that BN had no problem accessing the phonological form of either a morphologically complex or simple word in his mental lexicon. Using the gating task, we presented him with a sequence of morphologically simple (chapter 5) and complex (chapter 6) words and found that he recognized them in the same way as unimpaired listeners. That is, he maps the sensory input onto representations of lexical form and recognizes a word at the same point at which it is recognized by the control group. Using the auditory lexical-decision task (chapter 7), we also found that he could accurately discriminate complex and simple real words from simple and complex non-words (mean A' = .97). Taken together, these studies show that does not have difficulty in accurately identifying the phonological form of a suffixed word.

Results

Suffixed words/auditory-lexical decision

| | Percent correct and range [ ] | | | |
| | Real words | | Non-words | |
	Controls	BN	Controls	BN
Simple	100	97	100	100
Derived	97 [100–95]	90	100	94
Inflected	100	82	100	100

Prefixed words/auditory-lexical decision

| | Percent correct and range [ ] | | | | |
| | Real words | | | Non-words | |
	Controls	BN		Controls	BN
Opaque prefixed word	97 [100–90]	95	Prefixed	94 [100–83]	100
Trans prefixed word	98 [100–95]	85	Simple	99 [100–98]	100
Simple	97 [100–85]	100			

Accessing Lexical Content

BN had no difficulty using lexically represented syntactic or semantic information to constrain the development of higher-level structural representations—in this case, verb-argument structures. He heard utterances containing a test verb immediately followed by a target noun. We varied the relationship between the verb and the noun. In one case, the syntactic and semantic constraints on the verb enabled the appropriate verb-argument relationship with the noun to be constructed. In other conditions, the pragmatic, semantic, or syntactic relationship between verb and argument noun were violated. In all three violation conditions, BN's monitoring RTs to the noun were slower than when the relationship was normal. This was the pattern we obtained for unimpaired listeners. We took this as evidence that listeners use different types of lexically associated information to constrain the development of higher-level representations. In this respect, BN was indistinguishable from normal.

When BN listened to the sentences with the purpose of making a grammaticality judgment at the end of the sentence, his performance was slightly worse than that of the control group but still much better than chance ($A' = .87$).

Results

Verb-argument study/word monitoring

	Mean monitoring RTs (msec)			
	Normal	Pragmatic violation	Semantic violation	Syntactic violation
Controls	259	303	329	357
BN	487	531	537	570
	Differences between conditions (msec)			
	Control group mean	95% confidence limits		BN
Normal-pragmatic	44*	55−33		44*
Normal-semantic	70*	90−50		50*
Normal-syntactic	98*	126−70		83*

Verb-argument study/end-of-sentence judgments

	% correct judgment and range [ ]			
	Normal	Pragmatic	Semantic	Syntactic
End of sentence				
Controls	91 [100−83]	95 [100−83]	97 [100−92]	97 [100−88]
BN	75	84	88	78
Immediate				
Controls		98	98	98
BN		84	78	88

Constructing Higher-Level Representations

In the study described in chapter 10, where BN heard normal prose, anomalous prose, and scrambled strings, his monitoring RTs became progressively faster across normal and anomalous prose utterances, but not across scrambled strings. This showed that he could use syntactic, semantic, and prosodic information in the process of interpreting an utterance.

Results

Global sources of processing information

	Mean monitoring RTs (msec)		
	Normal prose	Anomalous prose	Scrambled prose
Controls	344	400	458
BN	559	589	647

	Controls: Mean RTs across word-positions (msec)		
	Early	Middle	Late
Normal prose	386	332	314*
Anomalous prose	439	394	367*
Scrambled prose	477	444	454

	BN: Mean RTs across word-positions (msec)		
	Early	Middle	Late
Normal prose	636	512	530*
Anomalous prose	638	543	585*
Scrambled prose	644	650	649

* = significant word-position effect

Processing Morphologically Complex Words

The first time we discovered any abnormalities in BN's ability to process spoken utterances was when they contained morphologically complex words. Since he had had no difficulty recognizing morphologically complex words in isolation (in the lexical decision and gating tasks) but only when they appeared in sentential contexts, this suggested that his problems were related to the accessing of the content, rather than the form, of a morphologically complex word. We discovered this when we tested him on the studies reported in chapters 12–15.

The first study (chapter 12) was designed as a general test of a patient's ability to process inflected and derived words in sentence contexts. We had BN listen to pairs of sentences where the second sentence of each pair contained a derived or inflected word immediately followed by a target noun. The test word was either appropriate or inappropriate for the prior context. In a third condition, we had a test word which was a non-word composed of a real word stem and suffix, but illegally combined. In contrast to the controls, BN's monitoring latencies were not significantly different in the three conditions, suggesting that he was not sensitive to the contextual appropriateness of the affixed word or to the illegal combination of stem and affix in the non-words.

Results

Derived and inflected words in context

	Mean monitoring RTs (msec)		
	Appropriate	Inappropriate	Non-word
Controls			
Derived	218	286	319
Inflected	231	295	322
BN			
Derived	545	489	526
Inflected	434	458	471
	Differences between conditions and 95% confidence limits [ ]		
	Appropriate-inappropriate	Inappropriate-non-word	Appropriate-non-word
Controls			
Derived	68* [90–46]	33* [50–1]	101* [138–64]
Inflected	64* [82–46]	27* [39–15]	91* [111–71]
BN			
Derived	−56*	37*	−19
Inflected	24	13	37*

Derived and inflected words in context/end-of-sentence judgments

| | % correct response | | |
	Appropriate	Inappropriate	Non-word
Controls			
Derived	99	99	99
Inflected	98	100	99
BN			
Derived	76	33	38
Inflected	88	21	54

We obtained the same result when we tested BN on the identical materials, using the judgment task (Linebarger et al. 1983). BN's performance was very poor. He correctly rejected only 25 percent of the contextually inappropriate sentences and 46 percent of the sentences containing non-words, and he was equally bad with derived and inflected words (A' for derived words = .62; A' for inflected words = .71).

At this point the obvious question to explore was whether BN's problem was specific to morphologically complex words or whether it was part of a general problem relating the syntactic and semantic properties of all words to sentential representations. Did BN have particular problems evaluating the semantic and syntactic implications of the suffix of a morphologically complex word, or was this part of a more extensive problem in evaluating the syntactic and semantic properties of all types of morphemes? The results of the verb-argument study enabled us to rule out the possibility of a general deficit. In that study, the inflection on the test verb was always contextually appropriate whereas the stem could be semantically and/or syntactically inappropriate for the context. For BN, as well as a control group, RTs for each type of anomaly were significantly slower than for the undisrupted condition.

These results showed, first, that the word-monitoring task as used by BN is sensitive to various types of linguistic violations. This means that BN's insensitivity to the types of linguistic violations involving morphologically complex words was not simply because he could not perform the task in the same way as unimpaired listeners. Second, the results show that when the inflection is consistent with the context but the stem is contextually inappropriate in one way or another, BN's RTs increase significantly. This shows that he is sensitive to the contextual appropriateness of the semantic and syntactic information carried by stems and suggests that he has specific problems with inflectional and derivational morphemes when they occur in sentential contexts. But what aspects of derivational and inflectional morphemes? Syntactic, semantic, or both?

To investigate this issue, we tested BN on two further studies, one examining the syntactic role of inflected words in utterances (chapter 13) and the other examining their semantic role (chapter 14). To determine whether BN has problems in processing inflections when they serve a purely syntactic role in an utterance, we had him monitor for target words in utterances with the structure: NP + [V + inflection] + NP, where the second NP was the target word. The nature of the inflection on the verb determined whether the verb was transitive or intransitive, and this in turn set up a structural preference for either an NP or a PP to follow the verb. When the suffix is [-ing], the verb is transitive and an NP is the preferred continuation. When the suffix is [-ed] the sentence is in the passive voice, the verb is intransitive and a PP is the preferred continuation. If BN can access the syntactic properties of the inflected verb and integrate them into the sentence representation, then monitoring RTs to targets following transitive verbs should be faster than those following intransitive verbs, just as they are for unimpaired listeners. But we found no differences in his RTs in the two conditions. This shows that he is unaffected by the structural implications of inflectional suffixes.

Inflections as syntactic devices

	Mean monitoring RTs (msec)			
	Consistent	Inconsistent	Differences	95% confidence limits
Controls				
Context	228	282	53*	87−23
No context	255	322	67*	94−40
BN				
Context	374	378	4	
No context	382	387	5	

The next question we asked was whether BN is also insensitive to inflectional suffixes when they play a semantic rather than syntactic role in an utterance by marking tense. To test this, we constructed sentence-pairs containing an inflected verb marked for tense. In such sentences, the inflectional suffix served an anaphoric or deictic role. The context sentence set up the present tense and the continuation sentence contained an inflected verb in the present or past tense. When the verb was in the present tense, the verb tense and context tense were consistent. But when the verb was in the past tense, then the verb tense was inconsistent with the tense set up by the context sentence. Here also, his RTs were not faster in the consistent compared to the inconsistent condition. This suggests that BN is unable to integrate the anaphoric properties of the inflectional suffix into the representation of the sentence context.

Inflections as tense markers

	Mean monitoring RTs (msec)			
	Consistent	Inconsistent	Differences	95% confidence limits
Controls				
Syllabic	213	265	52*	[64−40]
Nonsyllabic	223	234	11	[22−1]
BN				
Syllabic	358	282	−76*	
Nonsyllabic	375	370	−5	

Summary
The data so far suggest that BN has comprehension problems specific to the processing of morphologically complex words. However we need to consider one alternate possibility: that BN has problems with any type of word ending and not just with morphological suffixes. This possibility is supported by the results of the study described in chapter 15. This study was similar to all the morphology experiments, except that the test word was morphologically simple rather than complex. On some trials the ending of the morphologically simple word was changed so that it became a non-word (e.g., *nylon* became *nylup*). BN's monitoring latencies did not significantly increase in the presence of a non-word. Similarly, he showed no effect of contextually inappropriate real words when the appropriateness of the word depended upon its ending. So, for example, in a series of studies not reported in this book (Ostrin and Tyler, in prep.), we constructed pairs of sentences like:

(1a)   Mr Jones had an attack dog which he trained to be violent.

(1b)   Mr Jones had an attach dog which he trained to be violent.

(2a)   Sam ran into the college building to register for the course.

(2b)   Sam ran into the collar building to register for the course.

In both sets of sentences, the pairs of words (*attack/attach; college/collar*) are members of the same word-initial cohort (Marslen-Wilson 1987), which deviate toward their end. The amount of deviation varies from one segment (in 1) to an entire syllable (in 2). Although unimpaired listeners are sensitive to the deviation that results in a contextually inappropriate word, BN is not. His RTs are no slower in the inappropriate cases (1b and 2b) than in the appropriate cases (1a and 2a). This entire ensemble of experiments suggests that BN does not have a specific deficit involving the processing of bound morphemes. Rather, they imply that his deficit involves word-endings in general, irrespective of their morphemic status.

As yet, we have no definitive explanation for BN's inability to process the ends of words. However, we can plausibly account for his results within the framework of the cohort model (Marslen-Wilson 1987). According to the cohort model, when inimpaired listeners hear an utterance, they access the phonological form of each word on the basis of the acoustic-phonetic input. The sensory input initially activates all those form representations with which it is compatible. For example, when the listener hears *prop...,* among the set of form representations that will be activated are the words *properly, property, proper,* etc. As more of the speech input is heard, one word form will eventually emerge as the single best-fitting candidate. The speech input, if it is unambiguous, will always take priority over the sentential context in determining our percept of the word. So, listeners will hear *antidote* in (2b) even though it is contextually inappropriate.

BN may depend less than normal listeners on the sensory input and more upon the context in developing a representation of a spoken utterance. When he hears *prop* ... spoken in context he activates the normal set of word-candidates and accesses their semantic and syntactic context. However, when the word turns out to be *properly* spoken in the context:

(3)   John knew he could never buy a house with the way *properly* prices were going up.

The sensory information that makes the word contextually inappropriate (the end of the word) is overridden by the context so that BN "hears" the word that is a member of the cohort and compatible with the context (*property*). We are currently evaluating this hypothesis in further experiments.

An interesting aspect of these data is that the underlying cause of BN's language comprehension disorder does not appear to be an impairment in the representation of syntactic knowledge associated with bound morphemes. For this to have been the case, he should have shown selective difficulties with those bound (inflectional) morphemes thought to primarily play a syntactic role in utterances, and with the syntactic, as opposed to the semantic, properties of inflectional morphemes. Instead, he showed similar degrees of impairment for both the derivational and inflectional morphology.

Given that on gross measures of spoken-language comprehension BN appears not to have a significant comprehension deficit, this very specific problem with word-endings does not make it impossible for him to comprehend speech. The pragmatic context in which each utterance is spoken, its extralinguistic context, and the fact that he accesses the meaning of the stem of a morphologically complex word presumably compensates in part for an inadequately processed word-ending.

BN, then, does not conform to the standard description of an agrammatic patient. Although his speech production is classically nonfluent and "agrammatic," and he does have a comprehension deficit, it is not due to problems with syntax, either through the loss or the inaccessibility of syntactic knowledge. Rather, he has a specific problem processing the ends of words.

Summary Processing Profiles

Profile 3: PK (Anomic)

General Details
PK was born in 1945 and suffered a stroke in 1984. Before his stroke he was employed as an architect. His memory, as measured by digit span and matching tasks, is only slightly below normal. The results of standard aphasia tests give conflicting assessments as to whether he has a comprehension deficit. According to the BDAE his comprehension is essentially normal, whereas the Token test diagnoses him as having a severe comprehension deficit (see chapter 3). He does not seem to have problems with syntax, as measured by his performance on a grammaticality-judgment task that included sentences containing a variety of syntactic violations (e.g., subject-auxilliary inversion, verb complement clauses, and passives). He produces fluent spontaneous speech but has severe word-finding difficulties.

Accessing Lexical Form

Results

Phoneme discrimination

	Percentage of errors
Controls	1
PK	4.9

Simple words/gating task

	Mean hearing loss (db)	N correct (max = 20)	Isolation point (msec)	% cohort membership
Controls	9.8	20	325	
	[range: 7–15 db]			
PK	12.9	20	335	86

Simple words/auditory lexical decision

	% correct	
	Real words	Non-words
Controls	100	100
PK	100	100

Complex words/gating task

	% correct full forms	% correct stems	Isolation point/ derivation full forms (msec)	Isolation point/ derivation stems (msec)	Isolation point/ inflection full forms (msec)	Isolation point/ inflection stems (msec)
Controls	100	100	375	258	375	250
PK	89	83	350	180	390	170

Suffixed words/auditory lexical decision

	% correct and range [ ]			
	Real words		Non-words	
	Controls	PK	Controls	PK
Simple	100	100	100	100
Derived	97 [100–95]	95	100	91
Inflected	100	92	100	83

Prefixed words/auditory lexical decision

	% correct and range [ ]					
	Real words			Non-words		
	Controls	PK		Controls	PK
Opaque prefixed	97 [100–90]	100	Prefixed	94 [100–83]	95
Trans prefixed	98 [100–95]	95	Simple	99 [100–98]	95
Simple	97 [100–85]	90			

The process of contacting form representations of both simple and complex words is normal. He makes few errors in discriminating phonemes; those that he does make tend to be errors of place of articulation. In the gating studies, he recognizes simple and complex words at essentially the same point at which they are recognized by unimpaired listeners. And he is very accurate at discriminating real words, whether simple or complex, from non-words in the auditory lexical-decision tasks.

Accessing Lexical Content

Results

Verb-argument study/word monitoring

		Mean monitoring RTs (msec)		
	Normal	Pragmatic violation	Semantic violation	Syntactic violation
Controls	259	303	329	357
PK	512	560	620	599

	Differences between conditions (msec)		
	Control group mean	95% confidence limits	PK
Normal-pragmatic	44*	55–33	48*
Normal-semantic	70*	90–50	108*
Normal-syntactic	98*	126–70	87*

* = difference is significant.

In the verb-argument study, PK showed significant effects of all three types of anomaly, indicating that he was accessing the syntactic and semantic content of the verbs and integrating this information into the sentential context. His performance differed from normal in one respect: RTs to subcategory violations were not longer than those to selection-restriction violations. This suggests that when he is unable to construct the appropriate syntactic object, he does not attempt to evaluate the semantic implications of a verb and its argument.

Constructing Higher-Level Representations

Results

Global sources of processing information

	Mean monitoring RTs (msec)		
	Normal prose	Anomalous prose	Scrambled prose
Controls	344	400	458
PK	430	531	583

	Controls: Mean RTs across word positions (msec)		
	Early	Middle	Late
Normal prose	386	332	314*
Anomalous prose	439	394	367*
Scrambled prose	477	444	454

	PK: Mean RTs across word positions (msec)		
	Early	Middle	Late
Normal prose	491	411	382*
Anomalous prose	525	528	539
Scrambled prose	586	564	596

* = significant word-position effect

In this monitoring study where we vary prose type and word position, PK showed a word position effect in normal prose. That is, RTs became progressively faster throughout the sentence. However, unlike the control subjects he does not show the same word-position effect for anomalous prose. This is evidence that he has some kind of difficulty with syntax in the process of developing a representation of a spoken utterance.

Processing Morphologically Complex Words

Results

Derived and inflected words in context

	Mean monitoring RTs (msec)		
	Appropriate	Inappropriate	Non-word
Controls			
Derived	218	286	319
Inflected	231	295	322
PK			
Derived	483	506	576
Inflected	486	531	525
	Differences between conditions and 95% confidence limits [ ]		
	Appropriate-inappropriate	Inappropriate-non-word	Appropriate-non-word
Controls			
Derived	68* [90−46]	33* [65−1]	101* [138−64]
Inflected	64* [82−46]	27* [39−15]	91* [111−71]
PK			
Derived	23	70*	93*
Inflected	45*	−6	39*

Inflections as syntactic devices

	Mean monitoring RTs (msec)			
	Consistent	Inconsistent	Differences	95% confidence limits
Controls				
Context	228	282	53*	87−23
No context	255	322	67*	94−40
PK				
Context	414	445	31 ^	
No context	469	483	14	

^ = within confidence limits

Inflections as tense markers

	Mean monitoring RTs (msec)			
	Consistent	Inconsistent	Differences	95% confidence limits
Controls				
Syllabic	213	265	52*	[64−40]
Nonsyllabic	223	234	11	[22−1]
PK				
Syllabic	362	415	53*	
Nonsyllabic	341	394	53*	

PK has no difficulty accessing the form of a morphologically complex word, but he has some problems processing these words when they occur in sentence contexts. First, he shows no sensitivity to the contextual appropriateness of derived words. Derivations provide form-class information; they determine whether a word is a noun, a verb, or another part of speech. It may be that PK can not make use of this information. This may be part of the reason why he shows no word-position effect in anomalous prose.

Second, he appears to be only able to process inflected words when they play a semantic role in utterances. He shows no sensitivity to the syntactic aspects of inflections.

The Relationship between On-Line and Off-Line Tasks

Results

Verb-argument study/judgments

	% correct judgments and range [ ]			
	Normal	Pragmatic	Semantic	Syntactic
End of sentence				
Controls	91 [100−83]	95 [100−83]	97 [100−92]	97 [100−88]
PK	94	88	84	94
Immediate				
Controls		98	98	98
PK		91	81	88

Derived and inflected words in context/end-of-sentence judgments

	% correct responses		
	Appropriate	Inappropriate	Non-word
Controls			
Derived	99 [100–99]	99 [100–98]	99 [100–99]
Inflected	98 [100–99]	100 [100–99]	99 [100–99]
PK			
Derived	86	86	90
Inflected	83	92	100

The on-line monitoring and judgment data are consistent in the verb-argument study. PK can construct the appropriate higher-level representations and reflect upon them when necessary ($A' = .93$).

We see the same pattern in the processing of inflected words. That is, the monitoring results and the judgments show that he is sensitive to the contextual appropriateness of inflected words. However, the picture for derived words is somewhat different. He shows no sensitivity to the contextual appropriateness of derived words, as measured by the monitoring task, although he is able accurately to judge their appropriateness (A' for derived words $= .93$; A' for inflected words $= .93$).

Summary
The results of these studies suggest that PK suffers from a cluster of deficits, all of which can be considered to be primarily syntactic. He has difficulty exploiting the form-class information carried by derivations and the syntactic information carried by inflections. It is probable that his lack of a word-position effect in anomalous prose is due to his inability to use these and other types of syntactic information.

In this respect his comprehension deficits do not match his production deficit, as diagnosed by standard tests. On the basis of the standard tests, PK was classified as an anomic with severe word-finding problems. The samples of his spontaneous speech given in chapter 3, especially the sample of elicited conversation, support this diagnosis for production. There is no evidence in his spontaneous speech that he has anything other than a severe anomia. However, there is no evidence of an anomia in comprehension. If there was, we might plausibly assume that we would see some sign of it on the gating task, with PK having difficulty producing word-candidates in response to fragments and identifying words much later than the control subjects. But this gating performance was indistinguishable from normal.

Profile 4:   VS (Nonfluent)

General Details

VS was born in 1938 and suffered a stroke in 1978. She is a housewife. Her memory is slightly worse than normal. Her comprehension deficit was diagnosed as being severe on the Token test but minimal on the BDAE (see chapter 3). Her spontaneous speech is very restricted. She has difficulty producing more than single words or stereotypical phrases and she has some articulatory problems. Unfortunately, we could not test VS as extensively as we would have wished because she withdrew from the project.

Accessing Lexical Form

Results

Phoneme discrimination

	Percentage of errors
Controls	1
VS	13

Simple words/gating task

	Mean hearing loss (db)	N correct (max = 20)	Mean (msec)	% cohort membership
Controls	9.8 db [range: 7–15 db]	20	325 [range: 300–375]	
VS	21.7	16	390	74

Simple words/auditory lexical decision

	% correct	
	Real words	Non-words
Controls	100	100
VS	95	95

Complex words/gating task

	% correct full forms	% correct stems	Mean isolation point/ derivation full forms (msec)	Mean isolation point/ derivation stems (msec)	Mean isolation point/ inflection full forms (msec)	Mean isolation point/ inflection stems (msec)
Controls	100	100	375	258	375	250
VS	67	92	430	286	350	180

Prefixed words/auditory lexical decision

	% correct and range [ ]					
	Real words			Non-words		
	Controls	VS		Controls	VS
Opaque prefixed	97 [100−90]	76	Prefixed	94 [100−83]	95
Trans prefixed	98 [100−95]	85	Simple	99 [100−98]	95
Simple	97 [100−85]	95			

Although VS does not have a severe hearing problem, she found it very difficult to discriminate phonemes accurately. She made a large proportion of errors on all types of contrasts, whether word-initial or word-final.

This did not straightforwardly relate to her ability to access the phonological form of a word. She had no real difficulty accessing the form of simple words (chapter 5), but she did have some problems with complex words. This revealed itself, both in the auditory lexical-decision task where she performed slightly less well (A' = .92) than normals (NHL: Mean A' = .98; range = .95−1.0) and in the gating task with suffixed words (chapter 6). Here she correctly identified the full form of only 33 percent of the inflected words by word-offset, although she managed to recognize almost all of the stems. She tended to get the correct stem but add onto it the incorrect inflection. She was much more accurate in identifying the full form of a derived word (83 percent correct).

Accessing Lexical Content

Results

Verb-argument study/word monitoring

	Normal	Mean monitoring RTs (msec)		
		Pragmatic violation	Semantic violation	Syntactic violation
Controls	259	303	329	357
VS	448	533	549	599

	Differences between conditions (msec)		
	Control group mean	95% confidence limits	VS
Normal-pragmatic	44*	55–33	85*
Normal-semantic	70*	90–50	101*
Normal-syntactic	98*	126–70	151*

* = significant difference.

She was able to access the syntactic and semantic properties of words, as was shown by her sensitivity to all three types of verb-argument violations. The only way in which she differed from normal was in the extent to which her latencies were affected by the violations. They were slowed relative to the undisrupted baseline condition much more than those of the control group, as can be seen by the fact that her difference scores are beyond the confidence limits for the control group.

Constructing Higher-Level Representations

Results

Global sources of processing information

	Mean monitoring RTs (msec)		
	Normal prose	Anomalous prose	Scrambled prose
Controls	344	400	458
VS	487	566	621

	Controls: Mean RTs across word-positions (msec)		
	Early	Middle	Late
Normal prose	386	332	314*
Anomalous prose	439	394	367*
Scrambled prose	477	444	454

	VS: Mean RTs across word-positions (msec)		
	Early	Middle	Late
Normal prose	563	440	459*
Anomalous prose	584	583	530
Scrambled prose	581	647	635

In the prose experiment (chapter 10), VS showed a significant word-position effect only in normal prose, indicating that she was able to develop an interpretative representation spanning an entire utterance. Although the word-position effect was not significant in anomalous prose, her latencies did get faster as she heard more of an anomalous prose sentence, whereas they did not in scrambled strings. This suggests that the faster latencies in anomalous prose were not due to simple expectation. On the basis of this pattern of results we can say that she is able to develop higher-level representations of spoken utterances.

Processing Morphologically Complex Words

Results

Derived and inflected words in context

	Mean monitoring RTs (msec)		
	Appropriate	Inappropriate	Non-word
Controls			
Derivation	218	286	319
Inflection	231	295	322
VS			
Derivation	556	529	601
Inflection	506	537	547
	Differences between conditions and 95% confidence limits [ ]		
	Appropriate-inappropriate	Inappropriate-non-word	Appropriate-non-word
Controls			
Derivation	68* [90−46]	33* [65−1]	101* [138−64]
Inflection	64* [82−46]	27* [39−15]	91* [111−71]
VS			
Derivation	−27	72*	45
Inflection	31	10	41*

As mentioned earlier, VS had problems identifying the correct inflectional suffix in the gating task, although she almost always managed to get the correct stem. Her performance in the monitoring tasks showed that she was not sensitive to the syntactic and semantic implications of either inflected or derived words.

The Relationship between On-Line and Off-Line Tasks

Results

Verb-argument study/judgments

| | % correct judgments and range [ ] | | | |
	Normal	Pragmatic	Semantic	Syntactic
End of sentence				
Controls	91 [100−83]	95 [100−83]	97 [100−92]	97 [100−88]
VS	63	81	84	85

Derived and inflected words in context/end-of-sentence judgments

| | % correct responses and range [ ] | | |
	Appropriate	Inappropriate	Non-word
Controls			
Derivation	99 [100−99]	99 [100−99]	99 [100−99]
Inflection	98 [100−99]	100 [100−99]	99 [100−99]
VS			
Derivation	71	57	29
Inflection	88	31	25

In the verb-argument study, her monitoring performance was essentially normal, with latencies increasing when she encountered a sentence containing any of the three types of violation. The main way she differed from normal was that she showed a larger effect of the three types of violation than did the controls.

Her ability to judge whether a sentence contained an anomaly (mean $A' = .85$) was outside the normal range (NHL: range: .93−1.0) although it was still above chance. For the three kinds of anomaly, her judgments ranged in accuracy from 81−85 percent (A' range: .85−.83).

In the morphology study described in chapter 12, the monitoring and judgment data were consistent. She was insensitive to the contextual appropriateness of both derived and inflected words, whether measured by the monitoring or judgment task (mean $A' = .65$).

Summary
VS appears to have two main comprehension deficits. One involves morphologically complex words and the other involves her ability to reflect upon certain aspects of linguistic representations.

First, although she had no difficulty accessing the form and content of simple words, she did have some problems with complex words. She had difficulty mapping the sensory input onto the full-form representation of an inflected word and was unable to assess the contextual appropriateness of either derived or inflected words.

Second, VS's on-line performance suggests that, apart from her specific difficulties comprehending complex words, her ability to recognize words and use their syntactic and semantic properties to build higher-level representations appears to be intact.

However, her performance on various types of off-line tasks is worse than that of the normal controls. On the Token test, she scored 11/36 items correct, which is very poor performance, and on sentence–picture matching tests such as TROG (Bishop 1983) she barely scores better than chance. Her grammaticality judgments, although just outside the appropriate confidence limits, are much better than chance.

We see in VS, then, an example of a patient who shows much better comprehension performance when tested on a grammaticality-judgment task compared to other explicit tasks (e.g., sentence–picture matching). I argued in chapter 1 that these tasks involve different kinds of conscious awareness. The grammaticality task reflects the breakdown of a procedure that automatically percolates to the listener's awareness. The listener does not necessarily know what type of error has occurred. He or she merely becomes aware of the fact that the normal process has not been successful. We can constrast this type of task with one like sentence–picture matching where the subject has some degree of voluntary control over whether to reflect consciously on the picture and on the sentence in order to carry out the task. VS's results show that these different types of metalinguistic awareness can be differentially affected by brain damage.

Profile 5:   JG (Nonfluent)

General Details
JG was born in 1929 and suffered a stroke in 1980. Before his stroke he was employed as a groundskeeper. He has a moderate memory impairment, as measured by digit-span and digit-matching tasks. According to the Token test and the BDAE, he has a severe comprehension deficit. His spontaneous speech is hesitant and consists of short phrases with a number of verbal paraphasias.

Accessing Lexical Form

Results

Phoneme discrimination

	Percentage errors
Controls	3 [range: 0–5%]
JG	8

Simple words/gating task

	Mean hearing loss (db)	N correct (max = 20)	Mean isolation point (msec)	% cohort membership
Controls	13.7 db [1–24 db]	20	320 [range: 305–370]	
JG	22.1 db	20	370	85

Simple words/auditory lexical decision

	% correct	
	Real words	Non-words
Controls	99	100
JG	81	93

Complex words/gating task

	% correct full forms	% correct stems	Mean isolation point/ derivation full forms (msec)	Mean isolation point/ derivation stems (msec)	Mean isolation point/ inflection full forms (msec)	Mean isolation point/ inflection stems (msec)
Controls	100	100	442	267	408	258
JG	67	67	430	300	417	250

Suffixed words/auditory lexical decision

| | % correct and range [ ] | | | |
| | Real words | | Non-words | |
	Controls	JG	Controls	JG
Simple	99 [100–96]	81	100 [100–99]	93
Derived	99 [100–94]	90	99 [100–97]	52
Inflected	100 [100–99]	87	99 [100–96]	37

Prefixed words/auditory-lexical decision

| | % correct and range [ ] | | | | |
| | Real words | | | Non-words | |
	Controls	JG		Controls	JG
Opaque prefixed	98 [100–95]	85	Prefixed	92 [100–75]	91
Trans prefixed	99 [100–95]	90	Simple	95 [100–83]	97
Simple	99 [100–95]	80			

JG made a high proportion of errors (37 percent) on word-final consonants in the phoneme discrimination study. In the auditory lexical-decision
tasks, he was much better at discriminating simple ($A' = .9$) and prefixed ($A' = .93$) words than either inflected ($A' = .77$) or derived words
($A' = .84$). In the gating studies, he recognized both simple and complex
words at the point at which they were recognized by normal listeners.
When he failed to identify a word at all (e.g., he heard *sorted* as *forted*) this
was because he accessed the incorrect cohort due to his difficulty in making
various types of phoneme discriminations.

Accessing Lexical Content

Results

Verb-argument study/word monitoring

		Mean monitoring RTs (msec)		
	Normal	Pragmatic violation	Semantic violation	Syntactic violation
Controls	309	359	377	401
JG	467	478	513	483
		Differences between conditions (msec)		
		Control group mean	95% confidence limits	JG
Normal-pragmatic		50*	69–39	11
Normal-semantic		68*	93–53	46*
Normal-syntactic		92*	107–67	16

JG shows only an effect of semantic selection-restriction violations. He appears to be totally insensitive to either pragmatic or syntactic violations. This suggests that he is unable to access syntactic subcategory information attached to verbs, or, more likely, that he has difficulty using this as well as pragmatic information in the process of constructing a representation of an utterance.

Constructing Higher-Level Representations

Results

Global sources of processing information

	Mean monitoring RTs (msec)		
	Normal prose	Anomalous prose	Scrambled prose
Controls	344	400	458
JG	371	450	500

	Controls: Mean RTs across word positions (msec)		
	Early	Middle	Late
Normal prose	386	332	314*
Anomalous prose	439	394	367*
Scrambled prose	477	444	454

	JG: Mean RTs across word positions (msec)		
	Early	Middle	Late
Normal prose	441	331	342*
Anomalous prose	472	431	448
Scrambled prose	495	536	468

* = significant word-position effect

Local sources of processing information

	Mean monitoring RTs (msec)				
	Early	Late	Scrambled	Phonological disruption	Syntactic disruption
Controls	449	361	392	462	440
JG	597	550	576	584	563

	Differences between conditions (JG) and confidence limits (95%)			
	Early-late	Late-scrambled	Late-phonological disruption	Late-syntactic disruption
Confidence limits	127–49	54–6	129–71	123–34
JG differences	−47	26 ^	34	13

Once again, JG is insensitive to almost all of the linguistic manipulations we introduced. Although he shows a word-position effect in normal prose, suggesting that he is able to construct a meaningful representation spanning an entire utterance, he does not show a word-position effect in anomalous prose (the difference between the early and late conditions in anomalous prose is not significant and is not larger than the difference between early and late positions in scrambled prose). In addition, he appears to be unable to use local phonological or syntactic information in the process of interpreting an utterance.

These results are in accordance with the results from the verb-argument study in the following respect. JG shows a word-position effect in normal prose, but not in anomalous prose, suggesting that the word-position effect in normal prose is due to relations between the meanings of words. In the verb-argument study, we see the same kind of result. That is, he showed no sensitivity to syntactic violations, but he was sensitive to violations of semantic-selection restrictions. In a recent study not reported in this book, JG also shows robust semantic priming effects. Together, these results suggest that at least some aspects of lexical semantics may be preserved and that JG has difficulty using syntactic information.

Processing Morphologically Complex Words

Results

Derived and inflected words in context

	Mean monitoring RTs (msec)		
	Appropriate	Inappropriate	Non-word
Controls (NHL)			
Derived	290	348	378
Inflected	304	334	387
JG			
Derived	374	357	363
Inflected	332	353	369

	Differences between conditions and 95% confidence limits [ ]		
	Appropriate-inappropriate	Inappropriate-non-word	Appropriate-non-word
Controls (HL + NHL)			
Derived	63* [73−53]	28* [39−19]	91* [101−81]
Inflected	33* [45−21]	49* [64−34]	82* [101−63]
JG			
Derived	−17	6	−11
Inflected	21	6	37

Inflections as syntactic devices

| | Mean monitoring RTs (msec) | | | |
	Consistent	Inconsistent	Differences	95% confidence limits
Controls				
Context	289	311	22*	33−11
No context	388	402	14*	27−1
JG				
Context	324	339	15 ^	
No context	428	419	−9	

Inflections as tense markers

| | Mean monitoring RTs (msec) | | | |
	Consistent	Inconsistent	Differences	95% confidence limits
Controls				
Syllabic	261	283	22*	35−9
Nonsyllabic	265	293	27*	43−11
JG				
Syllabic	371	296	−75	
Nonsyllabic	308	341	33 ^	

JG shows no significant effects in this series of studies. Although the size of some differences were within normal confidence limits, the effects were always marginal and not very robust. In general, these results suggest that JG is insensitive to the contextual appropriateness of derived or inflected words.

The Relationship between On-Line and Off-Line Tasks

Results

Verb-argument study/judgments

| | % correct judgments and range [ ] | | | |
	Normal	Pragmatic	Semantic	Syntactic
End of sentence				
Controls	91 [100−83]	95 [100−83]	97 [100−92]	97 [100−88]
JG	81	69	75	88
Immediate				
Controls		98 [100−94]	99 [100−94]	94 [100−88]
JG		100	81	84

Derived and inflected words in context/end-of-sentence judgments

	% correct responses and range [ ]		
	Appropriate	Inappropriate	Non-word
Controls			
Derived	97 [100−99]	88 [95−71]	95 [100−81]
Inflected	98 [100−92]	93 [100−75]	93 [100−80]
JG			
Derived	86	29	38
Inflected	67	29	46

In the study investigating verb-argument relations, his monitoring RTs were only slightly affected by violations of semantic selection restrictions. He was also very poor at making immediate judgments (he suffered from a strong "no" bias) about whether a sentence contained an anomaly (A′ = .79). However, he was more accurate at making delayed-acceptability judgments (A′ = .88).

In contrast, in the morphology study, both his monitoring and judgment data were comparable. He showed no sensitivity to the contextual appropriateness of either a derived or inflected word, whether measured by the word-monitoring or judgment tasks (Mean A′ = .62).

Summary
JG's data suggest that he does not have major problems accessing the phonological form of a word spoken in isolation when we test this by means of the gating task. He occasionally has difficulty when he fails to access the correct cohort, but for the most part this is not a significant problem. However, he is less sensitive than normal listeners to the distinction between words and non-words, although his performance is still significantly better than chance.

The major way in which he deviates from normal is revealed in the word-monitoring studies, where he appears to be insensitive to almost all of the linguistic variables we introduced. There are four possible explanations for these results: he cannot perform the word monitoring task; he cannot access the syntactic and semantic properties of words; he is unable to use this information to construct the appropriate type of higher-level representations; and although he can build the necessary higher-level representations, he does this more slowly than normal listeners.

We do not have any data which conclusively rules out the first possibility, but the results of a study we have recently carried out with JG suggest that this is not the problem. In this study, JG heard a list of words and was asked to monitor for members of prespecified categories (e.g., a member of the category "fruit" or "color"). We measured his RTs to monitor for the category members and we also recorded his error rate. He rarely failed to press the response key when he heard a member of a pre-specified category and his latencies were within the normal range. This is clear evidence that he does not have problems monitoring for target words per se.

Considering the data from all of the studies, the last possibility is the most plausible account of his deficit. We can rule out the second and third on the basis of JG's end-of-sentence judgment data in the verb-argument study, where his performance is reasonably accurate. For this to be the case, he must be able to construct higher-level representations. The difference between the monitoring and end-of-sentence judgment data in the verb-argument study suggest that the process of constructing representations is slowed down in some way. A task that taps the rapid, on-line construction of representations (like the monitoring task) does not reveal any sensitivity to linguistic variables, whereas a task that taps into the final representation (the judgment task) does.

The fact that the anomaly detection data are worse than the judgment data and tell the same story as the word-monitoring data supports this interpretation.

The data reported here elaborate upon the Token test and the BDAE, on the basis of which he was diagnosed as a patient with a severe comprehension deficit. He does indeed have a severe comprehension deficit, and the on-line data suggest what the cause of the deficit might be.

Profile 6:   CH (Nonfluent)

General Details

CH was born in 1914 and before his stroke in 1980 worked as a glass worker. He died in 1988. His memory for digits was only very slightly below normal. On the Token test and the BDAE, he was diagnosed as having a moderate comprehension deficit. His speech output was very slow and hesitant, consisting of short, simple utterances.

Accessing Lexical Form

Results

Phoneme discrimination

	Percentage of errors
Controls	10% [range: 1–22%]
CH	19%

Simple words/gating task

	Mean hearing loss (db)	N correct (max = 20)	Mean isolation point (msec)	% cohort membership
Controls	37.9 db [range: 26–48]	18	405 [range: 340–445]	
CH	55.9	13	475	51

CH suffers from a profound hearing loss, which contributes to his difficulty in recognizing the form of a spoken word. He made a large number of place-of-articulation errors in the phoneme-discrimination test and he performed poorly on the gating task with simple words. This was primarily because he often misperceived the initial segment of a word (51 percent of the time) and therefore accessed the wrong cohort.

Accessing Lexical Content

Results

Verb-argument study/word monitoring

		Mean monitoring RTs (msec)		
	Normal	Pragmatic violation	Semantic violation	Syntactic violation
Controls	322	380	399	411
CH	359	389	408	419
		Differences between conditions (msec)		
		Control group mean	95% confidence limits	CH
Normal-pragmatic		58*	69–39	30*
Normal-semantic		77*	93–53	49*
Normal-syntactic		89*	107–67	60*

In the verb-argument study described in chapter 9, he showed that he could access the semantic and syntactic properties of verbs and use them to constrain permissible verb-argument relations. Although his difference scores were outside the normal confidence limits, his latencies significantly increased when he encountered each of the three types of anomaly.

Constructing Higher-Level Representations

Results

Global sources of processing information

	Mean monitoring RTs (msec)		
	Normal prose	Anomalous prose	Scrambled prose
Controls	359	436	489
CH	432	489	542

	Controls: Mean RTs across word positions (msec)		
	Early	Middle	Late
Normal prose	416	347	314*
Anomalous prose	482	423	402*
Scrambled prose	503	481	484

	CH: Mean RTs across word positions (msec)		
	Early	Middle	Late
Normal prose	531	388	378*
Anomalous prose	559	479	429*
Scrambled prose	571	521	533*

Local sources of processing information

	Mean monitoring RTs (msec)				
	Early	Late	Scrambled	Phonological disruption	Syntactic disruption
Controls	449	361	392	462	440
CH	527	474	486	684	563

	Differences between conditions (CH) and confidence limits (95%)			
	Early-late	Late-scrambled	Late-phonological disruption	Late-syntactic disruption
Confidence limits	127–49	54–6	129–71	123–34
CH	−53*	12	210*	89*

In the monitoring study where we varied the availability of different kinds of processing information across an utterance, he shows a significant word-position effect in scrambled strings. However, this does not invalidate the word-position effects found in normal and anomalous prose, since these are much larger (153 and 130 msec in normal and anomalous prose, respectively, vs 38 msec in scrambled prose).

In the phonological-phrases experiment, the word-position effect for anomalous prose was replicated. Moreover, he showed that, like normal listeners, he is able to use syntactic and prosodic information to build local phrases in the process of interpreting an utterance.

These studies together show that he is able to construct local and global representations of a spoken utterance.

Processing Morphologically Complex Words

Results

Derived and inflected words in context

	Mean monitoring RTs (msec)		
	Appropriate	Inappropriate	Non-word
Controls (HL)			
Derived	292	360	388
Inflected	315	351	397
CH			
Derived	373	424	417
Inflected	372	434	416

	Differences between conditions and 95% confidence limits [ ]		
	Appropriate-inappropriate	Inappropriate-non-word	Appropriate-non-word
Controls (HL + NHL)			
Derived	63* [73−53]	28* [39−19]	91* [101−81]
Inflected	33* [45−21]	49* [64−34]	82* [101−63]
CH			
Derived	51*	−7	44*
Inflected	62*	−18	44*

He had no difficulty processing inflected and derived words when they occurred in sentential contexts (chapter 12). We could not explore this in any more detail because CH died before we could test him on the other morphology or word-ending studies.

The Relationship between On-Line and Off-Line Tasks

Results

Verb-argument study/judgments

	% correct judgments and range			
	Normal	Pragmatic	Semantic	Syntactic
End of sentence				
Controls	86 [100–81]	76 [100–71]	98 [100–94]	98 [100–96]
CH	71	75	88	83

CH was tested only on one off-line test: the delayed-judgment task with the verb-argument materials (chapter 9). His performance in the off-line task was consistent with the results of the on-line monitoring task. That is, he was sensitive to all three types of anomaly (A′ = .89).

Summary
Although CH has severe hearing loss, which interferes with his ability to discriminate phonemes and to recognize words when they are spoken in isolation, this does not affect his ability to process words when they are spoken in utterances. He shows essentially the normal pattern in all the word-monitoring tasks designed to tap on-line language comprehension. This contrasts with his performance on standard tests of comprehension (e.g., Token test and BDAE), which suggests that he has a mild comprehension deficit.

What is the relationship between CH's comprehension and production abilities? On the basis of the comprehension studies we have tested him on, his language-comprehension system appears to be essentially intact. If we examine the samples of his spontaneous speech given in chapter 3, we can see that this is not true of his language production system. He has word-finding problems and his utterances are much shorter and syntactically simpler than normal. Thus, whatever functional disorder underlies his production deficit does not appear to affect his ability to comprehend spoken language.

Profile 7:   GS (Nonfluent)

General details
GS was born in 1927 and suffered a stroke in 1978. Before this she was employed as a clerk. Her memory for digits is slightly below normal.

According to the Token test and the BDAE she does not have a comprehension deficit. Her spontaneous speech is slow and hesitant and confined to short, simple utterances.

Accessing Lexical Form

Results

Phoneme discrimination

	Percentage of errors
Controls	10% [range: 1–22%]
GS	10.3%

Simple words/gating task

	Mean Hearing loss (db)	N correct (max = 20)	Mean isolation point (msec)	% cohort membership
Controls	37.9 db [range: 26–48 db]	18	405 [range: 340–445]	
GS	29.5	18	385	92

Simple words/auditory lexical decision

	% correct and range	
	Real words	Non-words
Controls	99 [100–95]	99 [100–98]
GS	95	98

Complex words/gating task

	% correct full forms	% correct stems	Mean isolation point/ derivation full forms (msec)	Mean isolation point/ derivation stems (msec)	Mean isolation point/ inflection full forms (msec)	Mean isolation point/ inflection stems (msec)
Controls	73	73	438	300	388	230
GS	78	78	440	270	422	225

Prefixed words/auditory lexical decision

	% correct and range [ ]				
	Real words			Non-words	
	Controls	GS		Controls	GS
Opaque prefixed word	97 [100–90]	85	Prefixed	83 [100–67]	98
Trans prefixed word	96 [100–90]	85	Simple	92 [98–81]	98
Simple	99 [100–95]	95			

GS has a significant hearing impairment, which no doubt contributes to her difficulty in being able to discriminate phonemes. She makes a large proportion of errors on contrasts involving place of articulation, whether they occur at the beginning or end of a word.

Her hearing loss does not appear to affect her ability to process words, simple or complex, when they occur in isolation. She is able accurately to discriminate words from non-words (A' = .95) and her performance on the gating task with simple and complex words is essentially the same as normal.

Accessing Lexical Content

Results

Verb-argument study/word monitoring

	Mean monitoring RTs (msec)			
	Normal	Pragmatic violation	Semantic violation	Syntactic violation
Controls	322	380	399	411
GS	457	573	572	622

	Differences between conditions (msec)		
	Control group mean	95% confidence limits	GS
Normal-pragmatic	58*	69–39	116*
Normal-semantic	77*	93–53	115*
Normal-syntactic	89*	107–67	165*

There are no major impairments in her ability to access the syntactic and semantic properties of words in the process of interpreting an utterance.

The only notable aspect of her performance is that her ability to process an utterance is more affected than unimpaired subjects by the presence of an anomaly.

Constructing Higher-Level Representations

Results

Global sources of processing information

	Mean monitoring RTs (msec)		
	Normal prose	Anomalous prose	Scrambled prose
Controls	359	436	489
GS	437	571	647

	Controls: Mean RTs across word positions (msec)		
	Early	Middle	Late
Normal prose	416	347	314*
Anomalous prose	482	423	402*
Scrambled prose	503	481	484

	GS: Mean RTs across word positions (msec)		
	Early	Middle	Late
Normal prose	523	383	405*
Anomalous prose	589	581	543
Scrambled prose	665	651	626

* = significant word-position effect.

Local sources of processing information

	Mean monitoring RTs (msec)				
	Early	Late	Scrambled	Phonological disruption	Syntactic disruption
Controls	449	361	392	462	440
GS:	691	660	675	750	692

	GS: Differences between conditions and confidence limits (95%)			
	Early-late	Late-scrambled	Late-phonological disruption	Late-syntactic disruption
Confidence limits	127–49	54–6	129–71	123–34
GS	−31	15	90*	32

In the prose experiment, GS showed the word-position effect in normal prose with latencies becoming progressively faster throughout the utterance. However, there was no word-position effect in anomalous prose; the size of the effect was 46 msec, which was comparable to that in scrambled prose (39 msec) and much smaller than that in normal prose (118 msec). This implies that she was unable to use either the syntactic or the prosodic information within the utterance to develop a structural representation.

The results of the study described in chapter 11, where we introduced various kinds of disruptions at a local level within utterances, is consistent with the hypothesis that it is syntactic rather than prosodic information which she is unable to use. In this study, she was insensitive to syntactic disruptions within phonological phrases but she was affected, just like unimpaired listeners, by disruptions in prosody. This suggests that her monitoring latencies were faster overall in anomalous prose than in scrambled strings because she is able to use prosodic information to structure the speech input into phonologically coherent sequences.

Processing Morphologically Complex Words

Results

Derived and inflected words in context

	Mean monitoring RTs (msec)		
	Appropriate	Inappropriate	Non-word
Controls			
Derivations	292	360	388
Inflections	315	351	397
GS			
Derivations	507	475	544
Inflections	482	542	553
	Differences between conditions and 95% confidence limits [ ]		
	Appropriate-inappropriate	Inappropriate-non-word	Appropriate-non-word
Controls			
Derivations	63* [73−53]	28* [39−19]	91* [101−81]
Inflections	33* [45−21]	49* [64−34]	82* [101−63]
GS			
Derivations	−32	69*	37
Inflections	60*	9	71*

Inflections as tense markers:

| | Mean monitoring RTs (msec) | | | |
	Consistent	Inconsistent	Differences	95% confidence limits
Controls				
Syllabic	229	264	35*	55−15
Nonsyllabic	262	257	−5	11−3
GS				
Syllabic	366	418	52*	
Nonsyllabic	378	499	119*	

In the first morphology experiment, she showed no effect of the contextual appropriateness of derived words. Taken together with her normal performance with derived words in lexical decision and gating, we can conclude that she can access the form but not the content of a derived word. In contrast, she had no difficulty processing inflected words in sentential contexts.

The Relationship between On-Line and Off-Line Tasks

Results

Verb-argument study/judgments

| | % correct judgment and range [ ] | | | |
	Normal	Pragmatic	Semantic	Syntactic
End of sentence				
Controls	86 [100−81]	76 [100−71]	98 [100−94]	98 [100−96]
GS	96	75	79	71

Although her performance was outside the confidence limits established for the control group, she was still much better than chance at judging whether a sentence contained an anomaly (A′ = .82). Her pattern of results on the on-line monitoring and delayed-judgment tasks was similar, indicating that she was sensitive to all three types of verb-argument violations.

Summary
Although GS has a significant hearing loss, this does not seriously impair her ability to access the form of either a simple or complex word. She is also

able to access the content of words without difficulty. She does, however, have some problems with syntax. This is revealed in the lack of a word-position effect in anomalous prose and an insensitivity to word-order violations within local structures. This does not interfere with her ability to process inflected words when they appear in utterances, but she does have difficulty processing derived words.

This pattern of impairment stands in contrast to her performance on standard tests of comprehension. On these tests she was assessed as not having a significant impairment. This contrast illustrates the value of probing a patient's comprehension deficit in detail using on-line tasks of language processing.

Profile 8:   JW (Nonfluent)

General Details

JW was born in 1933. Before his stroke in 1981, he was employed as a fitter with British Rail. His digit span is considerably smaller than that of un-impaired subjects. According to the Token test, he has a severe comprehension deficit, but on the BDAE his comprehension deficit was diagnosed as being less severe. He has very restricted speech output and rarely produces more than single words.

Accessing Lexical Form

Results

Phoneme discrimination

	Percentage of errors
Controls	10% [range: 1–22%]
JW	22%

Simple words/gating task

	Mean hearing loss (db)	N correct (max = 20)	Mean isolation point (msec)	% cohort membership
Controls	37.9 db [range: 26–48 db]	18	405 [range: 340–445]	
JW	34.2	19	380	80

Simple words/auditory lexical decision

| | % correct | |
	Real words	Non-words
Controls	99 [100−95]	99 [100−98]
JW	86	86

Complex words/gating task

	% correct full-forms	% correct stems	Mean isolation point/ derivation full-forms (msec)	Mean isolation point/ derivation stems (msec)	Mean isolation point/ inflection full-forms (msec)	Mean isolation point/ inflection stems (msec)
Controls	73	73	438	300	388	230
JW	78	92	450	325	410	340

Suffixed words/auditory-lexical decision

| | % correct and range [ ] | | | |
| | Real words | | Non-words | |
	Controls	JW	Controls	JW
Simple	99 [100−95]	86	99 [100−98]	86
Derived	99 [100−92]	86	98 [100−97]	76
Inflected	99 [100−96]	87	97 [100−95]	75

JW has a significant hearing loss, which may account for why he makes a large number of errors on the phoneme-discrimination task. However, in the gating task his performance was relatively normal; his mean IPs were very similar to those of the control group. In the lexical-decision tasks, his performance was only slightly worse than normal (mean A′ = .91). Although he made fewer correct decisions than the control subjects, he was still significantly more accurate than chance.

Accessing Lexical Content

Results

Verb-argument study/word monitoring

		Mean monitoring RTs (msec)		
	Normal	Pragmatic violation	Semantic violation	Syntactic violation
Controls	322	380	399	411
JW	510	551	579	579
		Differences between conditions (msec)		
	Control group mean	95% confidence limits		JW
Normal-pragmatic	58*	69–39		41^
Normal-semantic	77*	93–53		69*
Normal-syntactic	89*	107–67		69*

On the basis of the verb-argument study, we can conclude that he is able to access the syntactic and semantic content of words and use them in the process of developing a representation of a spoken utterance.

Constructing Higher-Level Representations

Results

Global sources of processing information

	Mean monitoring RTs (msec)		
	Normal prose	Anomalous prose	Scrambled prose
Controls	359	436	489
JW	483	580	617

	Controls: Mean RTs across word positions (msec)		
	Early	Middle	Late
Normal prose	416	347	314*
Anomalous prose	482	423	402*
Scrambled prose	503	481	484

	JW: Mean RTs across word-positions (msec)		
	Early	Middle	Late
Normal prose	549	511	390*
Anomalous prose	580	587	574
Scrambled prose	614	641	593

He showed the typical word-position effect in normal prose but not in anomalous prose. This suggests that he cannot use syntactic information in the way in which normal listeners do to constrain the development of an interpretative representation of an utterance.

Processing Morphologically Complex Words

Results

Derived and inflected words in context

	Mean monitoring RTs (msec)		
	Appropriate	Inappropriate	Non-word
Controls			
Derived	292	360	388
Inflected	315	351	397
JW			
Derived	380	385	368
Inflected	356	417	419
	Differences between conditions and 95% confidence limits [ ]		
	Appropriate-inappropriate	Inappropriate-non-word	Appropriate-non-word
Controls			
Derived	63* [73−53]	28* [39−19]	91* [101−81]
Inflected	33* [45−21]	49* [64−34]	82* [101−63]
JW			
Derived	5	−17	−12
Inflected	62^	2	63

^ = within confidence limits.

Inflections as tense markers

	Mean Monitoring RTs (msec)			
	Consistent	Inconsistent	Differences	95% confidence limits
Controls				
Syllabic	229	264	35*	55−15
Nonsyllabic	262	257	−5	11−3
JW				
Syllabic	334	322	−12	
Nonsyllabic	340	379	39	

He shows no effect of the contextual appropriateness of derived or inflected words. The difference of 60 msec between contextually appropriate and inappropriate inflected forms, although seemingly large, did not even approach significance because of the long and variable RTs.

The Relationship between On-Line and Off-Line Tasks

Results

Verb-argument study/judgments

	% correct judgments and range [ ]			
	Normal	Pragmatic	Semantic	Syntactic
End of sentence				
Controls	86 [100−81]	76 [100−71]	98 [100−94]	98 [100−96]
JW	94	34	41	44
Immediate				
Controls		88 [100−81]	89 [100−69]	86 [94−75]
JW		84	97	84

Derived and inflected words in context/end-of-sentence judgments

	% correct responses and range [ ]		
	Appropriate	Inappropriate	Non-word
Controls			
Derived	98 [100−95]	91 [95−81]	94 [99−89]
Inflected	97 [100−88]	90 [100−67]	98 [100−96]
JW			
Derived	86	53	43
Inflected	92	21	42

JW's ability to detect anomalies as soon as he heard them was quite good. In contrast, his end-of-sentence judgments were poor (.79) and well outside the control group's confidence limits (.93–1.0). The immediate judgment data patterns with the on-line-monitoring data. According to the results from both types of task, he is sensitive to violations of verb-argument structures. However, when he gets to the end of a sentence, he is unable to distinguish reliably between those that contain anomalies and those that do not. His poor end-of-sentence judgments may be related to his poor digit span. Although there is no necessary correlation between digit span and language comprehension (Butterworth, Campbell, and Howard 1986), in JW's case digit span may be symptomatic of a STM deficit that affects his ability to comprehend spoken language.

His monitoring and delayed judgment data were consistent in the morphology study. On both tasks he showed that he was insensitive to the contextual appropriateness of a derived or inflected word.

Summary
JW's ability to access both the form and content of simple and complex words seems relatively intact. He is able to process the speech input as he hears it and build higher-level representations. However, he does have problems with some aspects of syntax: he does not show the usual word-position effect in anomalous prose, and he is insensitive to the contextual appropriateness of derived and inflected words. These two may be linked in that they both rely, to a certain extent at least, on form-class information being correctly used by the processing system. JW may suffer from a functional deficit involving the use of syntactic information in the process of interpreting an utterance.

The data from the end-of-sentence judgment tasks are consistent with the data from standard comprehension tests in that they both show that JW has a comprehension deficit. However, they are not very specific about the nature of that deficit. The word-monitoring studies have the advantage of being able to pinpoint the deficit as primarily involving syntactic aspects of processing information.

Profile 9:   DE (Nonfluent)

General Details
DE was born in 1954 and was involved in a motorscooter accident in 1970 which left him with left-hemisphere damage. Although he scores slightly below normal on the digit-matching and digit-span tasks, his memory for events and for language is excellent (as determined by informal testing). According to the Token test and the BDAE, he has a moderate comprehension impairment. His speech production is severely restricted. He rarely produces more than single words which tend to be morphologically simple.

Accessing Lexical Form

Results

Phoneme discrimination

	Percentage of errors
Controls	1
DE	3

Simple words/gating task

	Mean hearing loss (db)	N correct (max = 20)	Isolation point (msec)	% cohort membership
Controls	9.8 db [range: 7–15 db]	20	325 [range: 300–375]	
DE	7.0	20	300	96

Simple words/auditory lexical decision

	% correct	
	Real words	Non-words
Controls	100	100
DE	86	100

Complex words/gating task

	% correct full forms	% correct stems	Isolation point/ derivation full forms (msec)	Isolation point/ derivation stems (msec)	Isolation point/ inflection full forms (msec)	Isolation point/ inflection stems (msec)
Controls	100	100	375	258	375	250
DE	83	100	390	200	402	250

Suffixed words/auditory lexical decision

	% correct and range [ ]			
	Real words		Non-words	
	Controls	DE	Controls	DE
Simple	100	86	100	100
Derived	97 [100–95]	82	100	100
Inflected	100	91	100	100

Prefixed words/auditory lexical decision

	% correct and range [ ]					
	Real words				Non-words	
	Controls	DE			Controls	DE
Opaque prefixed	97 [100–90]	85	Prefixed		94 [100–83]	100
Trans prefixed	98 [100–95]	70	Simple		99 [100–98]	100
Simple	97 [100–85]	85				

DE has no problems accessing the phonological form of a simple or complex word. In the gating and lexical-decision tasks his performance was essentially normal. He was very accurate in discriminating words from non-words (mean A′ = .96) and he recognized a word at roughly the same point as the relevant control group. The only way in which his performance differed from normal is that occasionally in the gating task he recognized the stem of a word but added to it the incorrect suffix.

Accessing Lexical Content

Results

Verb-argument study/word monitoring

		Mean monitoring RTs (msec)		
	Normal	Pragmatic violation	Semantic violation	Syntactic violation
Controls	259	303	329	357
DE	227	329	280	316
		Differences between conditions (msec)		
	Control group mean	95% confidence limits		DE
Normal-pragmatic	44*	55–33		102*
Normal-semantic	70*	90–50		53*
Normal-syntactic	98*	126–70		89*

In both the word-monitoring and judgment tasks, he was sensitive to all types of verb-argument violation, indicating that he can access lexical content. He was, however, abnormally sensitive to sentences containing pragmatic violations. The effect of this in the word-monitoring task was to increase latencies well above the normal range.

Constructing Higher-Level Representations

Results

Global sources of processing information

	Mean monitoring RTs (msec)		
	Normal prose	Anomalous prose	Scrambled prose
Controls	344	400	458
DE	258	358	409

	Controls: Mean RTs across word positions (msec)		
	Early	Middle	Late
Normal prose	386	332	314*
Anomalous prose	439	394	367*
Scrambled prose	477	444	454

	DE: Mean RTs across word positions (msec)		
	Early	Middle	Late
Normal prose	305	265	205*
Anomalous prose	355	379	370
Scrambled prose	388	427	412

Local sources of processing information

	Mean monitoring RTs (msec)				
	Early	Late	Scrambled	Phonological disruption	Syntactic disruption
Controls	449	361	392	462	440
DE	511	496	482	484	549

	Differences between conditions (DE) and confidence limits (95%)			
	Early-late	Late-scrambled	Late-phonological disruption	Late-syntactic disruption
Confidence limits	127–49	54–6	129–71	123–34
DE	−15	−14	−12	53*

DE did not show a word-position effect in anomalous prose, suggesting that he is unable to use syntactic (or perhaps prosodic) information to construct a representation spanning an entire utterance. However, this does not imply that he is unable to use any kind of syntactic information, in that we also found that he is able to use syntactic word-order information to build local structures.

In contrast to his problems with syntax, he appears to have no difficulty using semantic information to construct a meaningful representation of an utterance. Presumably, this is why we see a significant word-position effect in normal prose.

Processing Morphologically Complex Words

Results

Derived and inflected words in context

	Mean monitoring RTs (msec)		
	Appropriate	Inappropriate	Non-word
Controls			
Derived	218	286	319
Inflected	231	295	322
DE			
Derived	247	254	262
Inflected	223	225	257
	Differences between conditions and 95% confidence limits [ ]		
	Appropriate-Inappropriate	Inappropriate-non-word	Appropriate-non-word
Controls			
Derived	68* [90−46]	33* [65−1]	101* [138−64]
Inflected	64* [82−46]	27* [39−15]	91* [111−71]
DE			
Derived	7	8^	15
Inflected	2	32^	34*

^ = within confidence limits.

Inflections as syntactic devices

	Mean monitoring RTs (msec)			
	Consistent	Inconsistent	Differences	95% confidence limits
Controls				
Context	228	282	53*	87−23
No context	255	322	67*	94−40
DE				
Context	257	260	3	
No context	334	333	−1	

Inflections as tense markers

	Mean monitoring RTs (msec)			
	Consistent	Inconsistent	Differences	95% confidence limits
Controls				
Syllabic	213	265	52*	64−40
Nonsyllabic	223	234	11	22−1
DE				
Syllabic	239	235	−4	
Nonsyllabic	202	237	35	

DE appears to have no difficulty in accessing the form of either a derived or inflected word, but he does have problems accessing its content. When he heard sentences containing inflected or derived words, his latencies did not significantly increase when the word was contextually inappropriate.

The Relationship between On-Line and Off-Line Tasks

Results

Verb-argument study/judgments

	% correct judgments and range [ ]			
	Normal	Pragmatic	Semantic	Syntactic
End of sentence				
Controls (old)	91 [100−83]	95 [100−83]	97 [100−92]	97 [100−88]
DE	72	91	88	91
Immediate				
Controls (old)		98 [100−96]	98 [100−95]	98 [100−97]
DE		94	94	88

Derived and inflected words in context/end-of-sentence judgments

	% correct responses and range [ ]		
	Appropriate	Inappropriate	Non-word
Controls			
Derived	99 [100−99]	99 [100−99]	99 [100−99]
Inflected	98 [100−99]	100 [100−99]	99 [100−99]
DE			
Derived	71	62	76
Inflected	79	67	71

In the verb-argument study, although his performance was just outside the range for the control group, he was reasonably accurate at judging whether a sentence contained an anomaly in both the immediate (A' = .88) and delayed conditions (A' = .89).

His judgments in the morphology study were above chance (A' = .78), but considerably less accurate than in the verb-argument study and also well outside the control group's confidence limits. This is consistent with the monitoring data. The results of both tasks confirm that he has problems processing complex words in utterance contexts.

Summary

DE's speech production conforms to the standard description of a nonfluent agrammatic aphasic. According to recent descriptions of the underlying cause of this deficit as involving a general problem with syntax, we might expect him to have analogous problems with syntax in comprehension. The results of the studies described in this book provide some support for such a prediction. He appears to have difficulty using syntactic information in the process of interpreting an utterance, although he is able to construct local phrases on the basis of syntactic word-order information.

In contrast, however, to the results of the on-line studies, his grammaticality judgments are reasonably accurate, particularly in the verb-argument study, where 88 percent of the time he accurately labeled a sentence containing a subcategory violation as ungrammatical (A' = .9). We also see it in another grammaticality-judgment test we have run him on, which includes syntactic violations of verb-complement clauses, subject-auxilliary inversion, and passives. He correctly judges such sentences to be ungrammatical 88 percent of the time (A' = .94).

The other way in which DE differs from normal is in his increased sensitivity to the pragmatic coherence of an utterance. We saw in the monitoring version of the verb-argument study how his latencies increased well above those of the control group when he heard an utterance which violated pragmatic coherence constraints. We did not observe the same kind of effect in the judgment version of the study because his judgments were so accurate that his performance was at ceiling. Perhaps his ability to use semantic and pragmatic information compensates for the difficulties he has with some aspects of syntax. In informal conversation, DE certainly appears to have no difficulty in comprehending what is said to him. It may be that in many conversational interactions, the extralinguistic context, combined with his ability to extract the semantic and pragmatic implications of an utterance, are sufficient for him to engage in normal conversational interactions. It is only in the context of experimental testing situations that the extent of his comprehension deficit becomes apparent.

The other way in which DE's comprehension deviates from normal revolves around his difficulties in processing the ends of words. The fact that he showed no sensitivity to the contextual appropriateness of morphologically complex words in any of our studies initially led us to conclude that he had a morphological processing deficit. There was a considerable amount of evidence supporting this conclusion. Apart from the studies reported in this book, Ruth Ostrin and I have tested DE on additional experiments in which we manipulated the relationship between the stem and the affix of a morphologically complex word. In some cases the addition of a suffix led to a phonological change in the stem, as in the phonologically opaque *consumption*, whereas in others there was no change in the stem, as in the phonologically transparent *consumable*. We found that when DE was asked to monitor for the target word *chocolates* in the following contexts, he showed no difference among the three conditions.

(1a)   John could consume chocolates at an incredible rate.

(1b)   John could consumable chocolates at an incredible rate.

(1c)   John could consumption chocolates at an incredible rate.

Similarly, we manipulated the semantic relationship between the stem and the complex form; that is, whether it was semantically opaque (e.g., *witness*) or transparent (*witty*). Again, when DE was asked to monitor for the target word *bench* in the following contexts, he showed no difference among the three conditions.

(2a)   Jane sat on the marble bench.

(2b)   Jane sat on the witness bench.

(2c)   Jane sat on the witty bench.

Unimpaired subjects, however, did produce different RTs in the various conditions. Their latencies were slower when the complex word occurred in an inappropriate (1b, 1c, 2c) compared to an appropriate (1a, 2a, 2b) context.

The obvious conclusion to draw was that DE had problems processing morphologically complex words in utterances. However, a series of studies on morphologically simple words challenged this view. In these studies, we varied the appropriateness of the test word but this time we did so, not by changing the suffix but by varying the end of a morphologically simple word. So, for example, we can change the last syllable of *captain* so that the word is *captive*. When *captain* is contextually appropriate and *captive* is not, the RTs of normal subjects increase in the contextually inappropriate condition, whereas DE's do not.

In this long series of experiments, then, we can find no evidence that DE processes the ends of real words—whether the ending is morphological or not. These findings challenge the widely held view that "agrammatic" patients have problems specifically with bound morphemes and suggest that a totally different explanation is need to account for the pattern of data. One possible explanation is that DE is so dependent upon the pragmatic context when interpreting an utterance that he relies less than normal listeners on the acoustic-phonetic input. Thus, when two words start with the same sound sequence and are therefore members of the same cohort, the one that is most compatible with the context will be the one he "hears." The context will override disconfirming sensory information. If this is the appropriate characterization of DE's deficit, he is very different from normal listeners who rely heavily on the sensory input when processing spoken language.

A different possibility is that the processes involved in analyzing multisyllabic words in context are slowed down in some way. We are currently evaluating these alternative explanations.

Profile 10:   FB (Fluent)

General Details

FB was born in 1921 and suffered a stroke in 1979. Before this he was employed as a solicitor. He has a severe hearing impairment, but reasonably normal memory for digits (within the normal range). According to the Token test he has a severe comprehension deficit, but the BDAE diagnosed him as having only a mild deficit. His spontaneous speech is fluent but relatively semantically impoverished, and he has word-finding problems.

Accessing Lexical Form

Results

Phoneme discrimination

	Percentage of errors
Controls	10% [range: 1–22%]
FB	19%

Simple words/gating task

	Mean hearing loss (db)	N correct (max = 20)	Mean isolation point (msec)	% cohort membership
Controls	37.9 db [range: 26–48 db]	18	405 [range: 340–445]	
FB	37.9 db	13	470	68

Simple words/auditory lexical decision

	% correct and range [ ]	
	Real words	Non-words
Controls	99 [100–98]	99 [100–98]
FB	100	90

Complex words/gating task

	% correct full forms	% correct stems	Mean isolation point/ derivation full forms (msec)	Mean isolation point/ derivation stems (msec)	Mean isolation point/ inflection full forms (msec)	Mean isolation point/ inflection stems (msec)
Controls	73	73	438	300	388	230
FB	39	58	450	400	417	175

Suffixed words/auditory lexical decision

	% correct and range [ ]			
	Real words		Non-words	
	Controls	FB	Controls	FB
Simple	99 [100–95]	89	99 [100–98]	83
Derived	99 [100–92]	90	98 [100–97]	70
Inflected	99 [100–96]	71	97 [100–95]	75

Prefixed words/auditory lexical decision

	% correct and range [ ]				
	Real words			Non-words	
	Controls	FB		Controls	FB
Opaque prefixed	97 [100–90]	95	Prefixed	83 [100–67]	97
Trans prefixed	96 [100–90]	90	Simple	92 [98–81]	90
Simple	99 [100–95]	100			

FB has some difficulty accessing the phonological form of a word. He makes a large proportion of errors on place contrasts (both word-initial and word-final) in the phoneme-discrimination test, and in two gating studies he failed to recognize a significant number of the words even by the last gate. His poor performance in the gating studies was largely due to the fact that he frequently failed to identify the initial phoneme of a word and therefore accessed the wrong cohort. He had some difficulty discriminating suffixed words from non-words in an auditory lexical-decision task (A′ = .86), but he was more sensitive to the word/non-word distinction for prefixed items (A′ = .97).

Accessing Lexical Content

Results

Verb-argument study/word monitoring

		Mean monitoring RTs (msec)		
	Normal	Pragmatic violation	Semantic violation	Syntactic violation
Controls	322	380	399	411
FB	436	477	534	497
		Differences between conditions (msec)		
	Control group mean	95% confidence limits		FB
Normal-pragmatic	58*	69−39		39*
Normal-semantic	77*	93−53		96*
Normal-syntactic	89*	107−67		59*

His monitoring latencies increased when he encountered all three types of verb-argument violation. In this respect his performance was the same as that of the control group and indicated that he could access and use the semantic and syntactic content of lexical representations.

Constructing Higher-Level Representations

Results

Global sources of processing information

	Mean monitoring RTs (msec)		
	Normal prose	Anomalous prose	Scrambled prose
Controls	359	436	489
FB	465	513	569
	Controls: Mean RTs across word positions (msec)		
	Early	Middle	Late
Normal prose	416	347	314*
Anomalous prose	482	423	402*
Scrambled prose	503	481	484
	FB: Mean RTs across word positions (msec)		
	Early	Middle	Late
Normal prose	510	448	439*
Anomalous prose	542	512	485
Scrambled prose	585	574	548

* = significant word-position effect.

He showed a significant word-position effect only for normal prose. Although latencies decreased as more of an anomalous prose utterance was heard, they did so by a similar amount as in scrambled prose, indicating that the effect was due to expectancy rather than structure. This suggests that he can construct higher-level representations of an utterance, presumably by relying primarily on the meaning relations between words and the prosodic information in the utterance.

Processing Morphologically Complex Words

Results

Derived and inflected words in context

	Mean monitoring RTs (msec)		
	Appropriate	Inappropriate	Non-word
Controls			
Derived	292	360	388
Inflected	315	351	397
FB			
Derived	430	459	460
Inflected	420	430	461
	Differences between conditions and 95% confidence limits [ ]		
	Appropriate-inappropriate	Inappropriate-non-word	Appropriate-non-word
Controls			
Derived	63* [73−53]	28* [39−19]	91* [101−81]
Inflected	33* [45−21]	49* [64−34]	82* [100−63]
FB			
Derived	29	1	30*
Inflected	10	31*	41*

Inflections as syntactic devices

	Mean monitoring RTs (msec)			
	Consistent	Inconsistent	Differences	95% confidence limits
Controls				
Context	289	311	22*	33−11
No context	388	402	14*	27−1
FB				
Context	407	453	46*	
No context	475	458	−17	

Inflections as tense markers

| | Mean monitoring RTs (msec) | | | |
	Consistent	Inconsistent	Differences	95% confidence limits
Controls				
Syllabic	229	264	35*	55–15
Nonsyllabic	262	257	−5	11––3
FB				
Syllabic	408	394	−14	
Nonsyllabic	408	405	−3	

He was insensitive to the contextual appropriateness of derived words; his monitoring latencies were essentially unchanged by the presence of a contextually inappropriate derived word. The picture for inflected words was slightly different. He was able to access the syntactic properties of inflected words and use them to constrain the syntactic structure of the utterance, but only when there was a supporting context and when the syntactic structure highly constrained the appropriate form of the inflection.

The Relationship between On-Line and Off-Line Tasks

Results

Verb-argument study/judgments

| | % correct judgments and range [ ] | | | |
	Normal	Pragmatic	Semantic	Syntactic
End of sentence				
Controls	86 [100−81]	76 [100−71]	98 [100−94]	98 [100−96]
FB	69	94	75	94
Immediate				
Controls		88 [100−81]	89 [100−69]	88 [94−75]
FB		75	78	81

Derived and inflected words in context/end-of-sentence judgments

| | % correct responses and range [ ] | | |
	Appropriate	Inappropriate	Non-word
Controls			
Derived	98 [100−95]	91 [95−81]	94 [99−89]
Inflected	97 [100−88]	90 [100−67]	98 [100−96]
FB			
Derived	91	38	52
Inflected	71	17	50

In the morphology experiment, the judgment data are comparable to the monitoring data. Both tell the same story: FB has problems in processing morphologically complex words when they occur in contexts ($A' = .64$).

In the verb-argument study, the monitoring data and both sets of judgment data also show the same pattern of effects. They suggest that FB can access the syntactic and semantic content on verbs and use them to constrain the development of verb-argument structures.

Summary
FB's problems in developing the appropriate phonological representation, which leads to difficulties in mapping the speech input onto the correct form of a word, do not appear to seriously impair his ability to access at least the lexical content of verbs and use it to construct, on-line, some types of structural relations. He is also able to develop a meaningful representation spanning an entire utterance. However, he does have difficulty accessing both the form and the content of morphologically complex (suffixed) words.

FB's pattern of comprehension performance does not conform to the standard picture of a fluent patient as someone who has a severe comprehension deficit. His ability to construct an immediate representation of the speech input is only partially impaired. It is clear from the data presented here that he can build some type of meaningful representation of an utterance. Where he does have difficulty is on standard tests of comprehension, such as the Token test. On the basis of data from this type of task we would say that he had the severe comprehension deficit typical of Wernicke patients, but the results described here suggest that much of his comprehension ability remains intact.

Chapter 17
Concluding Comments

In this chapter I will discuss some of the more general issues which have been raised by the research described in earlier chapters. The first issue I will discuss is how the approach described in this book differs from much of the current work in aphasiology.

Cognitive Neuropsychology

One of the reasons we study language deficits in patients with brain damage is in the hope that these deficits can tell us something about the anatomical basis of language and about the way the normal language system functions. Early research mostly focused on the anatomical basis of language. The questions people asked were usually about localization of function and how language deficits might be correlated with damage to particular regions of the brain. During the past 10–15 years, the emphasis has shifted so that now there is just as much interest in functional deficits—irrespective of how those deficits might be related to brain structure. This approach has recently been given a name: "cognitive neuropsychology" (coined, I believe, by Max Coltheart).

Cognitive neuropsychology is the study of cognitive deficits for the express purpose of developing and constraining models of normal function. The idea is that if what you are interested in is developing models of normal performance, behavioral deficits in and of themselves provide one appropriate type of data. There is no need to relate these deficits to lesion site.

The cognitive-neuropsychological approach to the study of aphasic deficits assumes that language deficits inform us about the structure of the normal system. That is, they tell us about the components of the language-processing system—whether comprehension or production—and how they are related. If a patient has difficulties processing the syntax of an utterance, for example, but seems to have no problems in extracting its meaning, the claim is that this dissociation is evidence for two separate subcomponents of the language-processing system, a syntactic component and a semantic component. This analysis works well when the subcomponents relate to linguistically motivated knowledge representations. In that case, the linguistic and the psychological data neatly converge, and the patient data can be interpreted within an independently motivated model of normal language performance.

For some time it seemed as though this approach was successful in moving along the development of theories about normal language comprehension and production. However, problems arose when the subcomponents, motivated on the basis of the patient data, proliferated in number and type. I will illustrate this point with two concrete examples, dyslexia and agrammatism.

Dyslexia is the study of reading deficits, mostly involving problems in the reading of single words. In the 1970s a number of people started relating disorders of reading to John Morton's model of word recognition, known as the logogen model (Morton 1969). It consists of a set of components (represented by boxes in graphic descriptions of the model) with connections between the boxes. The contents of the boxes were originally motivated by data from experiments on single-word reading in normal subjects, but the data from patients with reading problems led to a refinement of their contents so that the number of boxes increased according to each new specific deficit. Whenever a patient exhibited a problem that had not been previously observed and could not be accounted for in the current conception of the model, either another box was added to accommodate that particular deficit or the connections between boxes were adjusted in some way. Each patient's deficit could be "explained" within the model by either a disruption of information from a particular box or the disruption of connections between boxes.

Although this approach has produced many elegant experiments and sophisticated theorizing and has helped to clarify the range of processes involved in normal reading, it suffers from a major problem—knowing when to stop generating new boxes to accommodate the patient data. It is not clear what explanatory adequacy this kind of methodology has if each new deficit can be explained by adding another box or deleting a connection or two.

The study of agrammatism has suffered from the same kind of problems. Originally agrammatism, defined as a syntactic deficit primarily involving the selective omission of the closed-class morphology, was considered to be one aspect of the general aphasic disorder known as Broca's aphasia. Patients were classified as suffering from Broca's aphasia primarily on the basis of their spontaneous speech. If their speech was hesitant and dysprosodic, if it consisted of short phrases which were syntactically simple and, critically, if it contained very few closed class items, then patients would be classified as suffering from the symptom complex known as Broca's aphasia. The cluster of deficits they exhibited were considered to have an underlying cause. They were all due to problems with the syntactic component of the language system. Although the primary diagnosing deficit in Broca's aphasia was always based on a patient's deficits in speech production, many, although not all, Broca patients also showed a similar problem in comprehension. That is, they were unable to process the syntactic aspects of utterances.

The syntactic basis of the deficit in Broca's aphasia was contrasted with the semantic basis for the deficit in Wernicke's aphasia. A patient suffering from this type of aphasia was claimed to have no problems with the syntactic aspects of processing, but to have problems with semantics. This dissociation between syntax and semantics in the two types of patients was taken as evidence for the existence of two separate subcomponents, semantic and syntactic, in the language-processing system.

This neat dichotomy dissolved somewhat when it was found that not all Broca patients had difficulty with the closed-class morphology. Some patients produced short, simple sentences but with closed-class elements intact, whereas others produced quite long and relatively complex utterances but omitted a large proportion of the closed-class elements. On the logic of this approach, dissociations of this type require the postulation of another component in the processing system—in this instance one responsible exclusively for the production and comprehension of closed-class elements.

The situation became even more complicated when Miceli et al. (1989) found that patients unambiguously categorized on the basis of an analysis of their spontaneous speech as agrammatics varied extensively in the degree to which they omitted different types of closed-class items. One patient might omit a large proportion of prepositions but very few clitics, while another patient might do the reverse. On the logic of this type of research, this pattern would be taken as evidence of separate subcomponents within the closed class and therefore an even more modular system. (This is not how Miceli et al interpret these data. They use them as evidence against homogeneity of the symptom complex known as agrammatism).

There are, I believe, three major problems with the standard cognitive-neuropsychological approach. First, specific deficits are assumed to tell us about the modular subcomponents of the language system. They either provide evidence for existing components or suggest new ways of further subdividing existing components. Each time a patient is found with a deficit that has not been observed before, then a new component is postulated. This leads to a proliferation of components within the system and reduces the explanatory adequacy of the models. This is because, in some sense, the predictive power of the models is reduced. A new deficit does not necessarily impinge on the model. It does not have to result in any modification of the model. One just needs to add another component or manipulate another connection between components in order to account for the patient data.

The second main drawback of this approach is that it encourages a research strategy in which people focus on individual subcomponents of the system rather than trying to understand how the system as a whole functions. Researchers tend to look for evidence, for example, of a selective semantic deficit or a selective deficit for the closed-class elements or a selective deficit in single-word reading. Although they may test the patient on a variety of experiments to try to investigate the deficit in detail, they nevertheless rarely investigate a whole range of processes in a single patient to see how the system as a whole functions and to determine which other aspects of the system are not functioning normally and which remain intact.

The third main disadvantage with this approach is that by assuming an essentially modular approach to the study of language deficits, it is natural that people have been more interested in representation than process. Researchers have tended to think that when a patient had a particular type of language deficit, this meant that the knowledge representation within the relevant component had either been disrupted or lost altogether. It is only quite recently that people have started thinking about process as well as representation, and this naturally inclines one to ask whether a particular deficit is due to a problem in accessing information or to problems with the way that information is represented (e.g., Shallice 1988).

When one starts to consider process as well as representation, one takes a rather different perspective on aphasic deficits, and it is one such perspective which I have attempted to illustrate in this book. The approach to the study of aphasic deficits which I have discussed focuses on both the mental processes and representations involved in spoken language comprehension and how they function in the development of an incremental interpretation of what the listener hears. It also attempts to take the entire comprehension system into account rather than focus on a single subcomponent. What are the advantages of this psycholinguistic approach to the study of aphasic deficits?

The Advantages of the Psycholinguistic Approach

The most obvious advantage is that it generates a processing profile for each patient covering a wide range of language comprehension processes. We thus obtain an estimate of preserved and impaired performance on a variety of different aspects of comprehension. This puts us in a better position to generate a comprehensive picture of the language-comprehension abilities of an individual patient.

To understand the nature of an individual patient's deficit, we need to determine which aspects of the comprehension system are impaired and which are functioning normally. If we focus only on the ways in which one aspect of the system is impaired (even if we study the fine detail of its functioning) and ignore the impact which that part of the system has on other parts, we run the risk of developing a distorted view of the underlying nature of a patient's deficit.

This broad-based view contrasts with much of the current work in cognitive neuropsychology. As I have argued above, the common assumption underlying much of this research is that the language-comprehension system can be viewed as consisting of a set of modular subcomponents. Damage to one subcomponent may be independent of any other subcomponent, and therefore it is possible to study any single subcomponent in depth and ignore the rest of the system. I believe that this basic assumption is false. There is good evidence to believe that, even if the language processing system is structured in this modular way, there is considerable interdependence among components. Therefore, if investigations of language disorders focus on one component (e.g., syntactic processing, word-recognition processes, morphology) to the exclusion of all others, we may not develop the appropriate characterization of a patient's deficit. One consequence of such an approach is that there will be little chance that the therapy which we design for an individual patient will be successful.

For many years, it was unclear whether specific therapies were successful in improving a patient's problems with particular aspects of language comprehension. But as Black, Nickels, and Byng (in press), among others, have ably demonstrated, when we develop a picture of a patient's preserved and impaired language comprehension abilities across a wide range of processes, therapy can be successfully tailored to the needs of an individual patient.

The other potential problem with focusing on selective components of the comprehension system is that it may lead us to develop inaccurate models of normal language-comprehension processes. There is, by now, a considerable amount of research showing the cooperative integration of different sources of processing information during language comprehension (e.g., Bates and MacWhinney 1989). For example, we know that the sentential context can, in some sense, compensate for an ambiguous speech signal (Grosjean 1980; Marslen-Wilson and Tyler 1980; Warren 1978). Similarly, in the case of anaphor resolution, the lexical specificity of the anaphoric device decreases as the constraining context increases (Marslen-Wilson, Tyler, and Levy 1982). These findings and others suggest that the normal language-processing system is organized to allow a cooperative integration of different sources of processing information with respect to the primary perceptual goal of interpreting an utterance within its discourse context. This means that the appropriate analysis of the input need not be fully specified with respect to each and every processing source. Given a system organized in this way, we cannot meaningfully investigate a single aspect of its structure because, in some sense, we cannot understand how each part functions without seeing how that part functions within the system as a whole. On this view, a patient's deficit would not necessarily result in any radical change in his or her language-processing system. Rather, the same structural organization of the system may function to compensate for an inadequately specified source of processing information. Unless we look at the system as a whole, we cannot see how the process of compensatory adaptation occurs.

What Are Strategies?

There has been much talk in cognitive neuropsychology about the extent to which a patient can compensate for a deficit by means of strategies. The argument typically goes as follows: A patient suffering from language impairment x can compensate for this by using compensatory strategy y such that his or her behavior is better than would be expected as a result of impairment x (see Caplan 1987; Kolk and van Grunsven 1985). My problem with this kind of account is that it is not clear what a strategy is. Is it something the patient, realizing that she has a problem, consciously employs? Or is it, as I argued earlier, something automatically brought into play as a result of a particular process breaking down? The distinction here is between strategies that are assumed to be under voluntary control and those that are not. If they are under voluntary control, the question is whether the patient has options as to which kind of strategy to employ. Presumably she would have options—but within limits. There might well be a set of strategies that could be employed given various factors involved, such as the particular type of speech input the patient is listening to or the demands of the task. On the other hand, if strategies are automatically invoked when a particular process breaks down, we would expect the same strategy to be activated on every occasion.

This distinction between different strategies, although important for the interpretation of patient data, is rarely discussed. The term "strategy" tends to be used in different ways, although the implicit assumption is that there is a commonly understood definition. Moreover, there is little discussion of the extent to which different tasks may or may not be carried out strategically, although it is clear that some tasks are more susceptible to strategic processing than others.

One advantage of using on-line tasks is that if, as we have claimed, they primarily tap the automatic processes involved in language comprehension, then they should be minimally affected by strategies, at least those under voluntary control. To understand the nature of a patient's deficit, we need to use a combination of on-line tasks and tasks that are susceptible to known strategies. This will allow us to distinguish the effects of brain damage on the core processes within the language system and the way in which strategies affect those processes.

Patient Performance and the On-Line/Off-Line Distinction

I have made much of the distinction between on-line and off-line tasks. In a sense this distinction forms the raison d'être of the entire approach. What do the different patterns of preserved and impaired performance on each type of task tells us about a patient's deficit? What are the possible patterns of performance, ignoring for the moment possible differences between the different off-line tasks?

- Poor on-line and good off-line performance
- Poor performance on both on-line and off-line tasks
- Poor off-line and good on-line performance

1. Should it be possible to find a patient whose on-line processes are impaired but whose off-line processes look normal? The answer to this is complex because, to a large extent, it depends upon the nature of the on-line impairment. If a procedure is completely non-operational, then the grammaticality judgments that call upon that procedure should also be impaired. However, performance on grammaticality judgments may be better than the on-line data would suggest. This is because other metalinguistic and general cognitive processes can be recruited by the subject. However, in general it should not be possible for a patient to show *normal* grammaticality judgments in the presence of abnormal on-line processes.

There is one proviso. A linguistic process may be operational, but slowed down. In this case, on-line processes and representations as measured by means of the word-monitoring or some other on-line task would be abnormal, whereas off-line performance may be quite good. We have a couple of examples of this in our data. The clearest case is that of patient JG, who shows no sensitivity to a number of linguistic variables when tested on the word-monitoring task. However, in some experiments his grammaticality judgments, although worse than those of the control group, were well above chance (JG A' = 0.87; range of control group A' = 0.93−1.0). JG illustrates the importance of using both on-line and off-line tasks to study language comprehension deficits. If we had only used one type of task to tap processing, we would not have been able to conclude that his ability to process spoken language was slowed down in some way. The contrast between the two types of task was crucial in clarifying the nature of his deficit.

In the real world outside the laboratory, patients whose on-line processes are impaired may—depending on the nature and extent of the impairment—be able to function quite well in communicative interactions. This is because they will assume that what they hear is intended to make sense and try to interpret it in the most pragmatically coherent way.

2. If a patient's underlying deficit is quite extensive—suppose, for example, that he or she cannot construct any type of structural representation, not even a local verb phrase or noun phrase—then it is unlikely that the patient will be able to develop a pragmatically plausible interpretation of the utterance. In such a case, we would expect to find poor performance in both on-line and off-line tasks.

3. The patient RH is an example of someone who performs essentially normally on on-line tasks. I have discussed this patient at some length in chapter 16. He clearly has no difficulty constructing intermediate representations of an utterance as he hears it. However, when tested on tasks requiring him to make some kind of explicit response to an utterance, either in the form of a sentence–picture match or a judgment, he performs very poorly. RH's performance on these tasks compared to his normal performance on the word-monitoring task lends credibility to the distinction between on-line and off-line tasks. It suggests that there is a valid distinction to be drawn between linguistic processes and representations of which the listener can and cannot be aware. RH's pattern of preserved and impaired performance on these tasks suggests that the intermediate representations and the processes involved in their construction remain unimpaired, while conscious access to the final representation is impaired. The data suggest that RH can develop the appropriate representations of an utterance; his problem lies in being unable to gain access to them for the purpose of making explicit decisions about them.

RH is not the only patient we have encountered who exhibits this kind of implicit/explicit distinction. We have seen a number of patients like this. One of the interesting points about these patients is that they do not all have similar production deficits. JW, for example, is a nonfluent speaker whose on-line monitoring performance, although showing some specific abnormalities, was similar to normal, while his performance on off-line tasks (sentence–picture matching and judgment tasks) was very poor. RH and JW, then, show the same kind of dissociation between performance on implicit versus explicit tests of comprehension. The fact that JW does not show the normal pattern in all of the on-line studies he has been tested on does not undermine this claim. The important point is that, in a study where we use exactly the same materials and probe with two different tasks, one implicit and the other explicit, we obtain normal performance in one case and abnormal in the other.

Although both patients show the same explicit/implicit dissociation in language comprehension, they differ markedly in their language production. RH produces fluent speech which is, essentially, semantically empty, whereas JW produces very little speech. What there is is mostly confined to single words. These two patients illustrate that the implicit/explicit distinction in language comprehension is not related to a patient's production deficit. Perhaps this is not surprising. We might plausibly expect that the comprehension processes and representations reflected in on-line tasks are those that might be more closely related to the processes and representations involved in language production. Both are automatic and not normally available to conscious awareness. However, when speakers try consciously to control what they say (as is the case in some kinds of experimental tasks and may be the case for some aphasic patients (cf. Kolk and van Grunsven 1985), then we might find a closer correspondence between explicit tests of language comprehension and a patient's production deficit.

Finally, there is the issue I raised in chapter 1 concerning the ways in which off-line tasks differ. The distinction is exemplified by the difference between the grammaticality judgment and sentence–picture matching tasks. Both require conscious awareness on the part of the listener but in one case (grammaticality judgment) the listener becomes aware that an automatic procedure has failed, and in the other (sentence–picture matching) the listener is required to reflect explicitly on the sentential representation in order to carry out the task. Can we find evidence of this distinction in the patient data? The answer is yes, in the form of patient VS.

VS is an example of a patient who performs much better on grammaticality-judgment tasks than she does on sentence–picture matching tasks. In most of the tests of on-line processing, her performance was comparable to normal. In particular, in the verb-argument study, VS showed a significant effect of all three types of anomaly (semantic, pragmatic, and syntactic) when tested using the word-monitoring task. Moreover, her ability to judge the grammaticality of the same sentences was well above chance ($A' = .82$), although worse than the control group's.[1] In contrast, VS's performance on both the TROG and a sentence–picture matching task, which is not reported in this book but was based on the Jones verbs test (1984) was very poor indeed (TROG: 50 percent correct; sentence–picture matching: 59 percent correct).

The results from VS suggest that tasks we loosely refer to as measuring off-line processes do not form a homogenous set. Rather, they relate in different ways to the language-comprehension system and therefore tell us different things about the breakdown of that system. To treat these different tasks as though they probe the same aspects of the system is to ignore the important differences between them and the insight these differences can bring to bear on the nature of a patient's deficit.

Variability among Patients

The patient data illustrate very clearly that even when patients can be unambiguously diagnosed as members of the same aphasic category (agrammatic, Wernicke, anomic), they rarely produce the same pattern of performance across a wide range of experiments. Whereas they might exhibit similar performance on some tests (e.g., the "Wernicke" patients RH and FB, or FB and WA), they never produce the same performance on all tests. This forces us to face the vexed issue of variability between patients (e.g., Caramazza 1984; Caplan 1987; Shallice 1979, 1989; Howard and Franklin 1988) and consider what such variability might mean both for the concept of diagnostic categories and for trying to specify the nature of a patient's underlying deficit.

Given this kind of variability among patients, the only way to preserve the concept of diagnostic categories is to say that they represent clusters of deficits and that, to be included in a particular category, each patient must exhibit some, but not all, of those deficits. To prevent this from being theoretically vacuous, one has to add the proviso that there is a core set of deficits each patient within that category must exhibit. This core set of deficits must then be explicable as arising from damage to a particular functional subcomponent of the system. This is exactly what happened in the case of agrammatism, when people debated for some time as to the appropriate definition of that category (Caramazza 1984; Goodglass and Menn 1985). Although the dispute still rages, it is generally agreed that, for a patient to be classified as an agrammatic, he or she has to have particular problems with closed-class morphemes—especially inflected morphemes—because of the syntactic role they play in utterances. But in this book, I describe data from two patients, BN and DE, both of whom would be classified as agrammatic and yet who appear to have different comprehension problems. Both patients initially looked as though they had the predicted deficit for bound morphemes, but further investigation showed that they also had difficulty processing the endings of multisyllabic words that were morphologically simple. It remains to be seen whether other agrammatic patients, when tested appropriately, will show similar deficits. Where DE and BN differ is in other aspects of language comprehension. DE has problems with various aspects of syntax and is unusually dependent upon the pragmatic coherence of an utterance, whereas BN appears to have no particular problems with syntax. Given the similarities and differences between these patients, should they still be considered as having the same underlying agrammatic deficit due specifically to problems with the syntactic role of the closed-class morphology?

Thus, the variability between patients makes it extremely difficult to group patients into meaningful categories if one uses the strict criterion that patients within a category have to exhibit the same core cluster of deficits and preserved functions within a particular cognitive domain. This means that the clinical classification of patients into different syndrome categories based on standard aphasia tests rarely helps to understand the nature of a patient's deficit. In fact, it may even muddy the waters because of the danger that one may look for evidence in support of that classification. This is not to say that clinical classification is without value. Historically, it has played an important role in relating behavioral deficits to organic deficits, and it continues to play an important role in assessment for clinical treatment.

In reporting detailed analyses of a number of individual patients across different aspects of language comprehension, we can look at the commonalities and differences between patients who can be classified as belonging to the same syndrome group. This enables us to see where patients within a group differ from each other and where they overlap, and where patients who belong to different categories are similar to each other. We may discover that the ways patients within the same group differ from each other are trivial and should be ignored, and that general commonalities emerge. Alternately, we can ignore the issue of syndrome category and concentrate instead upon trying to understand the extent to which the cluster of functional deficits which each patient exhibits are related to each other and to aspects of the normal model.

In doing cognitive neuropsychology with single case studies, we need to be able to discover the correct level of abstraction for explaining patient deficits. Unless some general picture emerges, we are left with the possibility that every patient will show a unique cluster of deficits. If this turned out to be the case, it would suggest that the system was infinitely fractionable. It would thus be difficult to continue to argue that data from brain-damaged patients bears on the structure and function of the normal system (cf. Shallice 1979).

Appendix A
Description of Control Subjects

In our control groups, we attempt to match our patient population as closely as possible in age, sex, and education. Most of our patients are either in their late 30s or early 40s, or are between 65 and 75 years. Therefore, we have a "mid-age" control group of eight subjects who are aged between 34 and 41 years (mean age is 37 years) and two groups of "old-age" control subjects. The members of one old-age group suffer from poor hearing whereas those in the other group have no significant hearing loss.

We distinguished between these control subjects on the basis of their hearing loss because so many older patients suffer from a significant degree of hearing loss. Since all of our research involves spoken language, degree of hearing loss may well interact with a subject's ability to perform in some of the studies. This may be a particular problem when slight distortions are introduced into the materials, as in the word-endings experiment reported in chapter 15. Subjects with poor hearing might perform badly in this task just because they cannot hear the words very well and thus cannot readily distinguish between an appropriate final syllable (*nylon*) and one that produces a non-word (*nylup*).

Moreover, degree of hearing loss might be particularly important in the processing of inflected words. Many morphologically complex words in English contain inflections which involve the sound /s/. Patients who suffer hearing loss typically have problems with speech sounds involving high frequencies, such as /s/. Therefore, if patients have problems with the word "paints," for example, this may not be because they cannot process inflected words, but rather because they cannot hear the inflection properly.

Our criterion for including a subject in the hearing-loss group was that he or she had to have more than 26 db impairment. The mean hearing loss in the loss group was 38 db (range: 26–48 db loss), and in the no loss group it was 16 db loss (range: 1–24 db). The mean age of the subjects in the loss group was 72 years (range: 68–78 years), and in the no loss group it was 70 years (range: 66–73 years).

We also have one control subject who is a recovered stroke patient. She has no detectable cognitive deficits resulting from the stroke. She is 69 years old and has a pronounced hearing loss (62.4 db). The date of birth, education level, and hearing loss of these control subjects are described in the tables below.

Old-Age Controls: Poor Hearing

	Date of birth	School leaving age	Hearing loss	Mean simple RT (msec)
Mr. D	1911	14 years	34 db	191
Mrs. K	1919	14 years	40 db	387
Mr. C	1921	16 years	37 db	160
Mr. G	1919	15 years	26 db	174
Mr. A	1913	16 years	47 db	450
Ms. M	1919	17 years	41 db	175
Ms. Ga	1914	17 years	28 db	310
Ms. R	1919	14 years	36 db	524
Ms. Fa	1920	17 years	42 db	248
Ms. W	1917	16 years	48 db	315
Mean			37.9	293
Range			26–48	160–524

Digit span/ match

	Digit span	Digit match: Total correct		
		4 digits	5 digits	6 digits
Mr. D	7	6/6	4/6	4/6
Mrs. K	7	6/6	4/6	5/6
Mr. C	7	4/6	6/6	6/6
Mr. G	6	6/6	6/6	3/6
Ms. M	4	6/6	6/6	6/6
Ms. R	7	6/6	6/6	5/6
Ms. Fa	7	6/6	5/6	5/6
Ms. W	7	6/6	6/6	4/6

Old-Age Controls: Good Hearing

	Date of birth	School leaving age	Hearing loss	Mean simple RT (msec)
Ms. A	1922	15 years	7 db	308
Ms. C	1922	16 years	1 db	303
Mr. F	1919	14 years	8 db	215
Mr. P	1923	14 years	14 db	183
Mr. S	1919	14 years	10 db	183
Ms. Fo	1916	19 years	16 db	154
Ms. S	1919	16 years	15 db	379
Mr. B	1917	17 years	18 db	228
Ms. Tw	1921	18 years	16 db	353
Ms. Gw	1921	14 years	22 db	357
Ms. Tu	1916	17 years	24 db	230
Mean			13.7	263
Range			1–24	154–379

Digit span/ match

	Digit span	Digit match: Total correct		
		4 digits	5 digits	6 digits
Ms. A	7	6/6	5/6	6/6
Ms. C	7	6/6	6/6	6/6
Mr. F	7	6/6	6/6	5/6
Mr. P	7	6/6	6/6	6/6
Mr. S	7	6/6	5/6	5/6
Mr. S	7	6/6	5/6	4/6
Mr. B	7	6/6	5/6	5/6
Ms. Tw	6	6/6	6/6	2/6
Ms. Gw	7	6/6	6/6	6/6
Ms. Tu	6	6/6	6/6	5/6

Recovered stroke patient: Ms T

Date of birth	1921
Date of onset	1986
School leaving age	14 years
Hearing loss	62 db
Mean simple RT	312 msec (compared to 293 msec for old-age controls with poor hearing)
Digit span	7

Digit match: Total correct

4 digits	6/6
5 digits	5/6
6 digits	5/6

Mid-Age Controls

	Date of birth	School leaving age	Hearing loss
Ms. A	1953	16 years	No hearing test
Ms. T	1948	16 years	11 db
Ms. F	1951	18 years	11 db
Ms. C	1947	16 years	No hearing test
Mr. H	1951	16 years	8 db
Mr. C	1946	18 years	7 db
Mr. R	1955	18 years	7 db
Mr. M	1950	16 years	15 db
Mean			9.8 db
Range			7–15 db

The two old-age groups and the recovered stroke patient have been tested on most of the studies described in this book, and in exactly the same way as the patients. For example, if an experiment requires four testing sessions, each separated by an interval of a month, then both the patients and control subjects are tested according to this schedule. In this way, we are able to develop processing profiles for individual control subjects as well as patients.

The group of eight mid-age controls were also tested in the same way as the patients and old-age controls. They were tested on many, but not all, of the studies described here. After many years of regular testing, a number of them were reluctant to continue. We decided that it was unnecessary to form a new group of subjects within the mid-age range after establishing that the error rates and monitoring latencies of the mid-age group were indistinguishable from those of the young control groups we used in all our studies. Thereafter, we used a variety of subjects, aged between 24 and 40 years, as controls for the younger patients, those who were under 45 years when tested.

We also tested young control subjects on all the studies while they were being developed for use with patients. Each experiment was initially tested on a group of young subjects from our subject pool (ranging in size from 20 to 40 subjects, depending on the study). These subjects were aged between 18 and 35 years. Each subject participated in a single study and was tested only on a single version of any experiment.

Appendix B
Notes about the Word-Monitoring Task

Methodological Considerations

In the word-monitoring task, as used in this book, subjects are presented with a printed word, which they are asked to read aloud. They then listen to a sentence and press a response button as soon as they hear that word in the sentence. Timing pulses (which the listener cannot hear) are placed at the onset of each target word. These pulses trigger a timing device that is stopped when the subject presses the response button.

We have found the word-monitoring task to be particularly useful in our work with patients. The task is sensitive to a large number of linguistic manipulations and enables us to examine a wide variety of on-line processes involved in spoken language comprehension.

In addition, almost all of the patients we have tested over the years can perform the task quite easily. They rarely miss the target word and they produce reasonably stable RTs. Although many patients produce RTs which are longer than those of their age-matched control group, this, in itself, is not a problem. Longer RTs are undoubtedly one of the general residual effects of brain damage, which frequently slows down psychomotor performance irrespective of the location of the damage (Benton and Joynt 1958; Dee and Van Allen 1973). We have data supporting this claim from a woman (born 1919) who has no detectable residual effects of a stroke she suffered in April 1986. She shows a normal BDAE profile, and she behaves as normal in a variety of word-monitoring studies. However, her latencies are considerably longer than a group of age-matched subjects who have not suffered strokes, and similar to those of many of our patients.

Furthermore, patients enjoy participating in the task. It has the advantage of not being a task where the patient's response is either correct or incorrect, and therefore doesn't make the patient anxious. There were, however, a number of ways in which the task had to be modified for use with patients.

First, we try, whenever possible, to use concrete nouns as target words because these are usually the easiest for patients to read. However, this is not always possible. One of the most important considerations when constructing our materials is that the target word should immediately follow the linguistic manipulation of interest. Sometimes this means that the target word cannot be a noun. However, we always ensure that it is either a noun, verb, or adjective.

We quite frequently encounter patients who are unable to read any target word—whatever its form-class. Whenever possible, we present these patients with a picture of the target word, which they are asked to name. In experiments where the target word is not a picturable object, we try to determine whether a patient knows the target word by a variety of means, such as mime and question-answering.

Second, in word-monitoring experiments, the target word the patient has to monitor for occurs in a number of different experimental conditions. We cannot avoid having the same word occur in all conditions. This is the only way we can eliminate the possibility that any differences we might find between conditions are due to differences in the patient's RTs to detect different words. Since the patient can not encounter the same word more than once in a single session (because of repetition-priming effects), this means that he or she has to be tested in a number of different sessions. We thus have to carefully counterbalance across different testing sessions so that on each session the patient hears one occurrence of each target word, and test items are distributed equally across all conditions.

Third, one of the problems with obtaining data for a single experiment over a long period of time, and with long delays in between each testing session, is that patients' monitoring performance may differ across sessions. Patients might produce generally slow responses at one session and much faster responses on another. One way of taking such changes into account is to look at the monitoring RTs for the filler items on each testing session. Since the filler items never vary across sessions, these can provide a baseline of the patient's speed of responding on any one occasion. In the ideal case, we should leave a long enough gap between testing sessions so that mean RT to the set of filler items remains constant over sessions. In practice, we have found that for most patients, this is achieved if we leave one month between testing sessions.

A fourth constraint on the design of the experiment is that it should be of a reasonable size so that it can be run in a small number of experimental sessions, each of which last no longer than 15–20 minutes.

Statistical Analyses of Word-Monitoring RTs

Reaction-time data from patients can be very variable (although they are not always so). We have tried a variety of ways of dealing with long and variable RTs, and have concluded that the following is the most conservative set of operations to perform on the data from an individual patient:

- Obtain the mean and standard deviation over the set of RTs in a condition, but excluding clear outliers—that is, RTs over 1500 msec.
- Take the mean $+/-2$ SD to be the minimum and maximum values. Set all RTs below the minimum to that value and all RTs above the maximum to that value.
- Calculate new mean and SD and set missing values to this mean.
- Use these "trimmed" data as input to an ANOVA.
- Planned or post-hoc orthogonal comparsions can be carried out to compare different conditions, if the required F values are significant.

It is important, when designing the experiment, that a sufficiently large set of test items are used. It is extremely difficult to obtain significant results if the data set is too small.

We treat the data from control subjects slightly differently. Although we analyze the data from an individual control subject in the same way that we analyze each patient's data, we also analyze each control group as a whole. For this type of analysis, we combine all the data, take the mean and SD, and treat extreme values as described above. The mean values for each item in each condition (collapsed across subjects) are then entered into an ANOVA. We also collapse RTs across items for each subject and enter these means into an ANOVA. We then calculate Min F' (Clark 1973) and carry out planned or post-hoc comparisons (when appropriate), using the error term derived from the Min F' analysis.

We also compute distributions of RTs both for individual patients and for the control group data, to ensure that they are not abnormally skewed, and confidence limits on sets of data to determine whether the patient's performance is outside the normal range.

Analyzing RT data for individual patients can occasionally be difficult in the sense that it is sometimes not clear whether an effect for a patient is different from normal. The most unambiguous outcome is where the patient shows an effect that is significant and where the size of the effect is within the confidence limits for the appropriate control group. However, some-times an effect is not statistically significant for an individual patient, but it is within the appropriate confidence limits. In general, I treat this as though the effect were not reliable. However, in dealing with RTs from patients, I believe we cannot be totally rigid in our interpretation of the data. We need to look for patterns of consistency across experiments so, for example, if a patient consistently shows small effects across related experiments that are not statistically significant although they are within the normal confidence limits, I discuss this as though the effects are reliable. However, if a patient shows only an occasional difference score that, although not significant, is within normal confidence limits, I treat this case as though the effect were not reliable.

General Points

When reporting the results for the individual patients, I have taken into account the entire body of data for that patient rather than discuss the results of a single experiment as though the other data did not exist. I have tried to make sense of the data from all the experiments together and therefore, at times, I may appear to go beyond a legitimate interpretation of the data from a single study. I believe that the approach I have taken is a defensible one. There is no doubt that carrying out RT studies with patients is difficult because we rarely obtain large effects. Therefore, we have to rely on the consistency between experiments and on the data as a whole, across experiments, telling a coherent story about the nature of the patient's deficit. This may occasionally necessitate elaborating on the results of a study that would not be defensible if they constituted the only data for that patient.

Notes

Chapter 1

1. In Marcel's (1983, 1988) terms, I am making the non-identity assumption.
2. Results from the gating task correlate quite well with those from other tasks—like word monitoring—we claim tap into intermediate representations (Tyler and Wessels 1983, 1985).
3. However, Freedman and Forster (1985) claim that only certain types of ungrammaticality affect performance (but see Crain and Fodor 1987 for a critique).
4. This task resembles phonemic cueing. However, in the gating task the experimenter has more control over the amount of sensory input that is presented to the subject.

Chapter 4

1. This is not an iterm-specific effect. In a supplementary test, we increased the number of nasal contrasts (both word-initial and word-final) and found the same pattern of results.

Chapter 7

1. The A' scores for the derived, inflected and simple words were as follows. JG: .84, .77, .89; FB: .87, .81, .92; JW: .88, .89, .95; RH: .86, .85, .94)

Chapter 8

1. VS was only tested on prefixed words due to her premature withdrawal from the project.

Chapter 9

1. For young controls the difference between pragmatic and semantic violations of 26 msec was only significant on a subjects analysis (p < 0.001). For both groups of old-age controls, the difference between pragmatic and semantic violations was not significant on either a subjects or items analysis.
2. We calculated A' (Linebarger, Schwartz and Saffran 1983) for both sets of controls to obtain a measure of their sensitivity to the violations. Both groups produced a mean A' of .97 (range HL: .95–1; range NHL: .96–1).
3. GS: .91–.93; JG: .9–.85; PK: .97–.94; BN: .89–.85; DE: .9–.88; CH: .87–.82; VS: .85–.83; FB: .89–.82.
4. The RTs are not a robust source of data because they are very variable. There are many reasons why this should be so. Subjects' criteria for deciding that they have encountered

an anomaly might well vary. This would lead them to respond rapidly on some occasions but much more slowly on others. Moreover, it is not possible to compare RTs to detect the three types of anomaly with those in the undisrupted baseline condition in that no RTs were collected for that condition. This was because subjects were asked to detect anomalies and none were present in the undisrupted sentences; therefore, there were no detection responses. The detection RTs, then, are only useful in that they give us a very general idea of the overall latency with which people perform the task.

5. Their mean A' was .92, with a range of between. .89 and .98.
6. Their mean A' was .95, with a range of .92–.98.

Chapter 11

1. We might have distorted the speech if we had merely spliced a period of silence into the speech wave.
2. To introduce some variety into the experimental materials, we used two types of phonological phrases in the study, NPs and PPs. To see whether there were any differences between them, we ran an ANOVA including this variable. It was not significant (F < 1), nor did it interact with the experimental conditions.

Part V (Introduction)

1. Patients who have particular problems with members of the closed class are often labeled "agrammatics." For a discussion of the validity of using this term to refer to a unitary language disorder, see Caramazza 1987 and Caplan 1987.

Chapter 12

1. All except one [-able] were monosyllabic.
2. The mean number of legitimate suffixes per base form was 2.6.
3. For Geo S the size of the difference between appropriate and inappropriate RTs was not significant, although it was within the confidence limits for the old-age controls.
4. The mean A' for the controls with poor hearing was .97 [range: .92–1.0] and for the controls with good hearing it was .98 [range: .91–1.0], indicating that they were very sensitive to the presence of either kind of disruption.

Chapter 13

1. A series of pre-tests established the syntactic appropriateness or inappropriateness of the target noun.
2. We selected 20 items on the basis of their consistency with the overall results.

Chapter 14

1. It was not possible to run an item analysis with syllabicity as a factor because no item appeared in all four conditions (syllabicity by consistency of inflection).
2. Although 60 msec appears to be a respectable difference, his RTs are extremely variable and therefore the effect does not approach significance.

Chapter 17

1. All patients (with the exception of PK) performed worse than the control group on the acceptability judgment task. This is, perhaps, surprising given that in most other respects some of these patients (e.g., CH) appear to be indistinguishable from normal. The judgment task appears consistently to underestimate a patient's comprehension abilities.

References

Anderson, S. 1982. Where's morphology? *Linguistic Enquiry* **13**, 571–612.

Aronoff, M. 1976. Word formation and generative grammar. *Linguistic Inquiry Monograph 1.* Cambridge, Mass., MIT Press.

Bates, E., and B. MacWhinney. 1989. Functionalism and the competition model. In B. MacWhinney and E. Bates, eds, *The Cross-Linguistic Study of Sentence Processing.* Cambridge: Cambridge University Press.

Berndt, R. 1987. Symptom co-occurrence and dissociation in the interpretation of agrammatism. In M. Coltheart, R. Job, and G. Sartori, eds., *The Cognitive Neuropsychology of Language.* London: LEA.

Berndt, R. and A. Caramazza. 1980. A redefinition of the syndrome of Broca's aphasia: Implications for a neuropsychological model of language. *Applied Psycholinguistics* 1, 225–278.

Bishop, D. 1982. *TROG: Test for the Reception of Grammar.* Abingdon, UK: Thomas Leach for the MRC.

Black, M., L. Nickels, and S. Byng. (In press). Patterns of sentence processing deficit: Processing simple sentences can be a complex matter. *Neuro-linguistics.*

Blumstein, S. E., W. E. Cooper, E. B. Zurif, and A. Caramazza. 1977. The perception and production of voice-onset time in aphasia. *Neuropsychologica* 15, 371–383.

Bradley, D. C. 1978. Computational distinctions of vocabulary type. Unpublished doctoral dissertation, MIT.

Bradley, D. C., M. F. Garrett, and E. B. Zurif. 1980. Syntactic deficits in Broca's aphasia. In D. Caplan ed., *Biological studies of mental processes.* Cambridge, Mass.: MIT Press.

Bresnan, J. 1982. *The mental representation of grammatical relations.* Cambridge, Mass.: MIT Press.

Butterworth, B., R. Campbell, and D. Howard. 1986. The uses of short term memory: A case study. *Quarterly Journal of Experimental Psychology* 38, 705–737.

Caplan, D. 1987. *Neurolinguistics and linguistic aphasiology: an introduction.* Cambridge: Cambridge University Press.

Caramazza, A. 1984. The logic of neuropsychological research and the problem of patient classification in aphasia. *Brain and Language* 21, 9–20.

Caramazza, A., R. S. Berndt, and A. G. Basili. 1983. The selective impairment of phonological processing: A case study. *Brain and Language* 18, 128–174.

Caramazza, A., E. Grober, and C. Garvey. 1977. Comprehension of anaphoric pronouns. *Journal of Verbal Learning and Verbal Behaviour* 16, 601–609.

Carlson, G.N., and M. K. Tannenhaus. 1988. Thematic roles and language comprehension. In W. Wilkins, ed., *Thematic Relations.* New York: Academic Press.

Chomsky, N. 1965. *Aspects of the theory of syntax.* Cambridge, Mass.: MIT Press.

Chomsky, N. 1981. *Lectures on government and binding.* Dordrecht: Foris.

Clark, H. H. The language-as-a-fixed-effect fallacy: A critique of language statistics in psychological research. *Journal of Verbal Learning and Verbal Behavior* 12, 335–359.

Coltheart, M. Deep Dyslexia: A review of the syndrome. In M. Coltheart, K. E. Patterson and J. C. Marshall, eds., *Deep Dyslexia*, London: Routledge.

Cooper, W., and E. Zurif. 1983. Aphasia: Information processing in language production and reception. In: B. Butterworth, ed., *Language Production*, **Volume 2**. New York: Academic Press.

Crain, S. 1982. Temporal terms: Mastery by age five. *Papers and Reports on Child Language Development* 21, 33–38.

Forster, K. I. 1979. Levels of processing and the structure of the language processor. In: W. E. Cooper and E. C. T. Walker, eds., *Sentence Processing: Psycholinguistic studies presented to Merrill Garrett*. Hillsdale, New Jersey: Lawrence Erlbaum Associates.

Foss, D. J., and M. A. Gernsbacher. 1983. Cracking the dual code: Toward a unitary model of phoneme indentification. *Journal of Verbal Learning and Verbal Behaviour* 22, 609–632.

Francis, W. N. and H. Kucera. 1982. *Frequency analysis of English usage*. Boston: Houghton-Mifflin.

Friederici, A. 1985. Levels of processing and vocabulary types: Evidence from on-line processing in normals and agrammatics. *Cognition* 19, 133–166.

Gee, J. and F. Grosjean. 1983. Performance structures: A psycholinguistic and linguistic appraisal. *Cognitive Psychology* 15, 411–458.

Goodenough, C., E. B. Zurif, and S. Weintraub. 1977. Aphasics' attention to grammatical morphemes. *Language and Speech* 20, 11–19.

Goodglass, H., and J. Berko. 1960. Agrammatism and inflectional morphology in English. *Journal of Speech and Hearing Research* 3, 257–267.

Goodglass, H., and L. Menn. 1985. Is agrammatism a unitary phenomenon? In M. L. Kean, ed., *Agrammatism*. New York: Academic Press.

Gordon, B. 1984. Lexical access and lexical decision: Mechanisms of frequency sensitivity. *Journal of Verbal Learning and Verbal Behavior* 22, 146–160.

Gorrell, P., S. Crain, and J. D. Fodor. 1989. Contextual information and temporal terms. *Journal of Child Language* 16, 623–632.

Grodzinsky, Y. 1984. The syntactic characterization of agrammatism. *Cognition* 16, 99–120.

Grosjean, F. 1980. Spoken word recognition processes and the gating paradigm. *Perception & Psychophysics* 28, 267–283.

Grossman, M., S. Carey, E. Zurif, and L. Diller. 1986. Proper and common nouns: Form class judgements in Broca's aphasia. *Brain and Language* 28, 114–125.

Hall, C. J. 1990, *Morphology and Mind*. London, Routledge.

Heilman, K. M., and R. J. Scholes. 1976. The nature of comprehension errors in Broca's conduction and Wernicke's aphasics. *Cortex* 12, 258–265.

Howard, D., and S. Franklin. 1988. *Missing the meaning: A cognitive neuropsychological study of processing words by an aphasic patient*. Cambridge, Mass.: MIT Press.

Jackendoff, R. 1972. *Semantic interpretation in generative grammar*. Cambridge, Mass.: MIT Press.

Jones, E. 1984. Word order processing in aphasia: Effect of verb semantics. In F. C. Rose, ed., *Advances in Neurology, vol. 42: Progress in Aphasiology*.

Kolk, H., and van Grunsven, M. J. F. 1985. Agrammatism as a variable phenomenon. *Cognitive Neuropsychology* 2, 347–384.

Kucera, H., and W. N. Francis. 1967. *Computational analysis of present-day American English*. Providence, R.I.: Brown University Press.

Lahiri, A., and W. D. Marslen-Wilson. 1991. The mental representation of lexical form: A phonological approach to the recognition lexicon. *Cognition* 38, 245–294.

Linebarger, M. C., M. F. Schwartz, and E. M. Saffran. 1983. Sensitivity to grammatical structure in so-called grammatic aphasics. *Cognition* 13, 361–392.

Luria, A. R. 1970. Traumatic aphasia. The Hague: Mouton.

Marcel, A. J. 1988. Phenomenal experience and functionalism. In A. Marcel & E. Bisiach, eds., *Consciousness in contemporary science*. New York: Oxford University Press.

Marslen-Wilson, W. D. 1973. Linguistic structure and speech shadowing at very short latencies. *Nature* 244, 522–523.

Marslen-Wilson, W. D. 1975. Sentence perception as an interactive parallel process. *Science* 189, 226–228.

Marslen-Wilson, W. D. 1984. Function and process in spoken word recognition. In H. Bouma and D. Bouwhuis, eds., *Attention and performance X: Control of language processes*. Hillsdale, N.J.: Lawrence Erlbaum Associates.

Marslen-Wilson, W. D. 1985. Speech shadowing and speech comprehension. *Speech Communication* 4, 55–73

Marslen-Wilson, W. D. 1987. Functional parallelism in spoken word recognition. *Cognition* 25, 71–102.

Marslen-Wilson, W. D., C. Brown, and L. K. Tyler. 1988. Lexical representations in spoken language comprehension. *Language and Cognitive Processes* 3, 1–17.

Marslen-Wilson, W. D., E. Levy, and L. K. Tyler. 1982. Producing interpretable discourse: The establishment and maintenance of reference. In R. J. Jarvella and W. Klein, eds., *Speech, Place and Action*. London: Wiley.

Marslen-Wilson, W. D., and L. K. Tyler. 1975. Processing structure of spoken language comprehension. *Nature* 257, 784–786.

Marslen-Wilson, W. D., and L. K. Tyler. 1980. The temporal structure of spoken language comprehension. *Cognition* 6, 1–71.

Marslen-Wilson, W. D., and L. K. Tyler. 1987. Against modularity. In J. Garfield, ed., *Modularity in Knowledge Representation and Natural Language Understanding*. Cambridge, MA: MIT Press.

Marslen-Wilson, W. D., and A. Welsh. 1978. Processing interactions and lexical access during word recognition in continuous speech. *Cognitive Psychology* 10, 29–63.

Marslen-Wilson, W., and P. Zwitserlood. 1989. Accessing spoken words: The importance of word onsets. *Journal of Experimental Psychology: H* 15 (3), 576–585.

Miceli, G., and A. Caramazza. 1987. *Dissociation of inflectional and derivational morphology*. Reports of the Cognitive Neuropsychology Laboratory, Johns Hopkins University.

Miceli, G., M. C. Silveri, C. Romani, and A. Caramazza. 1989. Variation in the patterns of omissions and substitutions of grammatical morphemes in the spontaneous speech of so-called agrammatic patients. *Brain and Language* 36, 447–492.

Morton, J. 1969. Interaction of information in word recognition. *Psychological Review* 76, 165–78.

Nespor, M., and I. Vogel. 1982. Prosodic domains of exernal sandhi rules. In H. van den Hulst and N. Smith, eds., *The structure of phonological representation*. Dordrecht: Foris.

Ostrin, R. K., and L. K. Tyler. (In prep.). Comprehending morphologically complex words: Suffixes or word-endings?

Patterson, K. E. 1979. What is right with "deep" dyslexic patients? *Brain and Language* 8, 111–129.

Patterson, K. E. 1980. Derivational errors. In M. Coltheart, K. E. Patterson, and J. C. Marshall, eds., *Deep Dyslexia*. London: Routledge.

Reichenbach, H. 1949. *Elements of symbolic logic*. New York: Free Press.

Salasoo, A., and D. Pisoni. 1985. Interaction of knowledge sources in spoken word recognition. *Journal of Memory and Language* 24, 210–231.

Scalise, S. 1984. *Generative Morphology*. Dordrecht: Foris.

Seidenberg, M., M. Tanenhaus, J. Leiman, and M. Bienkowski. 1982. Automatic access of the meanings of ambiguous words in context: Some limitations of knowledge-based processing. *Cognitive Psychology* 14, 489–537.

Selkirk, E. 1980. *On prosodic structure and its relation to syntactic structure.* Indiana University Linguistics Club.

Shallice, T. 1988. *From neuropsychology to mental structure.* Cambridge: Cambridge University Press.

Shallice, T. 1979. The case study approach in neuropsychological research. *Journal of Clinical Neuropsychology* 1, 183–211.

Shankweiler, D., S. Crain, P. Gorrell, and B. Tuller. 1989. Reception of language in Broca's aphasia. *Language and Cognitive Processes* 4, 1–33.

Swinney, D. 1979. Lexical access during sentence comprehension: (Re)consideration of context effects. *Journal of Verbal Learning and Verbal Behavior* 18, 645–660.

Swinney, D., E. Zurif, and A. Cutler. 1980. Effects of sentential stress and word class upon comprehension in Broca's aphasics. *Brain and Language* 10, 132–144.

Tyler, L. K. 1983. The development of discourse mapping processes: The on-line interpretation of anaphoric expressions. *Cognition* 13, 309–341.

Tyler, L. K. 1984. The structure of the initial cohort: Evidence from gating. *Perception & Psychophysics* 36, 417–427.

Tyler, L. K. 1985. Real-time comprehension processes in agrammatism: A case study. *Brain and Language* 26, 259–275.

Tyler, L. K. 1988. Spoken language comprehension in a fluent aphasic patient. *Cognitive Neuropsychology* 5, 375–400.

Tyler, L. K. 1991. The distinction between implicit and explicit language function: Evidence from aphasia. In: A. D. Milner and M. Rugg (Eds) The Neuropsychology of consciousness. London: Academic Press.

Tyler, L. K., and W. D. Marslen-Wilson. 1977. The on-line effects of semantic context on syntactic processing. *Journal of Verbal Learning and Verbal Behavior* 16, 683–692.

Tyler, L. K., and W. D. Marslen-Wilson. 1982. Conjectures and refutations: A reply to Norris. *Cognition* 11, 103–107.

Tyler, L. K. and W. D. Marslen-Wilson. 1986. The effects of context on the recognition of polymorphemic words. *Journal of Memory and Language* 25, 741–752.

Tyler, L. K., and P. Warren. 1987. Local and global structure in spoken language comprehension. *Journal of Memory and Language* 26, 638–657.

Tyler, L. K., and J. Wessels. 1983. Quantifying contextual contributions to word recognition processes. *Perception & Psychophysics* 34, 409–420.

Tyler, L. K., and J. Wessels. 1985. Is gating an on-line task? Evidence from naming latency data. *Perception & Psychophysics* 38, 217–222.

Van Riemsdijk, H., and E. Williams. 1986. *Introduction to the theory of grammar.* Cambridge, Mass.: MIT Press.

Warren, P. 1985. The temporal organisation and perception of speech. Unpublished doctoral dissertation, University of Cambridge.

Warren, P., and W. D. Marslen-Wilson. 1987. Continuous uptake of acoustic cues in spoken word recognition. *Perception & Psychophysics* 41, 262–275.

Warren, P., and W. D. Marslen-Wilson. 1988. Cues to lexical choice: Discriminating place and voice. *Perception & Psychophysics* 43, 21–30.

Webber, B. L. 1988. Tense as discourse anaphor. *Computational Linguistics* 14, 61–75.

Zurif, E. B., A. Caramazza, and R. Meyerson. 1972. Grammatical judgments of agrammatic aphasics. *Neuropsychologica* 10, 405–417.

Index